Advance Praise for *The Extraordinary Coach*

"Zenger and Stinnett use a strong, empirically-based approach to cut right to the heart of the (coaching) issue to provide something both situationally-relevant and contextually profound. The authors thread the needle between theory and anecdotal practice and provide perspective and tools that can benefit everyone from CEOs bent on changing culture to frontline managers plying their skills on the factory floor."
—Courtney Rogers, Executive Director, Human Resources and Talent, Amgen

"This book stands alone as one of the most practical, enlightening books about coaching ever written. In the book, Jack and Kathleen model their own coaching methods by helping the reader 'discover superior solutions' and 'make and implement better [coaching] decisions.' At a time when many organizations are searching for how to engage their employees, this timely book provides straightforward advice you can implement immediately."
—Elaine Biech, President, ebb associates inc, Author of *The Business of Consulting*

"A down-to-earth examination of the key principles and practices involved in coaching. (The authors') helpful treatment of this critical leadership skill begins with a context of research, moves to the realities of the workplace, and then settles into a series of practical guidelines and examples."
—Ronald E. Galbraith, Chairman/Chief Consulting Officer, onFocus|Healthcare

"A treasure of practical wisdom needed by all leaders. This book contains valuable information on the coaching process and success factors for behavioral change; combined with the high credibility of (the authors') research, the wisdom in this book is an important investment for today's organizations."
—Dr. Kathryn Kaminsky, Professor of Sustainable Leadership, Presidio Graduate School, San Francisco, California

"Put simply, the coaching framework this book builds 'works.' Well researched and grounded in solid data, it is far more than just an excellent coaching script and handbook, although it is that too. More importantly it leads the reader from the why–to the what–to the how–to the when of coaching. From what it takes to be the coach, to a wealth of powerful questions, to the extraordinary impact of coaching—it is all here. Leadership, mindset, and behavioral changes do not come easily for most, but for those leaders and organizations that are serious about achieving the amazing benefits of coaching, this book offers the complete package and is a 'must have.'"
—Jeffrey C. Smith, Certified Business Coach, Former Chief Human Resources Officer, Cincinnati Bell Inc.

"This book outlines a very powerful and practical sequence of coaching for leaders and professional coaches to use in their day-to-day work. The field of coaching has very little research and generally accepted standards. This book establishes a baseline in which anyone can evaluate their own coaching performance and develop improvement plans. I highly recommend this book as a core component of coaching classroom, plus on-the-job training and self-development programs."

—David Brookmire, Ph.D., President, Corporate Performance Strategies.

"A few years ago, Jack Zenger and Joe Folkman turned their detailed leadership behavior research into a terrific book, titled *The Extraordinary Leader*. It forever changed my views on the critical behaviors leaders need to fulfill their true potential and make a meaningful difference in their organizations. In *The Extraordinary Coach*, Jack Zenger and Kathleen Stinnett serve up a powerful, yet digestible, framework to help leaders become the coaches they aspire to be: relationship-based, collaboration-oriented, change-focused, and FUEL-ed for success! Leaders in all types of organizations, and at all levels, will benefit from this insightful work."

—P. Artell Smith, Vice President, Human Resources, Hewitt Associates

"*The Extraordinary Coach* is not your ordinary coaching guide for managers. With compelling evidence, Zenger and Stinnett deftly challenge our assumptions about how much–and how well–leaders actually coach their employees. *The Extraordinary Coach* offers effective and immediately usable coaching tools for managers who want their employees to truly excel."

—Catherine Robinson-Walker, MBA, MCC, President, The Leadership Studio®

"Coaching is an essential management activity for improving organizational performance and for people development. This book is a must-have for every manager. The authors provide practical answers to important coaching questions: why, how, and when. The online vignettes are a great learning tool."

—Tony Tasca, Ph.D., Retired Chief Human Resources Officer, Zain Group

"*The Extraordinary Coach* brims with very practical and timely advice distilled from decades of highly successful leadership development experience. I absolutely love this book. It really stands out with a unique combination of solid research, relevant and illustrative examples, and how-to applications. Jack and Kathleen's warm and conversational writing style makes reading *The Extraordinary Coach* feel like a personal coaching session with one of the wisest sages in the business. An absolute must-read for anyone leading others."

—Jim Clemmer, Practical leadership author, keynote speaker, and workshop/retreat leader

"This book is very helpful for leaders who want to be more coachlike in their leadership style. It gives an inside perspective often lacking in other leadership books."

—G. Lee Salmon, Executive Coaching Program Manager, Federal Consulting Group, U.S. Department of Interior

"*The Extraordinary Coach* is exactly what we have been looking for. The concepts are profound and practical. Every chapter answered my next question. This book provides the FUEL for our approach to creating a coaching culture at Associated Food Stores."

—Steve Jones, Manager, AFS University, Associated Food Stores

The
Extraordinary
COACH

How the Best Leaders
Help Others Grow

John H. Zenger
Kathleen Stinnett

New York   Chicago   San Francisco   Lisbon
London   Madrid   Mexico City   Milan   New Delhi
San Juan   Seoul   Singapore   Sydney   Toronto

The *McGraw-Hill* Companies

7 8 9 10 DOC/DOC 1 5 4 3

ISBN 978-0-07-170340-6
MHID 0-07-170340-3

McGraw-Hill books are available at special quantity discounts to use as premiums and sales promotions or for use in corporate training programs. To contact a representative, please e-mail us at bulksales@mcgraw-hill.com.

This book is printed on acid-free paper.

I dedicate this book to the countless leaders who enthusiastically coach their colleagues. They do an enormous amount of good. I also dedicate this book to my wife, Holly. Her sense of humor makes her coaching both pleasant and appreciated.

Jack Zenger

I dedicate this book to my parents, who have always believed in me and have given me a strong foundation upon which to grow, and to my partner, Dave, who endlessly supports me in pursuing the work and the life that I love. In addition, many individuals have contributed to my journey, provided opportunities for me to do the work I am called to, and shaped who I am today. This book is also for you.

Kathleen Stinnett

Contents

Foreword

When it comes to coaching for behavioral change "advice doesn't work." Lifted right from the pages of this book, these wise words ring clear and true to me after my many years as an executive coach to leaders around the globe.

What does work? Again, the answer can be found here in *The Extraordinary Coach*—coaching people to arrive at their own solutions so that they are committed to the outcome. These prudent words contain the foundation of my philosophy of executive coaching. The person has to want to change and be committed to change, or I don't waste my time. Extraordinary coaches know that if the person they are coaching doesn't want to be coached, the coaching isn't going to work.

Here are clear indicators that I recognize in individuals who are "uncoachable": (1) they don't think they have a problem and have no interest in changing, (2) they are pursuing the wrong strategy for the organization, (3) they are in the wrong job with the wrong company—it's just a bad fit, or (4) they think that everyone else has the same problem—it is impossible to help someone who doesn't think that he or she has a problem.

Once you have determined that the person is coachable, that he or she does want to change, how do you, as the leader, help her or him to grow? Through coaching, or, as Jack Zenger and Kathleen Stinnett define it in *The Extraordinary Coach*, with "interactions that help the individual being coached to discover superior solutions, make and implement better decisions, and expand awareness."

Coaching others can be one of the most rewarding experiences a leader can have in his or her career. However, it's not something to rush into blindly. A leader who is an adept coach can greatly enhance the organization's success; one who dabbles and doesn't take the process seriously can cause harm. Within the pages of this book, you'll discover what coaching is and what it isn't, and how you can learn the art and practice of coaching for leadership. Read it, devour it, practice it, and you, too, will be an extraordinary coach!

Marshall Goldsmith

Marshall Goldsmith is the million-selling author of *What Got You Here Won't Get You There, Succession: Are You Ready?,* and *MOJO: How to Get It, How to Keep It, and How to Get It Back If You Lose It.*

Chapter 1

Why Bother?
How Coaching
Pays Off

We meet a variety of people in the leadership development sessions we conduct. As the relationship evolves, they will often tell us how they genuinely feel, especially their skepticism about what we are presenting. Most of them are far too polite to express their innermost thoughts in the first hours without some specific encouragement, but we've found that it helps to get such feelings on the table and hit those questions head on.

In that spirit, allow us to predict what a significant number of readers may have in their mind—and that could well include you. We think it could be something like one of the following: "So what am I going to get out of reading this?" "What difference will it make in my organization if I implement everything that is in this book?" "Will it really be worth it?" "Is this just the latest management fad, or is there substantive evidence that it really works?"

We are going to answer those questions in stages. In Chapter 3, we present detailed statistical information regarding research we have conducted on the impact of coaching. Before drilling down to that level of detail, however, we would like to paint the bigger picture of the outcomes that will result from creating a coaching culture in the part of the organization in which you work. We assure you that these are not some theoretical views of what might happen. These conclusions are based on solid research and lots of experience in implementing them. Here's the big picture of what can happen and what outcomes coaching can provide.

1. GIVING NEW MEANING TO WORK

Organizations function best when workers feel that they are engaged in a useful cause, not merely performing menial tasks. Coaching provides perfect opportunities for the leader to communicate to each individual how that person's job contributes to the overall mission of the organization. While this message can be delivered partly in group meetings, it is best done in one-on-one coaching conversations. It is an essential message, though, because people today need meaning in their lives more than ever. The overall impact of being part of a family has declined in society. There has also been a general decline in the influence of religion in most people's lives. The net effect is that for a good many people, if their work lacks meaning and purpose, then their lives lack meaning and purpose.

2. ENGAGED AND COMMITTED EMPLOYEES

One powerful driver of productivity is the level of employee engagement and commitment. When people move from indifference to true passion for the mission of the organization, it has an incalculable impact on output.

There has been much discussion and debate about the various percentages of people who are highly engaged, not very engaged, neutral, or actively disengaged in their work. The differences in these employee attitudes have obvious consequences for a wide variety of performance outcomes. Think of the results you've seen from an employee who was highly committed to the organization and who delighted your most difficult customer compared to those from an uncommitted employee who seriously ticked off another long-term loyal customer. Managerial coaching shows strong evidence of increasing an employee's level of commitment and engagement.

3. HIGHER PRODUCTIVITY

One of the most appealing outcomes from coaching is higher productivity, using whatever metric your organization chooses. The measurable outputs from your people increase when they receive periodic coaching. The reasons are not at all mysterious. Coaching refocuses people on the most important objectives. It lets them know that their leader is paying attention to their performance. It helps them to develop better work habits, working both harder *and* smarter. All the known drivers of productivity can be increased through the leader's coaching.

All the known drivers of productivity can be increased through the leader's coaching.

Peter Drucker hypothesized that if an organization could increase employee productivity by 10 percent, the organization's profits would double. Whether or not these numbers are absolutely accurate, the bottom-line impact is hard to ignore. How could such a small increase in productivity affect profitability so greatly? The fixed costs of the organization have already been "paid for." If productivity were to increase by even 5 percent, almost all of the benefit would drop right to the bottom line.

4. STRONGER CULTURE

There is strong evidence that an organization's culture has a huge impact on its performance and productivity. By culture we refer to "how things get done around here" and how people treat one another in their daily interactions. Leaders influence organizational culture by the example they set and the behavior they reward or curb in their daily discussions with people. The climate and the culture are molded by the time leaders spend in having performance and career discussions with their direct reports.

5. STRENGTHENED BONDS BETWEEN SUPERVISOR AND EMPLOYEE

The effectiveness of leaders is controlled in large part by the strength of the bonds between them and the people that they lead. A distant, cool relationship between boss and direct report seldom has the strong impact on performance that a warm, positive relationship has. Coaching is an extremely effective tool to not only cement that bond but also continually enhance its strength. Coaching is the most tangible expression of the leader's personal commitment to the development of an employee. It sends a far more powerful message than merely budgeting money to allow an employee to attend some development program.

6. HEALTHIER INDIVIDUALS

Organizations are more effective when the individuals within them are psychologically robust. The most effective people possess high self-esteem and self-confidence. They are optimistic about the future. Rather than being filled with negative emotions, they approach issues from a positive point of view. When leaders invest in coaching, they greatly increase the probability that the individuals being coached will feel better about themselves and their performance.

7. RESILIENCE

Things seldom go exactly as planned. Problems arise. Potholes suddenly appear in the road. Nearly all leaders want their direct reports to recognize these challenges and meet them without the leader having to be there to micromanage them. It is especially important that employees not lose heart or conviction about the organization's mission or vision simply because a roadblock arises. Leaders would prefer not to be like the "plate spinners" who have to scurry about keeping every plate from wobbling and falling off the stick; instead, they would like people to create their own energy and have an inner ability not to be tipped over by challenges.

8. HEIGHTENED CREATIVITY

The coaching discussion is a perfect venue for the leader to convey the expectation and hope that each employee will approach issues with her own ideas and innovative approaches. The leader can convey that fresh thinking is not only welcomed but also expected. If coaching is a mutual exploration of better ways to approach challenging situations, rather than merely occasions when the boss gives direction or advice; then creativity may be enhanced.

9. INCREASED RISK TAKING AND EXPLORING

One of the strong criticisms of organizations today is that they are risk averse. People are afraid to try something new and different. People are stuck in ruts. Effective coaching consistently includes opportunities for the individual to explore new approaches, new work processes, and grand schemes for greatly improving the performance of the team. The leader/coach can not only encourage an employee to pursue such a project but also provide a safety net of support for that employee.

10. MINDSET OF AN OWNER VERSUS A HIRED HAND

Just as parents breathe huge sighs of relief when their children reach the stage where they start making wiser, well-thought-through decisions, so leaders wish their colleagues to develop along similar lines. Most leaders rejoice when a new colleague moves from requiring continual direction and hand-holding to the point where he takes the initiative to fix things and weighs the pros and cons before coming to a rational conclusion about the best course of action.

Many organizations that we work with state that they wish their employees took more initiative and were more innovative. Leaders long for their employees to be proactive and creatively take calculated risks to improve organizational performance. However, those same organizations and leaders rely on organizational systems to drive performance, and these organizational systems (performance

Coaching promotes greater reviews, merit increases, and bonus
ownership and commitment structures) often promote behav-
on the part of employees. iors that are not in alignment with
risk taking, innovation, and taking
initiative. Coaching promotes greater ownership and commitment
on the part of employees.

WHAT'S IN IT FOR YOU?

Clearly, the benefits of building a coaching culture and increasing
the effectiveness of coaching are great. There are both tangible
benefits (increased employee engagement and productivity) and
intangible benefits (improved culture and finding meaning and
purpose in work). While such gains are easy to describe from
an intellectual point of view, there is value in internalizing these
concepts and discovering the benefits through an inside-out
approach.

Here is the first of several worksheets that we will ask you to
complete, so that you can discover more through your own application. While it may be tempting to skip over this worksheet and
continue reading, if you do so you will short-circuit your own
learning, insights, and ability to apply these concepts and tools to
your own situation. So, please pause here and answer the following
questions, which invite you to consider the profound and personal
impact of coaching!

Personal Reflection

- Consider coaching you have received that had a positive impact on you, sent you on a different trajectory,
  provided you with confidence, encouraged you to try
  something new, or helped you solve your own problem.
  What difference has coaching made to you? What impact
  has coaching had at various times during your career?

Note: Many leaders struggle to think of coaching that they have received. If you fall into this category, you are not alone.

- What opportunities in your work history have you missed because you did not receive powerful coaching? *(Did you fail in a job in which you could have succeeded, had you received some coaching? Could the length of time it took you to reach full productivity have been significantly shortened?)*

- What impact do you hope to have on your direct reports, peers, and even senior leaders? What difference would you like to make with your colleagues?

Chapter Summary

1. You may be wondering what the difference is that coaching will truly make for you and your organization.

2. Coaching can provide meaning and significance to employees who may not have other avenues for feeling connected to a significant purpose.

3. Coaching has been shown to drive greater levels of engagement and commitment, which in turn leads to satisfied customers and productivity.

4. By actively coaching employees, leaders influence the culture they create and the bonds they form with employees. Coaching is a tangible expression of a leader's commitment to employees.

5. By providing coaching, leaders contribute to the health and resilience of their employees.

6. Employees' creativity and risk taking expand when they are encouraged to take ownership of their issues.

7. Coaching promotes greater ownership and commitment on the part of employees.

Chapter 2

Empty Cup, New Tea

Looking at Coaching in a New Way

A friend once made this profound statement, probably borrowed from a wise, ancient philosopher: "Empty cup, new tea." The friend was trying to convince a group of change-seeking participants that if they truly wanted "new tea" in their lives, they needed to "empty their cups" to make room for the changes. This is a simple but profound concept. And yet, how many of us try to take on something new—whether it is a behavior change, a new goal, a new relationship, or a bigger version of something that we already have in our lives—without asking ourselves the critical question, "What do I need to let go of to make room for this?"

"Empty cup, new tea" aptly applies to the notion of coaching and the concepts we will be discussing throughout this book. While many of the skills we will review in this book may not be entirely new to you, overall you will feel as though your cup is being filled with new tea. After all, the way we have combined the skills, tools, and concepts in this book will certainly differ from the way you have approached coaching in the past.

To make room for this new way of being and leading, you will need to identify what you are willing to pour out so that this new tea can fit into your cup.

WHAT NEEDS EMPTYING?

The list of things we suggest you jettison from your current mode of thinking include your problem-solving tendencies and those proven solutions that you have shared with others in the past. You may also ditch those ingrained habits for having conversations with your colleagues and employees.

If these statements seem slightly provocative, that is purely intentional. Perhaps now we have your attention. We are not suggesting that you can't refill your cup with some of these same things at a later point; we are just asking you to try different ways of utilizing these tools in your coaching conversations.

Unlearning some of the habits you've formed over many conversations and many years allows the new learning to take hold and primes you for a new way of approaching your leadership and coaching style. We acknowledge that unlearning old habits is much tougher than learning new ones.

Unlearning old habits is much tougher than learning new ones.

It is some of the hardest work we will ask you to undertake. Fortunately, the dividends are huge.

SO, WHAT GETS IN YOUR WAY? (DON'T CONFUSE HOW MUCH YOU KNOW WITH THE VALUE YOU ADD)

If you are like most leaders, you have been successful in your career, and you have gained experience from which others can benefit. Simply put, this is the problem. The very thing that has made you successful in your career to date—your hard-won experiences and lessons learned—can get in your way when you begin to coach your team members and peers. You know how to get the job done, and you are eager to share this wisdom with those around you.

In fact, you might even believe that this is what you are being paid for—to add value by giving advice and teaching your team members how to solve problems as well as you have solved them yourself. If you can provide your team members with good advice and useful suggestions, you will shortcut their learning curves, and they will get to a better solution more quickly than if they had to find the solution on their own. All of that sounds good in theory, until we really examine what we are trying to accomplish through coaching.

If we look at the very definition of coaching, it is really about growing and developing other people. In order to grow and develop, people need to think for themselves and make increasingly complex decisions in ever-changing environments. Through coaching, we want to help our direct reports, peers, partners, and bosses to solve problems on their own, with higher levels of sophistication, accuracy, and productivity. That's the ideal world.

In the real world, our very success can trip us up. We tend to give advice, and we hold an underlying belief that the way we can best add value (given our experience and wisdom and roles) is through helping others solve their problems. However, the very thing that we think will be helpful is often the very thing that shuts down our coaching conversations.

ADVICE DOESN'T WORK

Consider this: have you ever received advice from someone else that you have not taken? Chances are, you do not even need to think about this question before answering "yes." Now, think a bit harder and identify the last time someone gave you advice that you did not heed. Ask yourself, "Why didn't I take that advice?" Before reading further, take the time to identify why you didn't take the advice.

If you are like most people, your answers will include some of the following:

- I didn't respect/trust the person who was offering the advice.
- He didn't really understand my situation.

- She had her own agenda in mind.
- I had already tried what he suggested.
- What she suggested really wouldn't work in my situation.
- The advice was too simplistic; it didn't fully address the underlying issue.
- I had my own ideas, and I really wanted the other person to validate what I was thinking, not offer me something else to try.

We have asked hundreds of leaders how often they take the advice provided by others. From what we have seen anecdotally from these simple interviews, around three-quarters of the time advice typically isn't perceived as having value. And we can virtually guarantee that if it is not perceived as having value, the advice will not be taken.

For the reasons listed previously, people usually resist advice and seldom follow it. That does not mean that people never take advice—you can probably think of situations in which you have both given and received advice successfully. A friend may have given you a great suggestion to try, and you did. Or you offered a piece of advice to a colleague, and she took it and diligently implemented your idea. So, clearly, advice has its time and place—it just happens to be much later and more infrequently than you may currently be thinking. Most often the successes occur when one person has specifically asked for advice. We will talk about where and when your advice really can make a difference in the coaching conversation later (in Chapter 9, "Explore the Desired State"). For now, let's explore the muscle of advice-giving and how we have built our strength in this area.

Advice has its time and place—it just happens to be much later and more infrequently than you may be thinking.

SO WHY DO WE KEEP GIVING ADVICE?

Here are some of the many reasons for perpetuating our habit of giving advice.

Our Intentions Are Good

We hope that others judge us on our intentions, which underlie our behaviors. In reality, we can reasonably predict that others will *actually* judge us on our behaviors—what we say and do and, ultimately, how what we say and do make others feel. Our intentions cannot be seen or felt, and therefore, people will have to take the time to hunt for them if they get curious.

When we offer our advice, it is almost always with good intentions: we want to help others solve the problems they are facing. We can sense the frustration or tension that they (or we) are feeling, and we can identify the problem to be solved in their statements. So we jump in, not even noticing that when we offer advice, we have a greater probability of shutting down the conversation than of expanding it.

In fact, our efforts to be "helpful" actually work at cross-purposes to the focus of coaching: to grow and develop the coachee. When we are tempted to solve someone else's problem, we become a roadblock to that person's solving her own problem. Or, we frustrate the person and cause the conversation to shut down.

Here is a perfect example from Kathleen of how a simple suggestion can be frustrating:

> I travel all the time, often to multiple cities across multiple time zones in any given week. Invariably, I will call home and talk to my honeybunch, Dave, who will ask me how I am doing. Sometimes, if the week has been challenging and the travel pressures high, one of my responses is, "I'm tired." Invariably, he will suggest to me, "Why don't you take a nap at the airport?" (Beware of advice disguised as questions . . . they are often one and the same.)
>
> Here is what goes through my head when he says that: "Are you nuts? If I take a nap while I am waiting, I will *miss* my next plane. And oh, by the way, I don't fall asleep sitting up in airports. That would be impossible. That isn't going to help at all!" And sometimes, what goes through my head actually comes out of my mouth. And you can imagine what happens next: more advice. "Well, then take a nap on the plane."

Bottom line: I am *not* a napper. I never have been, and I never will be (or at least not in the foreseeable future). Dave is a superb napper. He loves napping (he calls it meditating). He can play a round of golf and plop into his chair for a power nap. He can get up early to take me to the airport, and reward himself with a nap. Therefore, when he hears that I am tired, he offers this solution—*his* solution—to me. And the conversation goes downhill from there. We have stopped trying to solve the problem of my being tired. We are both defending our ideas on why the other's ideas are not really workable.

We Are Pressed for Time

In our work coaching and training thousands of leaders, one of the most frequent complaints we hear from them is how time-starved they are. Regardless of their role or the industry in which they work, most leaders complain that while they recognize the value of coaching and developing employees, they have their own challenges in meeting deadlines and getting the work done. There also seems to be a common perception that "coaching takes too long." However, we believe that when it comes to coaching, you either "pay now or pay later."

When it comes to coaching, you either "pay now or pay later."

We also believe that coaching does not need to be formal, scheduled, and preplanned. In any moment, when an employee approaches his manager and asks, "What do you think we should do here?" a manager can turn that into a coaching dialogue by asking questions: "What do you think? What have you already thought about? Which one of those options do you like? What would be the pros and cons?" Now, we can guarantee that the manager most likely has an opinion and could have offered it. In fact, that is what the natural reflex probably is, given how most leaders have strengthened their "advice-giving muscles."

What if Dave had simply responded to my statement of "I am tired" with something like this: "That is completely understandable, given your travel schedule this week. Is that something you want to fix? What might be something you could do?" This simple response does three important things: (1) it acknowledges the state that I am in, (2) it checks to see if I even want to solve this "problem" (I might just be complaining), and (3) it puts the ball back in my court to fix.

Giving Fish Is Easy

Most readers have probably heard the adage "Give a man a fish, and you feed him for a day. Teach a man to fish, and you feed him for a lifetime." By offering advice, we are essentially offering our version of fish to our colleagues. By coaching instead, we will help grow the capacity of our colleagues, so that they can determine their own best actions to take.

If we can coach individuals to come up with their own solutions that they are committed to, this will ultimately be far more effective than a "better" solution we offer that they are less committed to. If we wanted to use a formula to demonstrate the difference suggested by this approach, we could measure the gain as follows:

Quality of solution $\times$ level of Commitment $=$ Benefit level

To make things easier, let's just say that the formula can be abbreviated to

Quality $\times$ Commitment $=$ Benefit

or

$$Q \times C = B$$

Scenario 1
In this scenario, we offer advice—a pretty good solution, but one that the employee is not totally committed to. Let's say that the quality of the solution is an 8 on a 1-to-10 scale, and the level of

commitment that the employee has toward implementing the solution is 4 on a 1-to-10 scale.

Given the formula $Q \times C = B$, we could realize a benefit of

$$8 \times 4 = 32$$

Scenario 2

In this scenario, we coach an employee to arrive at his own solution. Let's even say that given what we know and can predict, his solution is not as artful or sophisticated as our solution—it has some flaws or drawbacks to it. Therefore, let's say that the quality of the solution is only a 6 on a 1-to-10 scale. But, since the employee came up with the solution himself, he is far more committed to making it happen. Commitment climbs to an 8 on the 1-to-10 scale.

Now, applying our formula, we see that $Q \times C = B$ would give us

$$6 \times 8 = 48$$

The difference in the benefit (48 vs. 32) represents a 33 percent gain over the first scenario, even when we imagine that the solution would potentially be of lower quality. This, by the way, is probably a faulty assumption: the person closest to the issue is likely to be the one who can find the best solution. So, coaching could have even greater payoffs than this simple scenario depicted here.

With an eye toward teaching people how to fish, we will also pay attention to the long-term systems and patterns. We will talk more about this in Chapter 8, "Understand the Current State." While we can help someone fish her way out of a specific incident or challenge, we also want to make sure that she can fish in multiple scenarios.

Let's go back to the conversation about tiredness, traveling, and Dave. If he hears the complaint of "I am tired" every single time I am on the road, Dave might want to raise my awareness of the pattern of constantly being tired and complaining about it. A quick fix for one week of tiredness might not translate to fixing the underlying pattern or cause. A deeper or broader adjustment might be necessary.

WE CREATE OUR SYSTEMS, AND THEN THEY CREATE US

We live within systems. In fact, every relationship we have—whether it is with another individual or with a group of individuals—is a system. If we consider what happens in systems, we can see that most of them have a self-reinforcing dynamic. Most systems ultimately find an equilibrium in which each party develops a pattern of behavior that supports the other party in that system. Mary Beth O'Neill illustrates this system dynamic with two arrows, which naturally reinforce each other. Each arrow represents one side of the system, whether it is you and an employee, two partners, a child and a parent, or some other relationship.

Most systems ultimately find an equilibrium in which each party develops a pattern of behavior.

Parent-Child System

Let us look at the system dynamic using the parent-child system. A child who refuses to clean his room may find that if he waits long enough, his mother or father will pick up after him. Over time, both parties tacitly agree (perhaps without even being conscious of this agreement) that the parents will nag, the child will ignore the warnings, and the parents will ultimately do the work. When parents become frustrated because the child is not doing what the parents want, they rarely look at their own contribution to the equation (i.e., they ultimately step in and clean up the mess). Figure 2-1 is the two-arrow diagram showing the behavior that each side of the system engages in. The parent nags, and the child ignores the warning. Ultimately, the parents pick up the child's room.

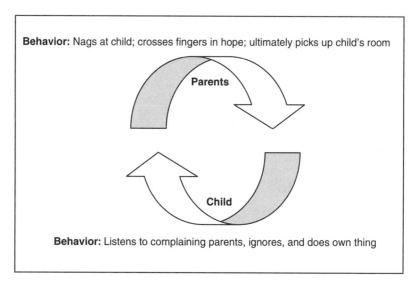

Behavior: Nags at child; crosses fingers in hope; ultimately picks up child's room

Parents

Child

Behavior: Listens to complaining parents, ignores, and does own thing

Figure 2-1 Parent-Child System

Manager-Employee System

Now, let us consider the same system paradigm as we look at the way many managers approach their employees. If the manager's behavior is to provide advice and solve her employees' problems, the systemic response from her employees is likely to include waiting to be told the right "answer" by the manager and/or going to the manager for advice on problems, as shown in Figure 2-2.

Because systems tend to be self-reinforcing, when employees come to us with their problems and we routinely solve those problems by offering our good advice, we will end up reinforcing this dependent system. Employees will expect managers to solve their problems and will also expect the managers to ultimately be responsible for their results (since it was the manager's advice that they followed). While this quick-fix approach will work in some situations, it typically does not help to grow and develop employees.

When we work with leaders, one of the questions we ask is, "What would you like your employees to be able to do?" Invariably, the answers come quickly and share common themes. Managers want their employees (and peers and bosses) to

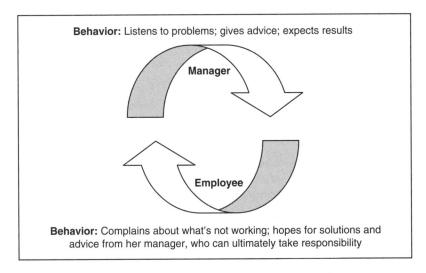

Figure 2-2 Manager-Employee System: Creating Dependence

- Solve their own problems.
- Think critically as they make decisions.
- Learn to make increasingly complex decisions, with higher stakes.
- Be productive.
- Be innovative.

When we compare this list to the way that employees in our system diagram might behave (complain about what is not working, hope for solutions and advice from the manager, who can ultimately take responsibility), we see that the two sets of behaviors seem almost incompatible. It is hard to imagine that a system that reinforces employees coming to their managers for advice would also encourage the same employees to solve their own problems and make critical decisions when the stakes are high.

Two Steps for Changing the System

The good news here is that if you can identify the system, you can change it. If you are able to identify the pattern of behavior that you and the other party have unknowingly established, you can begin to identify how to change the system. The simple process involves two steps:

1. Identify the change that you want to see on the *other* side of the system.
2. Identify the behaviors that *you* need to change to promote the new behaviors on the other side.

In our previous example, we have already done part of the work. You start by identifying the behavior that you want to see from the other side of the system. In this case, managers say that they want employees who are innovative and productive, and who use critical decision-making skills to solve their own problems.

Then, the second step involves asking the question, "What do *I* need to do to promote employees who are innovative and productive, and who use critical decision-making skills to solve their own problems?" Take time right now to really consider the answer to this question before reading further. How would you respond? How would you change the dynamic that has been established and reinforced by both parties?

Chances are, you have probably identified some of the following behaviors as part of a potential change in how you could approach the system:

- Ask questions to promote the employee's thought processes and decision-making skills.
- Ask the employee for her best thinking regarding how to proceed.
- Ask the employee what the advantages and disadvantages are to the solution he is considering.
- Define parameters for the types of decisions that need input and involvement from you and the types of decisions that the employee can make on his own.
- Encourage calculated risk taking.
- Be willing to support an innovative decision that might be "new" and untested.
- Be willing to endorse the employee's actions, even if you might have a "better" solution (remember the $Q \times C = B$ formula!).
- Reward employees for innovative behaviors—and results.

Figure 2-3 shows how this new dynamic might look instead.

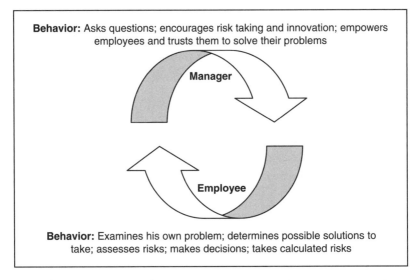

Figure 2-3 Manager-Employee System: Creating Empowerment and Growth

So What Happens When the System Changes?

Let's acknowledge that changing any behavior often requires a fair degree of effort, in addition to intention and commitment. This is true for you, and it will be true for your employees and others whom you coach. In fact, the process for making a behavior change is so well studied and documented that we will be spending a fair amount of time exploring this in Chapter 12: "Change Is the Yardstick."

For now, let's just say that if you begin to change the system you are in, you will probably experience some resistance from others in the system, even when the changes are clearly for the better. Why? Well, since systems tend to find an equilibrium that becomes self-reinforcing and fairly predictable, when you

If you begin to change the system you are in, you will probably experience some resistance from others.

make a change, you are in essence throwing the system out of its equilibrium. Do not be alarmed if you actually see *more* of the behavior that you are trying to change.

Any parent who has changed a technique with a child knows this pattern well. If the child is used to getting a strict admonition when she does something wrong, and the parent decides that silence is a better response, the child will often escalate the behavior to get the old, familiar reaction from the parent.

Managers who try to change their style of coaching with their employees often report back something like the following: "After a few minutes of my asking my employee questions, he finally said, 'Stop asking me questions! Just give me the answer. Tell me what to do.'"

Pouring out the tea may represent a challenge for either or both sides of the system. But it is helpful to remember how refreshing a new cup of tea might be.

Take a few minutes to complete the following worksheet, which will ask you to identify the system behaviors that you and your employees are demonstrating. You will then have a chance to determine the behaviors that might be required to shift the system dynamic that is currently in place. Try to complete this assessment as if you were a third-party observer, noticing each party's behaviors—yours and your employees'.

Reflection: Your Current Dynamic

Identify the patterns of behavior that you and your employees typically fall into. We have listed a small sample of potential behaviors and descriptions that you might adopt (see Figure 2-4); feel free to add your own to reflect your unique situation.

- ❏ Listening for the "problems" in what the other person is talking about
- ❏ Offering advice or suggestions (sometimes in the form of questions, too: "Have you thought about trying . . . ?")
- ❏ Telling them what I would do if I were in their shoes

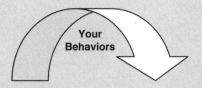

Figure 2-4 Your Current Behaviors

❑ Suggesting that they talk to someone else in the organization who can offer better advice

❑ Sharing my point of view regarding the pros and cons of the path being considered

❑ Avoiding employees who constantly complain about the same topics

❑ Being so busy and inaccessible that employees won't bring up issues unless they really need help from me

❑ Asking what support the individual is looking for regarding the problem at hand

❑ Asking what solutions the employee has already thought about trying

❑ Asking the individual for his assessment of the pros and cons of the path being considered

❑ Other: _____

Now, identify the behaviors or patterns you notice when you reflect on how your employees interact with you (see Figure 2-5). Select all that apply, or add your own.

❑ Complaining about problems that they are facing or "dumping" them in your lap to solve

❑ Asking you for advice or suggestions regarding how to resolve the issues at hand

❑ Presenting you with multiple possible solutions and asking you to choose the path that they should take

(Continued)

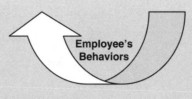

Figure 2-5 Current Employee Behaviors

❑ Avoiding talking to you or getting your opinion unless they absolutely have to
❑ Demonstrating a learned helplessness regarding the particular issue at hand
❑ Lacking the initiative to solve the problem directly or in a new manner
❑ Presenting the background of the situation, sharing their selected solution and rationale, and asking for confirmation or any different points of view
❑ Other: _____

While you may have selected many of the behaviors listed in the worksheet, it may be helpful to summarize the key dynamic that has been established between you and your employees. Would you describe the dynamic as "I order; they do" or "I give advice; they implement it" or "I empower; they take initiative"?

Now let us take the second step needed to change the dynamic. In the next worksheet, you will be asked to first identify the behaviors that you want to cultivate in your employees. Then, you will ask yourself which behaviors you need to demonstrate in order to promote the new change in the system.

Reflection: Desired Dynamic

What are the new behaviors that you want to foster in your employees (see Figure 2-6)? Check any that apply, and feel free to add additional behaviors.

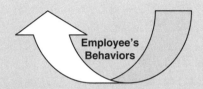

Figure 2-6 Desired Employee Behaviors

❑ Take more calculated risks
❑ Be more innovative in their approach to problem solving
❑ Take more initiative to determine the root causes of problems and address them
❑ Think more broadly and strategically; understand the impact on the business
❑ Provide the rationale and proposed solution to me when in doubt
❑ Think critically and make complex decisions, even when faced with ambiguity or incomplete information
❑ Other: _____

Now, what will you need to do differently to encourage your employees to act in the way you have just envisioned (see Figure 2-7)? Before you identify behaviors to demonstrate, respond to the next few questions, which ask you to reflect on your underlying beliefs and mental models regarding your role in coaching your employees.

1. What are your underlying beliefs about your employees—their potential, their contribution, and their interest in growing and developing themselves?

(Continued)

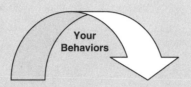

Figure 2-7 Your New Behaviors

2. How do you believe that you add value in your role in coaching your employees (and colleagues)? Are there other ways to add value that you have not tapped into yet?

3. What would you like your contribution to be? What role would you envision for yourself that would bring out the best version of yourself and your employees?

Given your responses, what behavior changes do you want to make to change the system you are in currently?

❑ Ask what support the individual is looking for regarding the problem at hand
❑ Ask what solutions the individual has already thought about trying
❑ Ask the individual for her assessment of the pros and cons of the path being considered
❑ Encourage risk taking and innovation
❑ Allow experimentation and solutions that might not have been your first preference
❑ Push the authority for larger decisions down to capable employees
❑ Reward and support positive improvements
❑ Other: _____

Good intentions do not necessarily align with good actions. Therefore, as we move through the various sections of the book, we will ask you to identify the steps you will take and the commitments you will make to become a better coach. We invite you to capture your next action steps in one document, so that you will have your own development plan in place when you finish reading this book. Based on the work you have just completed, as you have examined the system dynamics of your relationships, we would like you to capture the key learning takeaways and actions that you intend to take.

YOU THINK YOU ARE COACHING—DO *THEY?*

One of the interesting conclusions we have come to in our work and research is that managers believe that they coach far more often than their employees believe they do. One of our large telecom clients conducts annual employee opinion surveys to gather data regarding the performance of *Managers believe that they coach far more often than their employees believe they do.* managers and the overall organization. The company has described this phenomenon as reported by the employee opinion survey data:

- Managers believe that they are providing coaching to employees and score themselves high.
- Employees respond to the survey by stating that they receive little coaching from their leaders and score their leaders low on this element.

How can this be? What might explain this discrepancy in points of view?

If you apply these conclusions to yourself right here, chances are that you believe you are actively engaged in coaching your team members, and you wish that your manager would give you more valuable coaching, time, and attention.

When we work with groups of leaders and ask them how they currently coach employees and engage in coaching conversations, they usually list several activities and ways in which they provide coaching and development for their team members. We would like you to complete the same brief self-assessment in the worksheet provided here. Be honest with yourself: which activities do you engage in that support the growth and development of your employees? Check all of the boxes that apply, and add your own behaviors to the list if you do not see them here.

Ways I Coach My Employees Now

❑ Annual (or semiannual) formal performance review discussions
❑ Regularly scheduled one-on-one meetings
❑ Spot coaching: informal discussions related to issues that arise
❑ Providing performance feedback (positive and negative)
❑ Regular discussions regarding career development
❑ Regularly reviewing development goals and progress, and creating next steps
❑ Providing opportunities for skill expansions (stretch assignments, etc.)
❑ Being a "connector"—helping employees build networks with other useful people
❑ Supporting formal training and development efforts
❑ Other: _____

Chances are that you engage in some subset of these behaviors, taking more regular action on some of these items and giving less attention to others.

Now, we would like you to review the list you have checked and ask yourself whether the focus of each particular action is really on coaching your employees. A useful question to ask as the litmus test is, "Does this action grow my employees' capability or improve their performance?" Go ahead and do that now. Circle or place an extra check mark near the activities you engage in that truly grow your employees.

How You Compare to Others

Most managers we work with state that they have one-on-one meetings with their employees. When we ask what percentage of the time is spent on which types of discussions in these one-on-one meetings, most managers will conclude that approximately 85 to 90 percent of the time is consumed with project or task status updates. The employee updates the manager on where the project stands, the manager asks questions, and the employee shares the next steps or milestones on the horizon. If we pose the litmus test question, "Does this grow the employee's capability or improve his future performance?" we would probably have to honestly answer, "Not really." That leaves the remaining 10 to 15 percent of the time for the coaching part of the conversation.

Most managers also admit to holding performance review discussions but less frequently engaging in career development discussions. Few leaders have a system or process for regularly inquiring about and following up with development plans for their employees. In fact, many organizations we work with struggle with how to help employees build rich, robust, interesting development plans for themselves. It seems as though many folks—employees and leaders alike—go through the motions to comply with organizational system requirements but fail to really build development plans that will make a difference to the employee, or the organization, in the long run.

Most leaders provide feedback to employees, and almost all of the leaders we have worked with believe that they could do a better job here, and provide it more frequently.

So, if your answers align with what we see in general, you are in good company. Now the question to ask is whether you like the company you are keeping! If you are reading this book, you have probably already set a higher standard for yourself—wanting to improve your leadership effectiveness and the performance of those whom you are coaching. We believe you will be able to take some very practical, tangible actions and tools from this book that will make the difference to your coaching skills.

Make Your Coaching Visible

Now, assuming that many employees are not giving you the credit you might deserve for the time you are investing in coaching and developing them, the question to consider is whether there is value in making your coaching more visible to your employees. What would be the benefits to you, your team, and the organization if you truly created a coaching culture—one in which you expressly demonstrated coaching for the sake of growing and developing employees? What is the value of employees perceiving that you are investing in their growth and career potential?

While these may seem like rhetorical questions at the moment, we actually will share some of the interesting studies we have conducted that point to the real value of increasing our coaching effectiveness. You will read more about that in the next chapter. We will discuss how coaching actually builds relationships. We will also discuss the power of making your behavior changes visible, and how to do this, in Chapter 16, "Signaling the Lane Change."

Suffice it to say that most of us could make a powerful argument for the benefits of coaching. Investing in our employees by coaching them and expanding their capability will help us, them, and the organization.

WHAT WE BELIEVE: UNDERLYING TENETS OF OUR APPROACH TO COACHING

So, what are the key tenets that underlie our approach to coaching? Here are a few beliefs that form a framework for how we view coaching. In the chapters to come, we will explore how to make the application of these concepts tangible and practical.

1. People change when they feel the need to do so. Most of us will not change because someone else wants us to, unless the consequences of *not* changing are significant and important to us. When others request us to make changes that we do not genuinely want to make, any behavior change is likely to be either temporary or carried out as a result of a sense of compliance, not commitment.

2. Making major changes in our behaviors is not easy; in fact, change typically requires a great deal of effort. However, when people are committed to the change they want to make, it is absolutely possible. In fact, committing to the change is half the battle, and we usually have to weigh the pros and cons and see a clear balance in our favor before we will act.

3. It is critical to get the coachee involved in the conversation and the process. We cannot assume that what we want and desire will ever be what those we are coaching want and desire. Our best advice will seldom be as useful as their good ideas, as they will be executed with a higher level of conviction and commitment.

4. Since our coachees are closer to the issue, they are in the best position to determine what the solution might be. Evocation is better than education—if we can draw the solution out of our coachees, the results are far greater than if we assume the "teaching" and advice-giving role.

> *Evocation is better than education—if we can draw the solution out of our coachees, the results are far greater.*

5. You still get to have a point of view. Especially as a manager coaching your direct reports, you will have a point of view and want to bring it into the conversation. We are not asking you to stay silent while your coachee struggles or turns to you for guidance. However, we will explore why the right time to offer your insights is nearly always after the coachee's turn.

6. As a rule, collaboration and partnering are more effective than confrontation. However, when you have earned the right to do so (based on a trust-based relationship), challenging is an important part of the conversation.

Chapter Summary

- We need to empty our cups—our traditional ways of thinking about and having coaching conversations—to make room for new tea.

- We will want to expose and unlearn some of our habitual reactions and patterns of behaving with those we coach.
- What makes all of this difficult is that we have a lot to offer, and giving advice seems efficient, even though it isn't in the end.
- If we are truly trying to grow and expand the capability of our coachees, we must teach them how to fish.
- $Q \times C = B$. The quality of the idea, multiplied by the commitment to the idea, will ultimately produce the overall benefit.
- We live in systems; and most systems are self-reinforcing—until they stop working or we change them. Are you reinforcing a system that promotes dependence, or are you reinforcing a system that promotes expansive thinking, critical decision making, and empowerment?
- Making your coaching visible has its own payoffs—make sure that your employees see that you are making time for coaching and developing them. The rewards are immense.

Chapter 3

Pay Now or Pay Later

The Impact of Coaching

COACHING AND BUSINESS OUTCOMES

As promised in Chapter 1, this chapter begins with some research showing the impact of coaching on a variety of business outcomes. Figures 3-1 through 3-5 display the correlation between various levels of leaders' coaching effectiveness, as measured by a 360-degree feedback instrument that measures coaching competencies, and a variety of other outcomes.

Figure 3-1 compares varying levels of employee commitment with coaching effectiveness. What leader wouldn't want gung-ho, turned-on employees? Everything goes better when the organization is populated with such people.

As you ponder this and the following charts, one question that may arise is, "So are you saying that better coaching causes employees to be more committed and engaged?" The answer to that question could be, "No, the fact that things are correlated does not prove that one causes the other. It only proves that there is some strong connection between them. It may be that A doesn't cause B, but instead B causes A. Or it may be that something else that they share in common causes both."

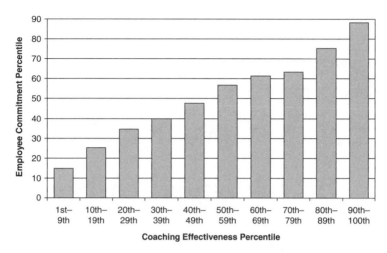

Figure 3-1 Coaching Effectiveness vs. Employee Engagement and Commitment

Employees whose managers are more effective at coaching express more satisfaction and commitment.

It is possible that highly engaged employees may be more receptive to coaching. Some may even specifically ask for coaching from their managers. Much of science, however, is based on discovering things that go together. We believe that there is good evidence to support the fact that effective coaching produces positive organizational outcomes.

One way of measuring commitment is by the level of effort put forth by the individual. Figures 3-2 and 3-3 are complementary. Figure 3-2 shows the correlation between leaders' coaching effectiveness and their employees' overall effort, while Figure 3-3 shows the relationship between coaching effectiveness and employees' expression of satisfaction with their level of involvement in the organization.

REDUCING TURNOVER

Organizations invest heavily in recruiting and training employees. Retaining talent is a central focus of most organizations, and it is common for organizations to have good measures of retention and employee turnover. But such measures are always after the

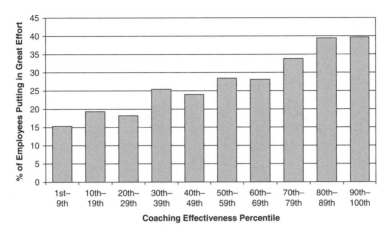

Figure 3-2 Coaching Effectiveness vs. Effort

Employees indicated the extent to which the company "inspires one to put forth a great deal of effort every day."

fact—turnover is measured only in hindsight. However, there is one measure that has been shown to be an excellent predictor of turnover. Ask employees about the extent to which they are thinking about quitting and going to another organization, and you will have an indication of how likely it is that those employees will quit. As a rough measure, in normal times, approximately one-half of

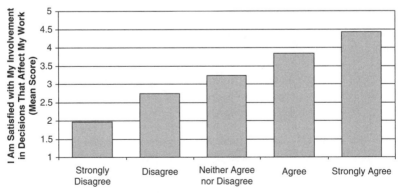

Figure 3-3 Coaching Received vs. Satisfaction with Involvement

Employees who receive coaching and feedback are more satisfied with their involvement.

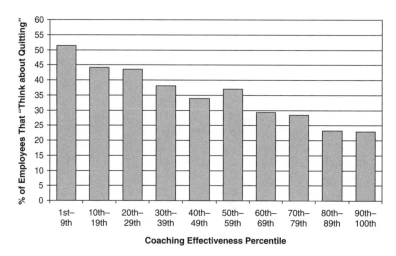

Figure 3-4 Coaching Effectiveness vs. Intention to Stay

Employees indicated the extent to which they "think about quitting" their current job.

the people who tell you that they are thinking about quitting will actually terminate within the next 12 to 18 months.

If the organization is seeking ways to minimize that talent erosion, the data in Figure 3-4 should be of interest. Note that more than half of the employees reporting to those people who are the least effective coaches are thinking about quitting. In contrast, less than one-fourth of those reporting to the best coaches were harboring those same thoughts of leaving.

In a word, improve coaching, and there is a strong likelihood that you will reduce turnover.

As Figure 3-5 shows, respondents' overall assessment of their supervisor appears to be strongly influenced by the degree to which they received coaching and feedback from that person. In a word, if you do not coach, then you are not doing a good job!

WHAT GETS IN THE WAY OF COACHING?

Many varied obstacles seem to get in the way of a leader's coaching. First, we would like to examine the things that leaders identify as the roadblocks to coaching. Then we would like to reflect on what

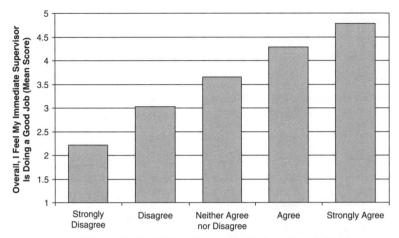

Figure 3-5 Coaching Received vs. Supervisor Performance

Employees who receive coaching and feedback rate their supervisors much more positively.

we sense are other subconscious, powerful barriers to coaching. We are inclined to believe that the latter are more likely the real roadblocks, whereas the statements that leaders make fall more squarely into the realm of excuses.

What Managers Say

Here are some of the factors that leaders claim get in the way of their ability to coach.

Time

When asked what gets in the way of coaching employees, managers invariably mention the pressure of time. The reality is that managers are working long hours. Their ranks have been thinned. They are stretched. Their schedules are packed. We are reminded, however, of the two men who are mopping up water from a floor. After working feverishly for hours, one of them finally says, "Let's stop mopping and go find what is leaking water."

Managers spend a good deal of time mopping up problems. Coaching is a way to turn off the spigot. It takes only a short leap of faith to say, "I'll take time to develop and coach my people because in the long run it will pay off more than virtually anything else I can do."

We think this is the classic example of "pay now or pay later." You can forgo changing the oil in your a car, rotating the tires, or doing other maintenance and save some time and money, but you know that in the long run, it will cost you more.

Furthermore, many leaders have the misconception that every coaching discussion has to be 50 minutes long. It need not be that way. Some topics may need only 15 or 20 minutes, and therefore they do not require as large an investment of time as some leaders fear. Time is something that everyone has been given in the exact same amount. We all simply elect to use it differently.

My Boss Doesn't Coach Me

There may be several messages embedded in this excuse. One could be, "I don't have to do it if my boss doesn't." Another could be, "I don't have any good role models." Indeed, it goes without saying that to some degree, we all mimic those in leadership roles in the organization. If we aren't getting coaching, we have a strong tendency to mirror and mimic that behavior. Our research indicates that the higher you go in an organization, the less frequently any real coaching occurs. Most boards of directors fail to coach their CEOs, and a good number have no formal performance review process.

My Employees Don't Need It

Some managers note that they have high-performing, mature employees who are self-sufficient. These people simply don't need coaching. Our observation is that the high-performing employees are often the people who gain the most from coaching. We never (and, yes, that is a sweeping word) hear people say that they don't want coaching from a boss whom they respect. On the contrary, an enormously high percentage express the desire to receive far more coaching than they do.

The Real Reasons (We Think)

Our belief is that there are several *real* reasons why leaders don't coach. We don't dismiss their avowed reasons entirely, but we suspect that the truth goes deeper.

Here are the things that we think truly get in the way.

Avoiding Potentially Uncomfortable Discussions

Part of human nature is to avoid things that are not pleasant. There is also some part of us that avoids having discussions that are unpredictable and thus might *become* unpleasant. While much of coaching should focus on the positive elements of a person's work and his future, there is often necessarily a dimension of talking about issues that are a bit awkward. This may be because the individual is prickly and contentious or, at the opposite end of the spectrum, sensitive and easily moved to tears.

Insecure about the True Value of One's Own Coaching

Some managers are not sure that they have sufficient wisdom, experience, or technical knowledge to be of great value to their subordinates. Our experience is that most leaders greatly underestimate the value of their own experience and perspective. Usually they have a broader and deeper understanding of the company culture that by itself is worth passing on. Conversely, as you will learn repeatedly in this writing, coaching is not about providing advice. It most often is an opportunity for a leader to unleash the potential of her employees.

Misunderstanding the True Nature of Good Coaching

Much of the discomfort with coaching stems from a serious misconception of what ideally should happen. They simply do not know how to conduct an effective coaching conversation. Many leaders associate the concept of coaching with the version they got from their high school athletics coaches. Most leaders think of it in terms of its being purely advice giving. We recognize that one of the big challenges we face in this book is somehow finding a way to help the reader leave behind some old conceptions of coaching, along with giving up some "telling and advice-giving" behavior that leaders feel is expected of them or is the correct behavior to be using.

Direct Reports Seldom Ask for It

Another reason is that leaders are fearful that employees will think that placing themselves in the position of "coach," which we have traditionally associated with someone who is older, more knowledgeable, more experienced, and possessing greater technical competence, is a mark of great conceit. It is infinitely easier to coach someone when she asks for it than when the coach has to initiate it. There are many ways in which the person to be coached could take a stronger role in initiating the discussion, and there is no question that this would help to make the coaching process flow more easily.

Personal Reflection: The Impact of Coaching

Take a moment to move the ideas in this chapter from the abstract into the concrete. Think of the members of your own team. Analyze the impact that coaching would have on them personally and on the team overall. Here are some questions to help you do that:

1. Identify your top performers and their contributions to the organization.

2. What would be the impact of losing these high performers?

3. As you consider these high performers and the potential impact of their loss, what is your assumption? Are they more likely to leave than some of the average or lower performers? (For what it is worth, our sense is that the best swimmers jump ship first.)

4. As you consider the research on the impact of coaching, how might your group be affected if you were perceived as a much more effective coach? What business effects would that have?

5. After reviewing the list of reasons why leaders do not coach more frequently, which, if any, do you think apply to you?

6. How might you overcome the barrier(s) that tend(s) to hold you back?

Chapter Summary

- Coaching effectiveness can be directly correlated with meaningful outcomes, including employee commitment, willingness to put in greater effort, satisfaction with involvement in work decisions, intention to stay (versus quit), and overall supervisor performance.

- Managers often cite reasons for not coaching. Common ones include "time" and "my boss does not coach me."
- We suspect that the real reasons for not coaching may be related to a manager's misconceptions of what coaching is, wanting to avoid tough conversations, or not having a clear game plan for coaching conversations.
- The impact of coaching is significant and can be measured. Coaching is not just something that is "nice to do"—it is a business imperative for managers.

Chapter 4

What Business Coaching Is and Isn't

Say the word *coaching* and an image immediately comes to mind. For some, the image is that of a wise sage offering profound insight about some weighty matter. For others, the term conjures up images of someone answering questions based on lots of experience, like the columnist in the newspaper who dispenses advice about the thorniest family problems. For still others, the word *coaching* triggers images of a person who is able to help others see things about themselves that they had not realized, like the NBA coach who watches his superstar from the sidelines and points out specific actions that the star should take in order to win the game. There are, of course, countless other images and variations of the ones we have just described.

Unfortunately, all of these images are largely incorrect when it comes to business coaching. As a matter of fact, they actually run counter to what we believe high-quality business coaches actually do. On occasion, a skilled business coach does give advice or offer suggestions; however, this is not the main thrust of what such a coach does. The best business coaches also act as a valuable mirror for their direct reports and help them to better assess what they are doing and how they are doing it. There is a time and a place when offering advice and making suggestions is appropriate, but it is not the main feature of good coaching.

COACHING DEFINED

Here is our definition of coaching: *"Interactions that help the individual being coached to expand awareness, discover superior solutions, and make and implement better decisions."*

Coaching allows the individual who is being coached—the coachee—to grow as a result of the process. While a coachee may grow after hearing a manager's advice and receiving direction, we believe that when a coachee comes to see her situation differently and discovers her own solution(s), she learns more in the process. She experiences a different level of commitment to the solution and the outcome, and she probably feels better about herself. Coaching helps individuals discover answers within themselves and helps them feel more personally empowered. The coach is also dedicated to helping to ensure the implementation and long-term follow-through of planned actions.

When a coachee comes to see her situation differently and discovers her own solution(s), she learns more in the process.

Mindset and Skill Set

We believe that coaching represents both a *mindset* and a *skill set*. The mindset comes into play for leaders who have a choice in how they guide conversations with employees. Leaders can either direct their employees' actions—in a fairly autocratic mode—or instead coach their employees to discover the best actions to take to move forward. A manager's mindset might be, "I can get more done by controlling and directing," whereas a coach's mindset might be, "I can get more done by growing my employees and gaining their commitment."

The mindset must precede the skill set. Unless a leader consciously chooses to coach—and chooses "growth" as a worthy objective of the coaching process and conversations—he will be less likely to fully employ the array of skills that support coaching.

What are those skills? The following list represents a good start on the list of behaviors that a leader may utilize through a coaching process:

- Clarify the outcome for the coaching interaction, and agree to the goal of the conversation or the overall process
- Listen deeply to what is said (and what is not said)
- Ask nonleading questions that expand the coachee's awareness
- Generate multiple alternatives or paths forward
- Explore the consequences of actions or decisions
- Elicit and describe a desired future state
- Negotiate performance goals and expectations
- Recognize potential and possibility
- Inspire others to stretch for goals beyond what they think is possible
- Solve problems collaboratively
- Provide ongoing support and encouragement
- Follow up to measure progress and continue the change process
- Hold the coachee accountable for agreed-upon commitments

While this list is not exhaustive, many leaders will notice one or two behaviors that they do not routinely use or even consider when coaching employees. In Chapter 6, "FUEL: A Framework, Not a Cage," you will have an opportunity to complete a brief self-assessment on how well you currently perform some of these behaviors.

Focus to Improve Current Performance and Future Capability

Finally, we believe that leaders utilize coaching most frequently *to improve performance and improve the future capability of others.* Note the two-pronged emphasis of coaching. It is about improving performance, but it does not stop there. It is also about the future. It is about the things that people do that fit with the culture and will help their long-term career progress or that may be getting in their way. Business coaching splits its emphasis between making things better today and helping the people being coached to prepare for larger roles and responsibilities years down the road.

Coaching Is a Change Agenda

The very nature of a coaching process, conversation, or relationship is that it is focused on change—growth and improvement. As

The very nature of a coaching process, conversation, or relationship is that it is focused on change—growth and improvement.

a result, coaching is an agenda for change. Coaching conversations should move the coachee forward, whether in thought or in action, in relation to the coaching issue(s) being discussed. Because coaching contains an agenda for change, coaching conversations are different from the conversations that many of us have with our friends or associates, where the focus is often on chatting or complaining.

WHAT COACHING IS NOT

We see coaching as being quite different from *mentoring*, where the mentor is usually a more senior person who is attempting to guide the "mentee" within the organization and convey wisdom that could well be lost in the next few years. The mentee may seek out a mentor based on the mentor's wisdom or experience, as the mentor has often already traveled the path that the mentee is seeking to travel. There is often a perceived hierarchy of power or information between the mentor and the mentee, with the mentor being older and wiser. By contrast, coaching may occur between a manager and his direct reports (in both directions) and also between peers. A coach does not necessarily need to have lived the experience of the coachee to be effective in helping to guide the coachee to a better solution.

It is also common for people to mistake coaching for *teaching*. The difference is that the teacher, by definition, possesses knowledge and information that the student lacks. The primary activity is the transmission of that information. The relationship between the teacher and the student is usually temporary and narrow, whereas the coaching relationship is longer-lasting and broad. While coaching may contain elements of teaching, it is far broader than merely conveying information.

Coaching also gets confused with *counseling*, and there are two probable reasons for that. First, coaching can focus on helping the individual to deal with difficult issues, which may remind people of the focus of counseling. Second, counseling often focuses on helping someone to change or reshape her behavior, and this can also be an objective of a good coaching discussion. So what is the difference? Counseling more commonly involves people who are experiencing some dysfunctional behavior or internal turmoil. It is often focused on healing past wounds and looking for the origins of dysfunctional behavior. Coaching, by contrast, is designed to include virtually everyone. Coaching takes a future focus, aiming to create a desired state and a series of actions to help achieve the desired state. It is less focused on the past and far more focused on moving forward into the future.

Are the lines between these various activities perfectly clear? Absolutely not! But the differences are sufficiently large that it seems wise not to unduly confuse them.

Differing Perceptions and Expectations

In our work, we have the occasion to interview and interact with large numbers of managers. Although it happens less frequently, we also have the opportunity to interview and interact with front-line workers who report to these managers. The differences in their perceptions of the same events could not be more dramatically different.

Managers will very often describe the regular one-on-one meetings they have with employees as coaching discussions. The employees, on the other hand, report that 90 percent of the time they spend with the manager focuses on project status updates and virtually never describe that event as coaching. We sense that several things will be required if employees are to consider such meetings as "coaching" discussions:

- Cover more than the current status of the projects in question.
- Include some discussion of the employee's career progress or ambitions.
- Be more formal and label the conversation as a "coaching" discussion.

- Let the employee have significant input in setting the agenda for these discussions.

In our interviews with the front-line workers, they would prefer to have 50 percent of the time spent on project updates and specific performance issues, and the other half spent on issues involving their growth and career development.

COACHING AS A MANAGEMENT STYLE

Coaching seems like a new idea to many managers. One reason for that could well be that societal values have changed dramatically and our leadership practices have been scrambling to catch up. Specifically, we are thinking of the dramatic shift in child-rearing practices. It seems that modern parents spend endless hours negotiating with their children, whereas their own parents and certainly their grandparents would have been highly directive. The Internet has democratized information so that everyone has access to all but the most guarded, classified information. Globalization has made diversity of backgrounds and styles a welcome practice and a business necessity.

Management practices have evolved to a small degree, but they have not kept pace with what has happened in society. Remarkably little has changed when it comes to the basics of management. If a middle manager in a firm had consumed some magic potion and fallen asleep 50 years ago and suddenly awakened (much like Rip van Winkle), there is a good chance that he could fit right into the management structure today if his company still existed. Let us paint a somewhat gloomy picture of what such a manager would find. Admittedly, this describes the less progressive organizations of today; unfortunately, however, many of these still exist. The multilayered company hierarchy would remain alive and kicking. Well-educated and very smart employees would still be taking orders from bosses who were frequently less up to speed on the technology than their direct reports. Important decisions would still be made by the senior executives, with only minor input from those below them. In meetings, people would continue to look to the most senior person in the room, who would do most of the talking, especially in the first half of the meeting. Direct reports might write down things that the leader says, but they would then go back to their offices and do little to implement those ideas, waiting to see if that direction would be sustained. The strategy of the organization would be determined by a handful of executives at the top, with minimal input from others in the organization. Competition between departments would often detract from the overall effectiveness of the organization.

At the same time, most of the other things surrounding this person would be dazzlingly new and almost impossible to comprehend. Typewriters would be gone, replaced by desktop computers, with which most professionals would create all their own correspondence. Secretaries would have vanished, replaced by executive assistants supporting a small number of very senior leaders. A large percentage of the total workforce would not have an office but instead would operate from their homes. Filing hard copies of papers would be a relatively rare occurrence. Most documents would be accessed digitally. Mail would have been largely replaced by digital messages transmitted over the Internet.

This newly awakened manager would hear people talk of the fax machine as almost a thing of the past, but he would not know what they were talking about because the fax machine didn't exist when he began his long nap. Depending on what the firm specialized in, he would see huge changes in manufacturing and the R&D (research and development) function. Globalization would have ensured that a large percentage of the firm's business was conducted overseas. Supply-chain management would all be new. The IT function would be entirely new. But, we repeat, in many of the basic management practices of the firm, it would be as if time had stood still and little had evolved.

Building upon a continuum of leadership approaches originally articulated by Robert Tannenbaum and Warren Schmidt,[1] Figure 4-1 shows a spectrum of leadership styles that leaders and coaches may adopt.

Most leaders tend to gravitate to an area on the continuum, usually without much thought or intention. They do not consciously choose their leadership style; instead, their leadership style is defined over time and by patterns of action. Interestingly, Tannenbaum

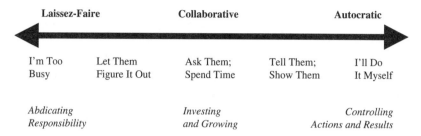

Figure 4-1 Continuum of Leadership Approaches

Work environments that seemed to function best were those in which there was the most felt and expressed control and influence. and Schmidt first articulated the various approaches to leadership (laissez-faire, collaborative, and autocratic) in 1958 and expanded on their original writings in 1973. Tannenbaum and Schmidt noted that the work environments that seemed to function best were those in which there was the most felt and expressed control and influence. We have added to their work by presenting the continuum in Figure 4-1 and adding descriptive elements.

Laissez-Faire Leadership: Who Is Driving the Bus?

What does laissez-faire leadership look like? This would be the leader who is "hands off" or even absent. Sometimes the laissez-faire leader has good intentions; many leaders adopt this style of leadership with their highest-performing employees, believing that the high performers do not need "managing."

If you ask who has control and influence in a laissez-faire system, it would seem on the surface that the employees must have them, since the leader seems to be abdicating them. However, if you ask these same employees how much control or influence they feel they have, they will quickly say things like:

- "I'm not sure how I am performing; there is little or no feedback."
- "There is no clear sense of direction, so I hope that I have been working on the right things."
- "I feel like I am drifting along, but no one is really paying attention."

Over time, it seems that employees who are given great latitude (or who are simply ignored) feel untethered and ungrounded. While there seems to be a move toward laissez-faire leadership for some high-potential employees and also for highly technical personnel, some of the recipients interpret this style as "benign neglect."

If this is your approach with high performers, or even your overall leadership style, we would challenge you to consider moving toward the middle of the continuum. Your highest performers are often the employees who are most interested in growth and development; treating them with a hands-off approach is a risky strategy indeed.

Autocratic Leadership: "My Way or the Highway"

What does autocratic leadership look like? It includes the highly directive leader who issues orders and commands and the leader whose guidance seems to suggest "my way or the highway." Who has influence and control in an autocratic system? The leader. Employees feel that they have very little of it, if they have any at all. Over time, this type of leadership system seems to promote compliance rather than commitment on the part of employees. Employees stop bringing forth their good ideas and new ways of thinking about things, as they know that their ideas will be shunned or overlooked.

In virtually every dimension of Western life outside of business, there has been a remarkable shift from autocratic relationships to much more collaborative interactions. This is true of marriages, parenting, education, and even our local political processes. Still, some business leaders have retained the autocratic style. Why? We will offer some possible reasons later in this chapter. But first, some have argued that the collaborative position is the one that requires the greatest effort and the healthiest egos.

Collaborative Leadership

What does collaborative leadership look like, and why does it work? You can probably conjure up the image of a leader working alongside her employees, genuinely focused on solving problems together. Leaders and employees partner, with no threats of power or need to use hierarchy to influence decisions. Leaders are willing to listen and be influenced, and employees, in turn, are more likely to contribute and feel a sense of ownership. Who has control and influence in a collaborative system? Both leaders and employees feel that their contributions matter and that they can influence both the processes and the end results. That is why the collaborative system works so well: both leaders and employees are invested in the process and the outcomes.

Coaching is the leadership practice that makes the collaborative leadership style work. As Gary Hamel has repeatedly argued, the underlying philosophy and leadership practices that are in vogue today were established in the early decades of the twentieth century, when the objective was to get semiskilled individuals to perform tasks repeatedly with ever-greater

> *Organizations need to become more inspiring and more human in order to meet the needs of the people who inhabit them today.*

efficiency. Organizations need to become more inspiring and more human in order to meet the needs of the people who inhabit them today. Hamel argues that the solution is for us to embrace less hierarchical structures and less mechanical procedures.

When a group of distinguished business leaders and social scientists met to contemplate how management could accelerate innovation, they came up with 25 recommendations. Among these were such things as

- Reduce fear and increase trust.
- Redefine the work of leadership away from being heroic decision makers to being architects of innovation and collaboration.
- Share the work of setting direction.
- Humanize the language and practice of business.

Why Do Elements of Autocracy Live On?

This is a very interesting question. The most plausible answer is that we have not developed a broad consensus among business leaders and the academic world about the new processes that should replace the old-style management. It is also possible that there are some elements of autocratic management that are hard-wired in the human brain. They are there to deal with emergencies, when the stakes are terribly high and time is extremely short.

Experiments in social psychology have clearly shown that when one person is given authority and control over someone else, it often brings out an extremely dark side. The highly respected Stanford psychologist Philip Zimbardo talks of the "Lucifer effect." It was Zimbardo who decades earlier had conducted an experiment in which college students were randomly assigned to be either jailers or prisoners. The experiment was ostensibly intended to analyze the emotional reaction of the prisoners, but it was really focused on the jailers' behavior. The student jailers became so vicious and abusive to the prisoners that the experiment was aborted after only one-third of the planned time had elapsed.[2]

What organizations clearly need today are leaders who don't succumb to getting caught up in their own authority, and we appear to be making some progress. Many people perceive the military as the last official bastion of autocracy, but nothing is further from the truth. Leadership styles in the military are probably at least as open and collaborative as those found in many private-sector companies, if not more so.

Michael Abrashoff, a former commander of the USS *Benfold* in the U.S. Navy, speaks eloquently of this as he reflects on his life after leaving the Navy:

> My organizing principle was simple: The key to being a successful skipper is to see the ship through the eyes of the crew. Only then can you find out what's really wrong and, in so doing, help the sailors empower themselves to fix it. . . . Moreover, subordinates may sidestep responsibility by reasoning that their managers are paid to take the rap.
>
> I began with the idea that there is always a better way to do things, and that, contrary to tradition, the crew's insights

might be more profound than even the captain's. . . . I asked everyone, "Is there a better way to do what you do?" Time after time, the answer was yes, and many of the answers were revelations to me.

My second assumption was that the secret to lasting change is to implement processes that people will enjoy carrying out. To that end, I focused my leadership efforts on encouraging people not only to find better ways to do their jobs but also to have fun as they did them.

I realized that no one, including me, is capable of making every decision. I would have to train my people to think and make judgments on their own. Even if the decisions were wrong, I would stand by my crew. Hopefully, they would learn from their mistakes. By trading pageantry for performance, we created learning experiences at every turn. We made sure that every sailor had time and was motivated to master his or her job; getting by wasn't good enough.

As a result, we had a promotion rate that was over the top . . . the new environment aboard Benfold created a company of collaborators who were flourishing in a spirit of relaxed discipline, creativity, humor, and pride.

What Makes the Middle of the Continuum So Difficult?

A great many leaders have never seen someone who operated from the middle of the continuum. Their bosses have most often been at one end or the other (although usually at the more autocratic end of the scale). In addition, the lion's share of leaders think that autocratic behavior is expected of them by those above them, those alongside them, and those reporting to them. Why else would they be receiving significantly higher salaries and enjoy so many other perks of office?

The more autocratic behavior displayed by the leader is often deeply ingrained in the organization. Policies and procedures reinforce it. The leader's signature is required to make purchases of a certain size or to contractually obligate the organization. With that power comes a feeling of commensurate privilege and entitlement. In a nutshell, it has been this way for a long, long time.

Because many leaders have never seen someone practice a middle-of-the-scale style of leadership, it feels like a very unnatural act. Asking direct reports for their ideas and taking those ideas seriously seems unnatural unless you've actually *been* one of the people who was asked. Trusting others in such a way comes naturally if you happen to be one of the few who has reported to such a leader.

Finally, it can be difficult to operate from the midpoint all the time. There are occasions when giving directives simply works better. There are other times when it is in everyone's best interest for the leader not to make the decision, perhaps because she does not possess the needed information. So a high degree of behavioral flexibility is required in order to lead in an optimum manner.

Personal Reflection: Your Leadership Approach

Consider the leadership continuum, shown again here.

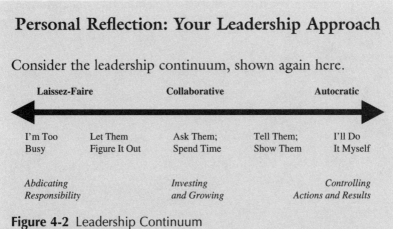

Figure 4-2 Leadership Continuum

1. Where would you place yourself on this continuum, in terms of your overall leadership approach? Please make a mark on the continuum in Figure 4-2 that represents your most habitual style of leading.

(Continued)

2. Now, ask yourself, from your employees' point of view, where would they place you on the continuum? Or would different employees place you in different spots along the continuum?

3. What do you notice about any differences? How do you feel about your selections?

4. What is your mindset for coaching? What benefits could you achieve by adopting a collaborative approach more often?

What would be the impact on

• You?

• Your employees?

• Your team?

• The business results you achieve?

Chapter Summary

- Coaching allows the individual who is being coached—the coachee—to grow as a result of the process.
- Both a mindset and a skill set are required if leaders are to coach well.
- Coaching focuses on both improving performance and growing the future capability of others.
- Coaching is an agenda for change; therefore, coaching conversations should lean toward action.
- While coaching shares some skills with other helping practices (teaching, mentoring, and counseling), the focus of coaching is distinct and looks toward the future.
- Management styles have not changed significantly over the years; we can still find managers who lead with an autocratic style.
- The most effective leadership style is the collaborative approach, which allows both employees and managers to influence and control decisions in the workplace.
- A high degree of behavioral flexibility is required in order to lead in an optimum manner.
- While there may be occasions when it is appropriate to be more autocratic or laissez-faire, the collaborative style tends to work the best.

Chapter 5

Does Your Coaching Rest on a Crumbling Foundation?

An instructive bit of research was conducted by the coaching firm CO_2 Partners. The question it posed to a large sample of people working in large organizations was, "Whom do you turn to for advice on problems at work?" The answers were

- *24 percent:* A peer in your organization
- *15 percent:* Another senior person at your job
- *14 percent:* A friend outside the workplace
- *13 percent:* Your mentor or coach
- *11 percent:* Your supervisor
- *7 percent:* Your spouse or partner
- *4 percent:* No one

Although this book is focused on helping managers to be more effective coaches with their direct reports, this process works only to the degree that the employee wants to talk with his manager. The data presented here show that only slightly more than 1 out of 10 people would turn first to their immediate supervisor if they had a problem. The rest go somewhere else.

If organizations are to succeed in building a coaching culture that centers around the manager-employee relationship, then this statistic is obviously a cause for concern. The research made no attempt to answer the "why not" question. We could speculate and probably come close to correctly hitting upon why this occurs. Some answers could include statements like

- I don't want to seem weak or unsure of myself in my manager's eyes.
- My manager probably won't know the answer.
- My manager will tell me which direction to take, and I don't want to be stuck with that directive.
- My manager isn't all that approachable on such matters.
- My manager always seems really busy, and she probably wouldn't take the time to help me.
- I need someone to discuss my problem with, not someone who will listen for two minutes and then tell me what to do without really understanding the issue.

Please add any of your additional guesses to this list. Whatever the reasons, though, something in the relationship between these employees and their managers stood in the way of the employee's going to her manager to discuss a problem.

SUCCESSFUL COACHING BEGINS WITH A RELATIONSHIP

It may seem obvious, but if coaching is to be a success, it must start with a relationship. Without that relationship, there is not likely to be any conversation of *If coaching is to be a success, it* substance. If the manager forces *must start with a relationship.* a conversation to occur, you can safely guess that it will start in a guarded and cautious way. In all likelihood, it will take a good length of time for it ever to become truly productive.

When researching dynamics similar to those shared by coaches and coachees, we came across other so-called helping professions (clinical psychology, social work, counseling, and psychiatry). Let's be clear that we are fully aware of the huge differences that exist between what those professions do and what a manager/coach does. But just as the deliverer of first aid can learn some valuable lessons from emergency room physicians, we think that business coaches can definitely learn some important lessons from those who have made helping others their career.

Two such people are Barry Duncan and Scott Miller. They have a Web site, www.talkingcure.com, that provides fascinating summaries of their research. They argue that 30 percent of the success of any therapeutic activity hinges on the relationship that the patient has with the therapist. If the patient doesn't like the psychologist, then it is not very likely that much good will come of the time they spend together. We think it practically goes without saying that this same principle applies to the manager-employee relationship. That relationship makes a huge difference in the success of the coaching time spent together.

Foundations of Success

One of Italy's famous landmarks is the Leaning Tower of Pisa. This is a notable building project, constructed in three stages over a period of about 200 years. Designed as a massive bell tower, the first floor of the white marble campanile was begun on August 9, 1173 with classical capitals leaning against blind arches.

Five years later, when construction began on the third floor, the tower began to slowly sink. Its instability was due to two factors:

- First, the foundation went down a meager three yards. This magnificent eight-story structure that was to rise 183 feet in the air and weigh 16,000 tons rested on a foundation that went down only 9 feet into the earth.
- Second, the soil on which it was built was extremely unstable.

The design was flawed from the beginning. Construction was subsequently halted for almost 100 years, and this allowed time for the underlying soil to settle. Without this, the tower would almost certainly have toppled. In 1198, clocks were temporarily installed on the third floor of the unfinished construction. The seventh story and the bell tower were finally completed in 1372, after 200 years. Since its completion, major remedial steps have been taken, some as late as 2008. These steps included excavating dirt from under the high end of the tower, adding lead weights to one side, and various other approaches to keep the tower from tilting further. Engineers and architects now believe that it will be stable for the next 200 years, but only after enormous and expensive retrofitting.

The integrity and endurance of every structure is a function of the foundation on which it is built. No matter how elegant the structure that protrudes above ground may be, the lack of an adequate foundation dooms it to failure. How much better it would have been to have invested more in building a solid foundation before beginning the aboveground construction.

Beyond the Foundation

The foundation of coaching is the relationship between the two parties involved.

The foundation of coaching is the relationship between the two parties involved.

Beyond the relationship, a number of additional activities can take place. For example,

- The coach can prepare extensively for coaching discussions.
- The coach can spend significant amounts of time coaching.
- The coach can ask powerful, insightful questions.
- The coach can work on being an active listener.

But all of these will fail to yield any benefits if the foundation of a solid relationship does not exist.

Reflection: Your Personal Memorable Coaching Experience

Think of a time when you received great coaching. What did the coach say or do? What were the attributes of that coach?

If you are like most leaders we work with, the qualities that came to you will include some of these:

- My coach genuinely cared about me.
- His interest went beyond my immediate job performance.
- She challenged me and believed that I was capable of accomplishing more than I thought was possible for myself.
- He was candid and straightforward; I knew where I stood with him.
- My coach didn't hold grudges; the past stayed in the past.
- She listened to understand my point of view.
- My coach helped me come up with my own solution; he asked me questions that allowed me to discover what I needed to do.

Almost all of the individuals we speak to confirm that they indeed had a good relationship with their coaches. Very few individuals share that they valued the coaching they received from leaders with whom they had a rocky relationship. And, most of the time, the number one attribute provided is "My coach genuinely cared about me." A trust-based relationship must be in place if coaching is to work.

HOW MANAGERS BUILD STRONG RELATIONSHIPS

A complete discussion of the ways to improve the relationship between a manager and his direct reports is something that is far beyond the scope of this book. Nevertheless, we want to offer a few suggestions.

- *Desire to connect.* The relationship starts with two emotionally healthy people who make a commitment to work well with each other. A marriage counselor, based on her long experience, made the insightful comment that in a marriage, the person who cares the least controls it. If either party is not committed to making the marriage work, then it won't succeed, and the person who cares the least is totally at the helm.

    That same principle applies to coaching relationships. If the direct report is not interested in either improving his current performance or enhancing his long-term career development (or preferably both), little or no growth will happen. Similarly, if the manager is not willing to invest the time and effort to assist the direct report, then her coaching will inevitably fail. Both parties have to be interested in creating a positive relationship. It takes two to tango.

- *Warmth.* If relationships were to be categorized along the single dimension of "warm vs. cold," there would be no question that the strongest coaching relationships would be clustered at the "warm" end of the scale. The leader who makes people feel secure and comfortable when talking about difficult topics will clearly be able to make the maximum contribution.

- *Flexibility.* The same relationship that is so effective with one direct report will not be as effective with another one. For those leaders who like to behave with consistency, this adds a new level of complication. The simple fact is that the type of relationship that works with one person often won't work with another. Talking about what each direct report desires and observing what works is the only way we know to make this succeed.

- *Creating feedback mechanisms.* One of the most useful techniques in making the relationship work is to utilize a variety of ways to increase feedback in both directions. Coaching works best when it operates as a two-way street. Both parties can benefit from the use of multirater feedback tools (360-degree feedback instruments). For those who are not familiar with this useful way to help leaders develop, here's the summary explanation. (For further information, please see the Notes section on page 297. You may see an example of a 360-degree feedback questionnaire on www.zengerfolkman.com in the Leadership Resource Center.) A questionnaire is given to the person involved in this development process, her direct reports, her peers, and her manager. The instrument asks questions about a number of leadership dimensions. Confidentiality and anonymity are preserved for the respondents. The term *360-degree* comes from this all-encompassing view of the participant's behavior. The results from these questionnaires are compiled into one report, which is then given to the participant for the purpose of helping her to develop her leadership skills.[1] We have developed a specific "coaching" 360 assessment that zeros in on a leader's skills in this specific area. This can be an extremely positive way to provide the manager with feedback from his senior manager, peers, direct reports, and other stakeholders in a safe, anonymous manner.

- *Use effective leadership practices.* How the leaders behave day after day with employees obviously makes an enormous impact on the relationship. The research of Zenger and Folkman shows that there are four competencies that most powerfully determine a leader's ability to establish strong coaching relationships. These four competencies are

    1. *Generates trust:* honors commitments; creates a safe environment; does what is right regardless of personal risk or consequences
    2. *Builds relationships:* understands and relates well to others; initiates positive interactions
    3. *Encourages collaboration:* helps coachees focus on unifying goals and working collaboratively with others
    4. *Personally supports the development of others:* invests time and effort in a coachee's development; provides coaching and looks for opportunities to grow others

- *Improve problem-solving skills.* It has been shown that one of the most predictive elements in the satisfaction and endurance of a marriage is the ability of the partners to solve problems together. When they are not capable of that, divorce is much more likely to follow. Being able to identify issues, collect information, look at alternatives, and finally choose one are all important elements of a successful relationship.

- *Social sensitivity.* Good relationships depend on communicating well with each other. A huge part of that communication goes beyond the spoken word and requires each person to pick up the small clues of tone of voice, facial expressions, pauses in speech, and overall body language. Some people estimate that 80 percent of the message comes from this host of subtle clues, not from the words spoken in a conversation.

AVOID BEHAVIORS THAT DESTROY RELATIONSHIPS

Books could be (and have been) written entirely about the behavior of bad bosses; however, that isn't our desire. A few points about these toxic behaviors seem especially relevant to the coaching process, though, and you'll find them here.

- *Maintain confidentiality.* Coaching conversations will often turn to personal and confidential issues. How you as a coach use that information will determine whether the coachee will ever share such data again. Never repeat personal information divulged by a coachee or a comment made about someone else that could spill back in a negative way. Assume that anything you repeat will be on the 6:00 p.m. news for the broadest consumption. If a coachee shares information that you feel compelled to share with others, make sure that you negotiate or ask permission to do so ahead of time. Not setting clear boundaries about what information is confidential and to be kept private can destroy any trust that has painstakingly been built.
- *Transparency versus hidden agendas.* Periodically ask yourself if the conversations you are having are directly focused on help-ing the other person to perform better today and to be better prepared for the future. If you find yourself wanting to lead the coachee down a particular path, state your reasons clearly. Explain why you are advocating for the solution you feel strongly about. People know when they are being manipulated or led, so if you have an agenda for the conversation, don't hide it.

- *Be fully present.* People can tell when you are really paying attention and when you are there in body only. How many times have you been in a conversation with someone when the e-mail alert sounds and your colleague's eyes shift to see what news has arrived? One person jokingly suggested coming to meetings toyless. "Toyless" refers to the practice of putting away the electronic toys, like smart phones, that keep you connected and distracted. If you look at the toys, you are not present for the person you are with. Such behavior is perceived as setting yourself above the rest, with the implicit message, "My time is more valuable than yours." When you are coaching over the phone, it is even more crucial that you have the self-discipline to remove distractions or temptations to split your focus. The research on multitasking is in: people cannot focus on two tasks simultaneously.

- *Keep your commitments.* Breaking commitments and not keeping promises is one of the most frequently cited behaviors that erode trust in relationships. When managers fail to follow through, their team members notice. The message that the manager unknowingly sends is "You are not as important as the things I choose to do instead."

Application

What actions do you need to take to begin building strong relationships with those you coach? Which behaviors do you need to eliminate, because they erode the trust and relationships that you are trying to build? In Table 5-1, list specific actions that you will take to build strong, trust-based relationships. Identify behaviors that you will stop, start, change, or continue.

(Continued)

Table 5-1 Relationship Building Behaviors

Behaviors or Actions To . . .			
Stop	Start	Change	Continue
Answering my cell phone in the middle of our conversations	Meeting in Joe's office instead of mine	Increase frequency of meetings; have one meeting per month be completely focused on Joe's agenda	Be direct and honest about organizational changes; continue holding confidences

Chapter Summary

- Successful coaching begins with a strong, trust-based relationship.
- The relationships you build with your employees form the foundation for effective coaching conversations.
- Coachees often cite a key attribute of their most memorable coaches: "My coach genuinely cared about me."
- Building strong relationships is not a mystery, and it starts with a genuine desire to connect.
- Too often coaches do not pay attention to behaviors that erode relationships, including not being present or being distracted by electronic gadgets and e-mail.
- Keep your commitments, keep your coachees' confidences, and begin paving the way for great coaching.

Chapter 6

FUEL: A Framework, Not a Cage

Most activities work better when there is a grand scheme guiding them than when they just sort of evolve in a haphazard way. An overarching design is absolutely necessary when it comes to complex tasks like building a house or manufacturing a wristwatch. When it comes to seemingly simpler tasks like having a conversation with a colleague, however, it can be tempting to just "wing it" and hope that there will be a positive outcome.

We would argue that coaching conversations are worth planning. They take up valuable time for both parties, so that time should be put to its most efficient use. At worst, such conversations can cause irreparable damage to the relationship between the coach and the coachee. At best, they can improve a coachee's performance and produce motivation and increased performance results.

Coaching conversations are worth planning.

Selection interviewing is a good parallel for coaching conversations. The typical job-selection interview, for example, has been shown to be only slightly better than pure chance at predicting job performance, and far inferior to a number of other methods that could be used in making a selection, such as cognitive testing or having the individual perform a simulated work task. Indeed, one

Table 6-1 FUEL Coaching Framework

Frame the Conversation	Set the context for the conversation by agreeing on the purpose, process, and desired outcomes of the discussion.
Understand the Current State	Explore the current state from the coachee's point of view; expand the coachee's awareness of the situation to determine the real coaching issue.
Explore the Desired State	Articulate the vision of success in this scenario, and explore multiple alternative paths before prioritizing methods of achieving this vision.
Lay Out a Success Plan	Identify the specific, time-bounded action steps to be taken to achieve the desired results, and determine milestones for follow-up and accountability.

observer described the typical selection interview as an "expensive source of vivid noise." However, when the selection interview is planned, follows a defined track, and uses well-crafted questions, that interviewing process becomes a much more powerful tool for selecting the right candidate.

Similarly, we would suggest that having a plan, following a defined track, and using well-crafted questions will greatly aid your ability to improve your coaching conversations. This chapter will explore the concept of FUEL—the road map for any coaching conversation (see Table 6-1). If your purpose in coaching is to help others grow and develop, this coaching conversation guide can provide the FUEL for the journey—both for you and for your coachee.

THE DIFFERENCE BETWEEN A FRAMEWORK AND A CAGE

After reviewing the FUEL coaching conversation process, a good friend and colleague of ours gave us a great description of it: "It's a framework, not a cage." Hearing this pithy expression started our thinking about the key differences between a framework and a cage (see Table 6-2). After going through this mental exercise, we felt that our friend was completely accurate in his assessment.

The next few chapters of this book are dedicated to exploring how to best use each step in this coaching conversation process.

Table 6-2 Differences between a Framework and a Cage

Framework	Cage
• Outline of a structure	• Rigid, inflexible
• Offers a form and guidelines	• Unbending, no exceptions
• Provides direction	• Locks things in
• Flexible, multipurpose	• Linear, single-purpose

While you won't use all of the steps in every conversation, we are convinced that the more you follow these general guidelines, the more productive your coaching conversations will be. Consider the FUEL model as a framework for holding coaching conversations, and let the coaching conversation guide introduced later in this chapter be your personal "track" to run on.

One other note: while we will explain these steps in a linear fashion, the actual flow of the conversation will seldom follow this exact track. It will invariably loop back onto itself. One phase will be protracted, and another will go quickly. We'll describe the most natural places where these loopbacks tend to happen in conversations.

Self-Assessment: How Coaching Conversations Work Now

Before we dive into our suggested template for coaching conversations, we would like you to complete a quick self-assessment regarding your current coaching conversations. You'll see that the 20 questions listed in the worksheet are grouped by the four steps of the FUEL model.

Rate each statement on a 1-to-5 scale, with 1 indicating that you rarely or never use that behavior and 5 indicating that the behavior is something that you almost always perform. Circle the response that describes your behavior most accurately. Please be candid as you complete this assessment. If you are unsure which rating to assign, ask yourself the question,

(*Continued*)

"If my coachees were asked to complete this assessment, how would they rate me?" You can use this virtual third-party opinion as a tiebreaker!

Frame the Conversation	Rarely/ Never				Almost Always
1. I prepare in advance for coaching by identifying the purpose, process, and desired outcomes for the conversation.	1	2	3	4	5
2. I ensure that I am focused on the most important behavior or issue to discuss, and I get agreement on this from the person I am coaching.	1	2	3	4	5
3. When someone comes to me with an issue, I ask the individual to define how I can best help or support her: what does she want from me in the conversation?	1	2	3	4	5

Understand the Current State	Rarely/ Never				Almost Always
4. I spend 25 percent or less of the time talking; the person I am coaching speaks 75 percent or more of the time.	1	2	3	4	5
5. I listen for more than just the words spoken; I truly pay attention to the emotional/energy state of the person as well.	1	2	3	4	5
6. I ask questions that promote greater awareness on the part of the person I am coaching. My questions expand the way he views the situation.	1	2	3	4	5
7. I help the individual to explore the consequences of making a change or staying in the current place.	1	2	3	4	5
8. When I provide feedback, I ask the individual to share her view of the situation before I share my own.	1	2	3	4	5
9. When I share my own observations of the situation, I provide factual, specific data and observations.	1	2	3	4	5

(*Continued*)

Explore the Desired State	Rarely/ Never				Almost Always
10. I take the time to fully understand what the desired state or end result is that we are trying to achieve.	1	2	3	4	5
11. I resist giving my advice before hearing fully what the person I am coaching is thinking about.	1	2	3	4	5
12. I invite the person I am coaching to identify several different paths forward before we begin prioritizing the best one(s) to take.	1	2	3	4	5
13. I explore the individual's motivation and level of commitment to making the desired change.	1	2	3	4	5
14. Together we explore the possible barriers or resistance that the individual might face in moving toward the goal.	1	2	3	4	5

Lay Out a Success Plan	Rarely/ Never				Almost Always
15. I help guide the person I am coaching in breaking down his desired goals into specific, discrete action steps.	1	2	3	4	5
16. I work to make sure that the action steps are time-bounded—that each step is tied to a specific deadline.	1	2	3	4	5
17. I help the individual I am coaching explore support resources.	1	2	3	4	5
18. I actively work to set milestones for follow-up and accountability beyond the coaching conversation.	1	2	3	4	5
19. I have a system for regularly following up with the individuals that I am coaching.	1	2	3	4	5
20. I seek out opportunities to check in with the individuals I am coaching to determine how they are progressing toward their plans.	1	2	3	4	5

MAKING SENSE OF YOUR SCORES

Well, how did you do? If you are like most leaders who complete this assessment, you probably scored fairly high on several behaviors and lower on many others. Virtually no one we have met has claimed to excel at all of the behaviors listed in this quick self-assessment. Nor do they need to!

From our research and study of the best coaches across multiple industries and countries, we see that the exceptional ones tend to excel in three to five critical competencies related to coaching. This is good news for all of us—we don't have to be perfect at our coaching craft to be truly exceptional and useful to our coachees. However, having a balance of strengths might ultimately be valuable for us to consider. We'll cover this concept later (in Chapter 18, "Growing Your Skills as a Coach"), when we provide a snapshot of the 14 evidence-based competencies at which the best coaches excel.

Now, back to you. Just answering the questions in this assessment may cause you to pause and reflect on areas that surprise you. Here are a few of the more common surprises we hear from leaders who complete this reflective exercise:

- I probably don't prepare as much as I could.
- I tend to dive into most conversations; I don't know that I really take the time to gain agreement regarding what my coachee wants or what the outcome of the conversation will be.
- I'm supposed to be talking less than 25 percent of the time? Really? I'm probably doing most of the talking in most of my coaching conversations.
- I tend to offer my advice pretty early in the conversation. Time is limited for both of us. I assumed that is what I was supposed to do.
- We don't explore multiple alternatives; we usually jump onto the first or most obvious solution that comes to mind.
- I haven't thought about determining how committed the other person is to really making a change. I figured she ought to be.
- I'm awful at follow-up! I don't have a system in place to loop back and hold people accountable.

- I think it is the coachees' responsibility to make sure that they do what they say they are going to do. I don't think I should have to follow up to make sure that they are staying on task.

If you relate to any of these statements, or if you feel that there are other areas of dissonance between the items in the self-assessment and how you currently coach, you are in good company. By the time you finish reading this book, you'll have a much better idea of the areas that you most want to work on improving.

While the items in the self-assessment might *imply* a process for holding coaching conversations, we want to offer an explicit framework to guide your dialogues. The Coaching Conversation Guide in Table 6-3 is a suggested process for holding virtually any coaching conversation. Because it is a framework and not a cage, you may find that you don't follow it in a linear fashion or utilize every step of the process. In fact, you may utilize only one or two key parts of the overall process when time is of the essence and you have just moments to talk with a colleague. Later in the book, we'll explain how you can use the spirit of coaching in an on-the-spot conversation, even if you have just a minute or two for a coaching dialogue.

As you review the Coaching Conversation Guide, you will see the following structure:

- In the left-hand column, you will see the substeps of the four elements of the FUEL model.
- In the right-hand column(s), you will see suggested possible questions to ask or statements to offer to guide that section of the conversation.

We suggest that you first review the guide by reading down the key FUEL headings, along with the substeps in the left-hand column. This provides you with the best outline for the overall conversation. Then reread the entire guide, this time including the various prompting questions or phrases in the right-hand column(s) to get a sense of how the overall conversation might go.

Table 6-3 Coaching Conversation Guide

Step 1: Frame the Conversation

(Set the context and focus for the conversation.)

Identify the behavior or issue to discuss.	*(If coach initiates the conversation)* I'd like to talk about . . . [the issue].	*(If coachee initiates the conversation)* What is the most important thing for us to focus on?
Determine the purpose or outcomes of the conversation.	*(If coach initiates the conversation)* • By the end of this conversation, I would like to accomplish . . . • What else would you like to make sure that we address?	*(If coachee initiates the conversation)* • What would you like to accomplish in this conversation? • How might I help you with this issue?
Agree on the process for the conversation.	• Here's how I thought we could proceed: . . . • How does that sound?	

Step 2: Understand the Current State

(Explore the individual's point of view before sharing your own.)

Understand the coachee's point of view.	• How do you see this situation? • What is happening? • What is working well? • What makes this challenging? • How might you have contributed to this situation? • How might others see the situation?
Determine the consequences of continuing on the current path.	• What impact is this having on you? On others? • What are the consequences if the situation doesn't change? • How does this influence your goals and what you are trying to accomplish? • What are the long-term implications?
Offer your perspective, *if appropriate.*	• Could I share some observations I have made? • Could I offer some other consequences to consider?

(Continued)

Step 3: Explore the Desired State

(Identify the target and generate multiple paths to achieve the end state.)

Understand the vision for success.	• What would you like to see happen here? • What would the ideal state look like?
Set goals and perform-ance expectations.	• What are your goals? What would you like to accomplish? • Here's how I see it: . . .
Explore alternative paths of action.	• What might be some approaches you can take? • What else might work? • Could I offer a couple of thoughts? You might want to consider . . .
Explore possible barri-ers or resistance.	• What are the major barriers preventing this change from happening? • Where would the biggest resistance to this change come from?

Step 4: Lay Out a Success Plan

(Create the detailed, actionable plan and follow-through that will lead to goal attainment.)

Develop and agree on an action plan and timelines.	• What specific actions will help you achieve your goal? • What will your first steps be? When will you start? • Who can help hold you accountable? • How will you stay focused on your goals and plans?
Enlist support from others.	• Who can support you in moving forward? • How can I support you? (Here's how I see my role: . . .)
Set milestones for follow-up and accountability.	• Let's review our plans: . . . • When should we touch base on this again?

As you review the Coaching Conversation Guide, ask yourself the following questions:

- If I were following this coaching conversation outline, how would the conversation sound?
- How would this conversation be different from the ones I'm currently having with employees and team members?

Chances are that you are noticing how many open-ended questions might be asked during the course of a coaching conversation.

You might also be noticing who is doing most of the work in solving the issue at hand—the coachee. You might even be wondering where all of your good advice and guidance fits into this equation. Finally, you might be wondering if this process will really work to solve the problems at hand efficiently. Please know that this framework has been proven to work and has been effective for thousands of leaders who have used it. What leaders find is that the process outlined in this conversation ensures that the coachees buy in and are committed to implementing the solution that they identify. Leaders do less "telling" and more "growing" their employees and colleagues by utilizing this framework.

When This Guide Might Be Applied

Coaching is a highly beneficial skill set that can be applied to a variety of problems or issues. As a leader in an organization, you are most likely to apply these skills in both performance discussions and career discussions with employees, with peers, or (this may surprise some readers) with those *above* you in the organization structure.

The Coaching Conversation Guide works whether the conversation is focused on

- Providing an employee with tough feedback related to a performance issue
- Inviting a team member to consider what worked and what didn't, for the purpose of continuous learning and improvement
- Discussing skill expansion and career growth opportunities with a direct report
- Solving a personal or performance dilemma related to a relationship or task problem

The Coaching Conversation Guide can be utilized whether you, as the leader, are initiating the conversation (wanting to explore a performance or career issue) or whether the employee is initiating the conversation (wanting to discuss a particular challenge or an opportunity at hand). If we consider the guide as a framework, it is easy to see how the various aspects of the FUEL model can be adjusted to meet the various differences in conversations.

As we move through the next few chapters, we will have a chance to see how to bend and mold the Coaching Conversation Guide—and how it sounds in real life. Having said that, though, we strongly encourage you to try it out for yourself several times, doing your best to follow the process as written. This is a tried-and-true process—we know it works from our own use of it. The process receives rave reviews from both coaches and coachees alike when it is applied in real-time applications in hard-nosed business settings.

We invite you to understand each step of the FUEL process thoroughly. That way, you can see the benefit of each of these steps more clearly. Better yet, you can apply this process to your own coaching conversations.

Chapter Summary

- It is worth planning coaching conversations so that the time spent in the conversations is used most productively.
- Experience shows that having a road map for coaching will help the coach best plan and conduct any conversations.
- The FUEL model provides a valuable framework, or set of guidelines to follow. As a framework (not a cage), it is malleable and flexible.
- While the FUEL model may appear to be linear, using this framework is actually more fluid in real life.
- The Coaching Conversation Guide provides a "track to run on" and allows the coachee to do most of the heavy lifting in the conversation.
- The Coaching Conversation Guide utilizes a series of open-ended questions that invite the coachee to identify the best solutions moving forward. That does not mean that the coach does not get to have a point of view, but we will explore later how you can best insert your own ideas into the conversation.
- The Coaching Conversation Guide represents a tried-and-true process, one that works regardless of whether the coach or the coachee initiates the conversation.

Chapter 7

Frame the Conversation

Setting the Target

In this chapter, we begin to really break down the FUEL process into discrete steps. In real coaching conversations, the steps will be more fluid than the way we present them here. However, we know that it is helpful to present ideas in bite-sized portions and in a more linear, step-by-step fashion so that they are clearer and more digestible. Once the basic ideas have been grasped, it becomes easier to work within them.

We start at the beginning of the conversation. The first step of the coaching process creates the target at which you aim the conversation. How many times have you been in a conversation or in a meeting with others where you were not exactly sure where you were heading or what end result you were trying to achieve? Too many times, if you are like most people.

In a resource-limited world, where time is of the essence, both coach and coachee naturally seek to maximize efficiency and not waste time. The first step of the coaching process, Frame the Conversation
(see Table 7-1), is a step that it is essential to do well because it makes certain that time is not squandered in talking about the

In a resource-limited world both coach and coachee naturally seek to maximize efficiency.

Table 7-1 Frame the Coversation

Step 1: Frame the Conversation		
(Set the context and focus for the conversation.)		
Identify the behavior or issue to discuss.	*(If coach initiates the conversation)*	*(If coachee initiates the conversation)*
	I'd like to talk about . . . [the issue].	What is the most important thing for us to focus on?
Determine the purpose or outcomes of the conversation.	*(If coach initiates the conversation)* • By the end of this conversation, I would like to accomplish . . . • What else would you like to make sure we address?	*(If coachee initiates the conversation)* • What would you like to accomplish in this conversation? • How might I help you with this issue?
Agree on the process for the conversation.	• Here's how I thought we could proceed: . . . • How does that sound?	

wrong things. Framing the Conversation provides the outline and focus for the conversation. It includes what issues will be discussed, what the end result will be (the outcomes that the coach and the coachee are aiming for), and any other useful boundaries and objectives, such as how much time either the coach or the coachee has, a proposed agenda for the conversation, and agreements on confidentiality. In essence, both coach and coachee are agreeing to be in the same conversation and being explicit about the exact nature of that conversation.

In addition to increasing the efficiency of the conversation, clearly Framing the Conversation reduces any potential tension that might exist for either party. Imagine an employee who is approaching her manager with a somewhat delicate issue having to do with another employee and is seeking some guidance or advice. If the manager were to ask the employee what she wanted to walk away from the conversation with, and then suggested a process for how to get there, the employee would probably already feel some relief. The employee could trust that she was in "good hands," knowing that the manager understood what was most important to resolve and was offering a road map for getting there.

Let's look at how this might sound with the coachee bringing forth an issue. Note that in the example in Table 7-2, the coach follows the general framework of the model, but uses slightly

Table 7-2

Step 1: Frame the Conversation

(Set the context and focus for the conversation.)

Identify the behavior or issue to discuss.	**Coachee:** Hey, do you have a few minutes? Something is really bugging me, and I would like to talk about it with you.
	Coach: What would you like to focus on? Give me an overview of the issue.
	Coachee: I'm really struggling with Ed. I keep finding myself needing information from him, and he doesn't respond. It seems as if he doesn't think my deadlines are important. When it comes to *his* deadlines, he hounds me and expects an instant response. But when I need something from him, I'm low on his priority list. I can send multiple e-mails and voice mails and still not get a reply.
Determine the purpose or outcomes of the conversation.	**Coach:** Well, that certainly sounds frustrating—and a bit lopsided. So, what would be most helpful to sort through in this conversation? What would you like to accomplish in this discussion?
	Coachee: I guess I'd like a reality check: am I being unreasonable in my expectations? I don't think I am. So, I guess I'd like to figure out a strategy to approach Ed so that I can get him to respond to my needs more quickly—and not have the conversation backfire on me.
	Coach: So, you'd feel good if you left with a game plan for approaching Ed, and perhaps some messages to take into a conversation with him?
	Coachee: Yes.
Agree on the process for the conversation.	**Coach:** Well, then, let's start with a very quick "reality check" and make sure that you *are* assessing the situation fairly. Then, let's identify what you would like to achieve through your communication with Ed, and perhaps identify some ways to broach the subject with him. We can even role-play this a bit. How does that sound?
	Coachee: Sounds good.
	Coach: So, let's start with the quick reality check.

different questions and statements to Frame the Conversation from those listed in the framework in Table 7-1.

After reading the dialogue in Table 7-2, you probably have an immediate reaction. Here are a few that we have heard:

1. My conversations certainly don't start this way. I don't take the time to clarify what the coachee is trying to accomplish and what would be most helpful to her.
2. This step certainly makes sense—clarifying what we are trying to accomplish in the conversation. I can see how that could make the conversation more focused—for both of us.
3. I'm not sure I would have the patience to do as much "listening" in the coach role; my tendency is to jump in.
4. It seems too formal to try to gain agreement regarding the focus and process.

This last reaction is understandable. Taking the time to gain these agreements has not been a common practice for most people. But let us dissect Framing the Conversation a bit more and look at the benefits of taking the time to do this step well. In essence, when you Frame the Conversation, you are creating an explicit agreement for the conversation. Some people call this step of the process "creating a contract," where you are agreeing on the expectations for the outcomes of this particular conversation or discussion.

MOVING THE CONVERSATION BEYOND A "COMPLAINT" OR A "CHAT"

The value of creating a contract is that it moves a conversation into the coaching mode, and away from being a "chat" or a "complaint," according to Pam McLean, CEO of the Hudson Institute of Santa Barbara (a coaching training organization). Think about this: how many times has a colleague approached you with a "complaint" about something that is not working well and with which she is frustrated? In an attempt

A contract moves a conversation away from being a "chat" or a "complaint."

to empathize or commiserate with that individual, you probably said something like, "Tell me more. . . . That is awful. . . . I can see why that is upsetting. . . . You are right. . . . Ed sounds like he is being completely unfair."

The two of you can spend a lot of time when both of you jump into the same boat and complain about Ed—and make him the bad guy. Of course, when we commiserate with others, our intentions are usually good—we want to help make our colleagues or friends feel better about their situation and to show that we understand their point of view. However, this probably doesn't help our colleagues to resolve the issue and gain new insight into their own contribution to the problem and how they might resolve it.

Psychologists used to encourage people to experience catharsis, which simply meant expressing their anger and frustration. "Let it all hang out" was the popular phrase. The assumption was that by such venting, the steam would be released and the people would feel better. But then researchers began to study what actually happened. They discovered that encouraging people to express their anger only made them *more angry*. Instead of making people feel better, it actually made them feel worse. They were more upset and angry than they would have been if they had chosen one of several other approaches.[1]

Alternatively, a colleague might approach you with a frustrating situation, and you might banter back and forth, sharing your own experience with similar situations. Time can pass while you are engaged in some friendly "chatting," and again, the coachee might not gain further insight into his situation or understanding regarding how to resolve the frustration.

By using some targeted questions in Framing the Conversation, the coach can quickly signal to the coachee that he intends to be helpful, but that he needs to understand what the coachee wants help with. Table 7-3 gives some additional questions to consider using as soon as a coachee approaches you with an issue on which she would like coaching. Building a repertoire of questions that work for you can be a great practice. Over time, you will identify the ones that work well and that seem natural for you. As you read the questions in Table 7-3,

Table 7-3 Questions to Frame the Conversation

Identify the behavior or issue to discuss.	• What would you most like to focus on? • That sounds like a big topic—is there a specific issue that you'd like to focus on? • What issue would be most important for us to talk about in the next 15 minutes? • We said we could talk about X, Y, or Z. Which would be most important to tackle today, given our time?
Determine the purpose or outcomes of the conversation.	• How can I help you with this issue? • What would be a useful outcome of this conversation? • What are you hoping that we can achieve in the next 30 minutes regarding this situation? • Help me understand what you'd like to make sure to accomplish in our discussion. • What would you like to leave with today?

you might even highlight or check those that would be most likely to feel comfortable for you at this step of the conversation.

Once you have completed the first two substeps of the framing step, the coach and coachee should be clear as to what the focus on the conversation is, and what they are jointly trying to accomplish. This becomes the initial *target* that you are now aiming for in your coaching conversation. If you consider this target, loosely, as a goal, you now need to come up with a game plan for getting to your goal. This is where the third step of Frame the Conversation comes in handy: agree on the process for the conversation.

THE COACH OWNS THE PROCESS; THE COACHEE OWNS THE CONTENT

The third substep of Framing the Conversation is "Agree on the process for the conversation." A useful guide to keep in mind, assuming that we are coaching individuals to draw their own conclusions and create their own best solutions, is that the coachee owns the "content" of what you are discussing, and the coach owns the "process." Another way to say this is that, ideally, the coach will be well versed in how to guide the conversation. The

The coachee owns the "content," and the coach owns the "process."

Table 7-5 Specific Example: Agree on the Process

Agree on the process for the conversation.	Understand the Current State	*Let's start with a very quick "reality check" and make sure that you are assessing the situation objectively.*
	Explore the Desired State	*Then, let's identify what you would like to achieve through your communication with Ed,*
	Lay out a Success Plan	*. . . perhaps identify some ways to broach the subject with him. We can even role-play this a bit. How does that sound?*

- How much time you have for the discussion
- How you will treat confidential issues (either ensure confidentiality or be explicit regarding who might need to be involved after the conversation, and so on)
- How you view your role and the coachee's role (your role is to ask questions and offer insights; the coachee's role is to take the lead and brainstorm possibilities, determine the best course of action, and so on)
- Any other defining parameters of the conversation (be candid, feel free to challenge, be forthcoming with feedback regarding what isn't working, and so on)

If the coach in the previous example were to expand on the process statement, perhaps the additional text would include something like this:

> I've got only 20 minutes right now, so let's start this conversation. If we need to pick up later, let's schedule some time before I need to leave for my next meeting. I want you to know that I will not convey any of this to Ed; I'm going to support you in figuring out how you can close the loop with him. If you need me to get involved directly, I will. But until we make that determination, I'm treating this as a private conversation between you and me.

Remember, the entire purpose of the step of Framing the Conversation is to ensure that both coach and coachee are agreeing to be in the same conversation at the same time, and to make explicit what that conversation will be about. Taking the time to make sure that both parties are on board with the parameters

Taking the time to make sure that both parties are on board will pay dividends in the time saved.

and goals of the conversation will pay dividends in the time saved during the conversation and in ensuring that the needed outcomes are achieved.

Consider this alternative example instead. I was coaching a high-potential leader over a period of nine months, and we spoke approximately every three weeks. I would routinely start the conversation by asking, "Cheryl, what would you like to focus on today? What would give you the most value, given the hour that we have now?"

On one occasion, Cheryl replied, "Well, since the last time we talked, you will not believe what has happened. I challenged a project that senior leaders wanted us to move forward with, and the backlash was unbelievable. One senior leader who disagreed with my approach reached out to my direct manager, saying that I wasn't qualified to be in my role. Instead of coming directly to me, my manager began a dialogue with my senior leader, and I heard about this indirectly through someone else. I can't tell you how upset I was that the person who took issue with what I said didn't approach me directly. And that my manager didn't even come talk to me—I had to hear about it through a different channel!"

In a moment of calm and clarity, I had the good sense to confirm, "So is this what you'd like to focus on today—how to work through this issue?" To my disbelief, Cheryl quickly answered, "No, I have figured that out. Actually, the issue has sorted itself out, really." Cheryl then continued, "What I'd like to focus on is a hiring decision that I'm about to make and how to make sure that I'm covering all bases in picking the right person." So off we went—on the *right* topic to discuss.

I often reflect on that conversation and wonder what would have happened if I had jumped in with Cheryl to say, "Wow! Tell me more. . . . That sounds awful. . . . Then what happened? What did he say? What did you do?" My guess is that we could have spent the better part of 20 or 30 minutes reliving that disconcerting situation for her, making the conversation a "chat" or "complaint" session rather than moving forward on an agenda in a meaningful coaching mode—focused on the future and taking action on something that was of real importance to her.

When the Coach Brings Up the Issue

So far, we have highlighted coaching conversations in which the coachee has presented the issue to the coach—something that he would like help on. What happens when the coach initiates the conversation? What changes are required in the process of Framing the Conversation?

You will follow the *same steps* of the conversation; the major difference is that you can *prepare* for these steps, since you will be able to identify what you might want to say in advance.

Let's look at the example in Table 7-6.

Table 7-6

Identify the behavior or issue to discuss.	**Coach:** Hey, Sam, I'm wondering if you have a few minutes to talk about how the Webinar with our key stakeholders went.
	Coachee: Sure. That would be good. I've got a meeting at 11, but we can talk until then.
	Coach: Great. I'd love to review how you think the session went, and what our partners are likely to take away from the discussion. I'd be happy to share my own thoughts and observations, too.
	Coachee: OK.
	Coach: Anything else that you'd like to make sure we talk about regarding the Webinar?
	Coachee: No. Or, well, I guess I'd like to know what you thought of the examples I used. I might have gotten a little creative with my slides there.
	Coach: Great. We can talk about your examples, too.

(Continued)

Determine the purpose or outcomes of the conversation.	**Coach:** Since you will be hosting many of these Webinars in the weeks to come, I thought it might be useful to explicitly identify what worked well—to make sure that we repeat those things—and also to identify anything that we could do differently to continually improve these for future audiences. Does that make sense?
	Coachee: Sure.
Agree on the process for the conversation.	**Coach:** Why don't we start with your own reflections and assessment: what do you think went well, and what would you do differently? Then I'll add my two cents, and if we identify anything that looks like a roadblock for future Webinars, we can brainstorm possible approaches together. How does that sound?
	Coachee: Good. And, remember, I'd like to get your reactions to the examples I used, too.
	Coach: Right. I'll share my reactions to your examples, and tell you which ones I thought worked really well. So let's start with how you think the session went.

As you can see, the coach follows the same process of contracting for the conversation. When the coach initiates the conversation—and thus the topic of the conversation—she will be able to articulate the behavior or issue to discuss, the outcomes of the conversation, and the process for the discussion. Even when the coach initiates the conversation, however, she will still want to make the framing step a two-way dialogue. The coach should ask the coachee if the topic or issue makes sense, if the coachee seeks any other (different) outcomes, and if the process for the conversation makes sense before proceeding.

Video Example

If you would like to see examples of a coach framing a coaching conversation, go to www.zengerfolkman. com and click on the Leadership Resource Center icon. You will find one or more examples of a coach helping to guide the beginning of a coaching conversation. In the example(s), the coach will ensure that both the coach and the coachee have a clear focus for the ensuing coaching conversation.

Who Should Drive the Agenda?

You might be wondering at this point who should drive the topic of the conversation. Both you and the person you are coaching, especially if he is one of your direct reports, will be equally able to identify potential coaching topics. If we focus specifically on the coaching role you play with direct reports, it would be easy to assume that you, as their leader, could drive the coaching agenda. We would like to suggest that you allow much more time for *their* agenda in your coaching work.

In fact, we can draw upon research from a related helping profession to convince us of the power of letting our employees drive the coaching agenda. According to Duncan and Miller (see www.talkingcure.com), when counselors asked their clients what they would like to accomplish in the current discussion, and paired this with a request for feedback at the end of the session, the counselors found that their attrition rates dropped by 50 percent and their effectiveness increased by 65 percent. While we will be the first to acknowledge that counseling and coaching are quite different beasts, we do think that it is interesting to connect these two dots here. When counselors invited their clients to determine the focus of the discussion and then invited feedback at the end ("Did we accomplish what you wanted? Was this a good use of time?"), clients were *far* more satisfied. This phenomenon can't be limited only to the world of counseling.

If we asked our direct reports more frequently, "What is most important for us to focus on?" and "Did we get to resolve your most pressing issues?" it is easy to imagine that our employees would be far more satisfied—and productive—than if we continuously took the lead in our coaching conversations.

Task Updates Do Not Equal Coaching Conversations

In our work with leaders, we find that many leaders are proud to announce that they regularly hold one-on-one conversations with each direct report. Whether these happen weekly, biweekly, or monthly, the vast majority of managers state that they regularly and routinely honor these one-on-one commitments and stick to them in their schedules. However, when we peel the next layer away and ask these managers what the conversations focus on, they are quick to highlight the major time investments:

- Task or project updates
- Communications regarding company business and/or department news that hasn't reached the employees yet
- Feedback regarding project milestones and accomplishments

In fact, leaders regularly state that approximately 80 to 90 percent of their one-on-one meetings are devoted to task or project update communications. Any remaining time is spent on developmental conversations that grow and expand the employee's capability.

Although task and project updates are critical and necessary to address with employees, we would like to challenge you to distinguish between project updates and true coaching conversations. If we define coaching conversations as those that expand the employee's awareness, thinking, and capability,

We define coaching conversations as those that expand the employee's awareness, thinking, and capability.

then a task status update typically will not fit this definition. Unless you approach these routine one-on-one meetings with a coaching mindset—and vigilantly seek opportunities to expand and grow your employees in the process—they are likely to turn into mere update reports.

If your coaching conversations *have* begun to feel closer to update reports—which is understandable—then a simple solution might be to continue holding these one-on-one meetings, but to set up *separate meetings* that focus on development and capability/career expansion. Even if these separate meetings happen only on a monthly, bimonthly, or even quarterly basis, your employees are likely to notice and benefit from the difference (and so are you).

SO WHAT DO WE TALK ABOUT?

Many leaders are perplexed when it comes time to determine how they can initiate a different kind of coaching conversation. There are typically two issues operating here that make this transition challenging for leaders:

1. How do I start having a different kind of conversation, since we are used to the typical way of doing business?
2. What can we talk about beyond the project or task updates?

If we recall what happens in a system dynamic, we will recognize that both parties are used to a particular way of interacting with each other. Therefore, if the standard one-on-one conversation has entailed the manager's asking about project status, accomplishments, and challenges, and the employee in turn reporting on project status, accomplishments, and challenges, it is quite easy to understand how both parties might find it difficult to venture into a different kind of conversation.

There are some variations on why this second challenge—determining what to talk about beyond project updates—is tough. Sometimes leaders report, "I have mature, experienced employees working for me—they don't really need 'development' per se." Or they explain, "I have Gen Y employees working for me, and when I ask them if they want to talk about anything else, they always say, 'No—I'm good.'" Regardless of any resistance to venturing into new territory that either you or your coachee may be feeling, it is important that you find ways to interact differently and engage in new conversations. One way to do this is with a checklist of potential coaching topics.

Coaching Topics Checklist

Utilizing a Coaching Topics Checklist like the one shown in Table 7-7 may be a good "door opener" to alternative conversations. We would recommend using this checklist as another framework and modifying and customizing it to fit your unique situation. The specific topics in Table 7-7 are far less important

Table 7-7 Coaching Topics Checklist

On the following checklist, please mark the three topics that are of most interest to you. If something important is not listed, add it to the list and mark that as your choice.

We'll use this list in the coming months as a tool for structuring our conversations.

	Low								High	
1. The progress I am making in my career.	1	2	3	4	5	6	7	8	9	10
2. The success I am feeling in my current position.	1	2	3	4	5	6	7	8	9	10
3. How I could contribute more to the organization in my current role.	1	2	3	4	5	6	7	8	9	10
4. How I could learn more while in my current role.	1	2	3	4	5	6	7	8	9	10
5. How I could expand my role and responsibility.	1	2	3	4	5	6	7	8	9	10
6. How to improve the way I work with other departments in this organization.	1	2	3	4	5	6	7	8	9	10
7. How my group could be more efficient and productive.	1	2	3	4	5	6	7	8	9	10
8. How to gain more technical competence in this industry.	1	2	3	4	5	6	7	8	9	10
9. Ways to improve the manner in which I get things accomplished.	1	2	3	4	5	6	7	8	9	10
10. How I could become more innovative in my role.	1	2	3	4	5	6	7	8	9	10
11. How to achieve better work/life balance.	1	2	3	4	5	6	7	8	9	10
12. How best to prepare for career opportunities in the firm.	1	2	3	4	5	6	7	8	9	10
13. How to handle a specific challenge I am facing in my work.	1	2	3	4	5	6	7	8	9	10
14. How to overcome any major weaknesses that those above me in the organization perceive me to have.	1	2	3	4	5	6	7	8	9	10
15. How to identify and magnify those important strengths that I possess.	1	2	3	4	5	6	7	8	9	10
16. Things I should know, but I'm not aware of.	1	2	3	4	5	6	7	8	9	10
17. Other:	1	2	3	4	5	6	7	8	9	10
18. Other:	1	2	3	4	5	6	7	8	9	10

than the essence that the checklist suggests—to propose possible topics of discussion that might be useful threads to follow as you continue conversations with your employees.

Let us quickly test the value and viability of using a checklist like this. Take a minute and *complete this form for yourself.* We've always found that leaders, like you, will latch on to at least one or two areas of interest to discuss with their managers or other colleagues. So, try this out for yourself. Complete this checklist as if you were being asked to identify possible coaching topics for yourself. *Do that now, before reading further!*

Chances are that you identified at least two or three areas that you have a relatively high interest in pursuing with an interested party (hopefully, your manager!). You may have also noted that none of the listed topics focus on the current project/status/task-at-hand updates. If you are like many leaders who have completed this checklist, you might be interested in actually engaging *your* manager in a conversation about one or more of these topics. We encourage you to take that initiative!

You might also imagine that such a Coaching Topics Checklist could serve as an ongoing checklist to return to as manager and employee meet regularly to discuss topics of interest to the employee. In fact, having a checklist like this one (customized to fit your environment) might provide the structure for checking in regularly on career and development discussions.

Both the manager and the employee share the ongoing focus for developmental conversations.

Either the manager or the employee might be responsible for bringing this checklist to scheduled coaching conversations, so that both the manager and the employee share the ongoing focus for developmental conversations.

Another Coaching Focus: Growing Performance Capability

Another potential framework on which to focus coaching efforts could be a competency model for effectiveness. Zenger Folkman has conducted a great deal of research into the competencies that distinguish the most effective individual contributors and leaders from the rest; its research is documented in the book *The Extraordinary Leader* (Zenger and Folkman, McGraw-Hill, revised 2009). Utilizing a competency model to form a framework for development discussions can be extremely useful in guiding conversations focused on growing the capability needed for current and future performance.

Drawing upon the Zenger Folkman research, the following leadership dimensions and related competencies have been proven to differentiate the best performers from the rest:

Character
  1. Displays high integrity and honesty

Personal Capability
  2. Has technical and professional expertise
  3. Solves problems and analyzes issues
  4. Innovates
  5. Practices self-development

Focus on Results
  6. Drives for results
  7. Establishes stretch goals
  8. Takes the initiative

Interpersonal Skills
  9. Communicates powerfully and prolifically
  10. Inspires and motivates others to high performance
  11. Builds relationships
  12. Develops others
  13. Engages in collaboration and teamwork

Leading Change
  14. Develops a strategic perspective
  15. Champions change
  16. Connects the group to the outside world

In addition to the Coaching Topics Checklist, both the manager and the employees can utilize a competency model framework as a basis for ongoing development discussions.

A Target for Success

One suggestion for using a competency model (like that just given) would be to invite your employee to identify those competencies that she feels are most critical for her role. At the same time, you would complete the same step.

Next, ask your employee to identify the competencies that she has the most interest in or passion for developing. Finally, look for overlap: where do your employee's passions and organizational needs overlap?

After interviewing thousands of employees and leaders, we have routinely found a small set of universal factors that are always present when individuals achieve peak performance:

- Competence
- Passion
- Organizational needs

If we view these as a Venn diagram, this model looks like Figure 7-1. This framework can offer yet another conversation framework for the manager who wishes to engage in a different or more robust development discussion with employees.

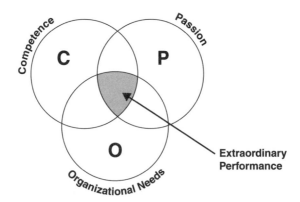

Figure 7-1 Ingredients of Extraordinary Performance

Application

Since you will often be the one to initiate or invite coaching conversations, we think it is useful to practice utilizing the steps of the Coaching Conversation Guide to prepare for your upcoming dialogues. We invite you, in Table 7-8, to consider how you might "rehearse" Framing the Conversation for a coaching conversation that you initiate with a colleague.

Table 7-8

Step 1 Frame the Conversation
(Set the context and focus for the conversation.)

	In Your Words
Identify the behavior or issue to discuss.	I'd like to talk about . . . [the issue].
Determine the purpose or outcomes of the conversation.	• By the end of this conversation, I would like to accomplish . . .
	• What else would you like to make sure that we address?
Agree on the process for the conversation.	• Here's how I thought we could proceed: . . .
	• How does that sound?

Chapter Summary

- By Framing the Conversation, both coach and coachee can maximize their efficiency and their precious resources—including their time!
- Framing the Conversation ensures that the coach and the coachee are agreeing to be in the same conversation, and makes explicit what that conversation will be about.
- Creating a contract for the conversation moves the conversation away from chatting and complaining.

- The coach owns the *process*, whereas the coachee owns the *content* of the conversation.
- The three steps of Framing the Conversation are
  - Identify the behavior or issue to discuss.
  - Determine the purpose or outcomes of the conversation.
  - Agree on the process for the conversation.
- Whether the coach or the coachee initiates the conversation and brings the topic forward, the three steps will be utilized to Frame the Conversation effectively.
- Research suggests that when the coachee is empowered to select the coaching conversation topics, and is later invited to provide feedback regarding the value of the session, the relevance and quality of the conversation (from the coachee's point of view) increase significantly.
- Task updates are not coaching conversations, even though many one-on-one conversations may focus on sharing project status updates.
- Utilizing a coaching topics checklist may provide a useful "door opener" for initiating different types of coaching conversations.
- Utilizing a performance competency model may provide another framework for inviting coaching conversations.
- Targeting the intersection of competence, passion, and organizational needs may be useful in aiming for developmental conversations.

Chapter 8

Understand the Current State

"So How Is That Working for You?"

Assuming that you have successfully completed the first step of the coaching dialogue, Frame the Conversation, you and your coachee will both be targeting the same focus and desired outcome for the conversation. You will have been explicit regarding what that conversation will be about. You are now ready to dive into the details of the current situation, so that you both understand the territory that you are trying to navigate.

Here are some ground rules and guidelines for approaching this step of the coaching conversation:

1. *Suspend your judgment and "knowing."* Chances are that a high percentage of what you believe to be true about the situation— either from preconceived notions or from drawing quick conclusions based on the coachee's description—will be inaccurate.

2. *Maintain a mindset of curiosity.* Your primary task during this phase is to shine a light, for the coachee, on the real issue that needs to be addressed. If you do this step of the conversation well,

your coachee will see her situation in a new light. And if she sees it in a new light, she will be able to choose different actions.

3. *Do not rush into action; take time for exploration.* If the problem could be solved easily, the coachee would have already solved it. The fact that he is wrestling with the issue suggests that the problem is not as readily apparent or the solution is not as neat and tidy as you might believe. Or perhaps the problem and the solution *are* obvious but the coachee is resistant to moving forward in solving the problem for a myriad of reasons. Understanding the Current State allows both of you to gain a clearer picture of what is truly going on—so that you ultimately solve the "right" problem.

4. *Resist giving advice.* Remember that your primary goal for coaching is to expand the thinking and capability of the person you are coaching. If you rush in too quickly to offer your advice, you short-circuit the learning and growth process for the coachee. Even if the coachee asks you for advice, *don't take the bait!* If, after moving through the next steps of the coaching conversation (see Table 8-1), the coachee is missing a critical

Table 8-1 Understand the Current State

Step 2: Understand the Current State	
(Explore the individual's point of view before sharing your own.)	
Understand the coachee's point of view.	• How do you see this situation? • What is happening? • What is working well? • What makes this challenging? • How might you have contributed to this situation? • How might others see the situation?
Determine the consequences of continuing on the current path.	• What impact is this having on you? On others? • What are the consequences if the situation doesn't change? • How does this influence your goals and what you are trying to accomplish? • What are the long-term implications?
Offer your perspective, *if appropriate.*	• Could I share some observations I have made? • Could I offer some other consequences to consider?

idea for proceeding, you can offer it as a possibility. So, for now, just sit tight and turn on your exploration lanterns.

The focus of Step 2: Understand the Current State is not to solve the problem at hand just yet but just to understand it better. In fact, *the true goal of this step of the coaching process is to expand the coachee's point of view into her own situation.* If she can truly understand what the issue is, why it's

> **The true goal of this step is to expand the coachee's point of view.**

particularly bothersome, and the consequences of changing (or not changing), she is likely to gain some insights into how best to proceed. One of the phrases we like to remember is *"awareness precedes change."* Since coaching is always focused on a change agenda, then in order to effect changes in behaviors or outcomes, we must create new awareness for the coachee.

WHY THIS STEP IS SO DIFFICULT FOR US

Like many of the substeps in coaching conversations, those in Step 2 seem relatively straightforward. However, most coaches will agree that this step of the process is perhaps the most challenging of all. Why is that the case? Here are some hunches:

- Many leaders want to jump right in and solve the problem. They "hear the problem" in what the coachee describes, and they believe that they do not need much more description to understand what is really going on.
- When leaders relate to the experience that is being described, they believe that they truly understand what the coachee is going through. (Often, however, the coachee's experience is quite different from the coach's own experience.) This "relating" to the problem actually prevents the coach from hearing the situation from the coachee's point of view.
- Most of us listen to the facts and issues being described as if they represent a fairly complete description of what is truly happening. We fail to listen at deeper levels for what is really going on—how

the coachee is affected by the situation, what the consequences are, and the emotional impact of what is going on. How much angst is this issue causing the coachee, and why? What stories has the coachee made up about what is going on, and how close are those stories to reality?

This step is like walking around the problem to look at it from different vantage points: it takes a bit of time and a great deal of discipline to do so, especially if we think we already clearly understand the issue and the optimum solution for it.

To illustrate how difficult it is to really suspend judgment and listen with an open mind, look at Table 8-2. We received an e-mail a few years ago, describing how a first-grade teacher in Virginia provided the beginnings of some well-known phrases to her first-grade class and asked the students to fill in the missing portion.

In the left-hand column in Table 8-2 are the "starter" phrases, and in the right-hand column are the students' responses.

If you are like most Americans, you probably guessed the "right" or more familiar answers to most of these phrases without

Table 8-2 Seeing Another Point of View

Starter Phrase	The Children's Responses
Don't change horses	until they stop running.
Strike while the	bug is close.
It's always darkest before	Daylight Saving Time.
Never underestimate the power of	termites.
Don't bite the hand that	looks dirty.
Love all, trust	me.
Where there's smoke, there's	pollution.
A penny saved is	not much.
Laugh and the whole world laughs with you; cry and	you have to blow your nose.
Children should be seen and not	spanked or grounded.
You get out of something only what you	see in the picture on the box.
If at first you don't succeed	get new batteries.
An idle mind is	the best way to relax.

even thinking too hard. "Don't change horses in midstream" and "A penny saved is a penny earned" are tried-and-true guiding principles passed from generation to generation, even if they no longer make the same sense in today's modern world. Still, you have probably heard most of these phrases repeated over and over again.

Now compare your own responses and answers to those provided by the children. Their responses are funny, and you can even see how they made sense. But please pause to note how quickly your mind formed the complete answer to each phrase, as soon as you saw the first few words. You probably did not even stop to think that there could be a completely different version of each phrase, once you recognized or identified the familiar pattern.

The same phenomenon happens when you are coaching others. If Terry complains about Andrew being difficult, and you also have the experience that Andrew can be difficult to work with, you immediately fill in your version of "problems with Andrew," and your mind immediately begins to think of solutions that might be useful for Terry to consider. Unfortunately, while your solutions probably work best for *your* particular flavor of "problems with Andrew," this is not necessarily the case for Terry's particular flavor of the same. The same is true of virtually any problem that you might hear someone else describe: problems with a colleague or project; work/life balance being out of whack; feeling undervalued, overworked, and underpaid; and so on.

You most certainly have experienced some version of what is being described. We want to emphasize, though, that your version is absolutely going to be different from the version of the person who is speaking. So, we want to encourage you to *begin exercising restraint with regard to filling in the rest of the picture too quickly.* Pay attention to feeling certain that you understand the situation and you know what is going on; this can be an early cue to remember that the coachee's reality is likely to look and feel differently to him.

Begin exercising restraint with regard to filling in the rest of the picture too quickly.

THE THREE STEPS OF UNDERSTANDING THE CURRENT STATE

So, let us dive into the finer points of each of the three steps contained in Understanding the Current State:

1. Understand the coachee's point of view.
2. Determine the consequences of continuing on the current path.
3. Offer your perspective, *if appropriate.*

Understand the Coachee's Point of View

We want to emphasize that, if done well, this substep will help the coachee see his situation differently from the way he saw it when he started. Will you, as coach, understand the coachee's point of view better after this step of the conversation is completed? Absolutely. But what will create even more value is if the coachee sees his situation and issue differently as a result of your good work in this phase.

So, how can that happen? We will answer that question for you in the next few pages. Let us start by asserting that you have two important roles during this phase of the conversation:

1. A mirror
2. An exploration guide

Your Role as a Mirror

One primary role that you play with someone you are coaching is that of being a mirror that reflects back to that person what her reality is. Consider why we look into mirrors. Almost every day, we will look at our reflection in a mirror at least once—and often far more frequently. Why? To see how others are viewing us, to make sure that what we *believe* we are projecting is actually what others are seeing, and to decide if anything needs to be adjusted based on what we see.

If you consider that your role is to be a human mirror to those whom you coach, you will want to be a reflective instrument:

- Let them know what you are hearing.
- Reflect back how they are describing their scenarios.
- Help to present an "objective reality" of the situation.

Coaching Conversation Guide, at a high level, *is* the process that the coach will guide the coachee through. The generic process after Framing the Conversation would be:

- Understand the Current State
- Explore the Desired State
- Lay Out a Success Plan

So, if a coach were going to use a generic process statement, he might say something like the italicized text in Table 7-4.

If this is what a coach offers in defining the process for the conversation, this is definitely a good start. However, the coach can customize this process statement and make it much more relevant to the actual specific outcome that the coachee is hoping to achieve. Going back to the example introduced in Table 7-2, the coach used the process statement shown in italics in the right column of Table 7-5.

You can see that the coach used language and a suggested process, or flow for the conversation, that closely reflected what the coachee wanted to focus on: the "reality check" and how to have a conversation with Ed that wouldn't blow up. In doing so, the coach truly tailored the structure for the conversation to meet the "target" that the coachee was aiming for.

There may be other elements that you want to address when agreeing on the process for the conversation. These might include things like

Table 7-4

Agree on the process for the conversation.	Understand the Current State	*Why don't we start with an overview of the current situation, so that we both have a clear picture of what is happening here?*
	Explore the Desired State	*We can explore what you would like to see happen and then brainstorm some alternatives for getting there.*
	Lay Out a Success Plan	*Then we can identify some specific actions to take and a timeline for moving forward.*

In order to truly be a reflective mirror, presenting objective reality, you cannot distort the image that comes back to the coachee. What does that mean for you? It means that you must not let your own biases creep into the reflection. If you do, you will be more like a mirror in a carnival fun house, distorting the image of the person standing in front of it. We do not want any wavy or broken mirrors that present the image in a distorted way! So, make sure that your reflection is true and accurate.

How can you do that? By listening well.

Listening Well

The best thing you can do when you are listening to your coachee explain a situation is WAIT. W.A.I.T., as in, Why Am I Talking? That's right, it's not always necessary to put your two cents in right away. While we are truly trying to Understand the Current State, we will be well served to remember this handy acronym. Remember, the coachee should be talking at least 75 percent of the time.

So, if the coachee is doing most of the talking, what are we doing? Listening. Now, that probably sounds obvious, but listening is one of the skills that few people ever master in their lives. While we may have a lifetime of practice in listening, our practice of this skill has not necessarily been perfect. My piano teacher used to say, "Practice does not make perfect. *Perfect* practice makes perfect. Practice only makes permanent." And so it is with listening. So what do we listen for?

Consider that most of what a coachee shares about his situation will be descriptions of the issue as he sees it—he will probably focus on events and even present his interpretation of those events as facts and truths about the situation. Most situations are like icebergs, with only 10 percent actually appearing above the water. If you have ever seen an iceberg up close, you know that it appears very substantial—it is hard to imagine that the vast majority of its mass is hidden and cannot readily be seen at the surface. The same is true of most coaching issues. What a coachee describes may often represent only the tip of his total situation.

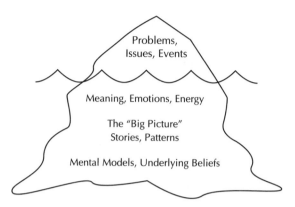

Figure 8-1 Listening at a Deeper Level

Drawing upon Robert Hargrove's model in *The Masterful Coaching Fieldbook,* you can see that we want to listen for many different layers beyond the surface layer that is often described (see Figure 8-1).

This model suggests that we must listen at deeper levels. We need to challenge our assumptions and conclusions. We want to listen for emotions that our coachee displays through her tone of voice and body language. We want to listen for patterns of behavior and thinking and to reflect those back to our coachee. And we want to use all of these as we reflect back to her—by being a mirror.

Listening for Emotions: Follow the "Emotional Bunny Trail"
If the client is discussing the situation at the top level—the part of the iceberg that appears above the water—the fastest way to take the conversation to a deeper level will be for you to listen to what is just below the surface: the emotions and feelings that the coachee is experiencing. You do this by watching and listening for any "pings"—any changes in the way in which the coachee describes his situation.

There are two ways to listen more deeply for emotions:

1. Listening for any emotion words (e.g., *scared, anxious, frustrated, thrilled, ecstatic,* or *mad*)
2. Watching and listening for nonverbal cues that would express emotional energy underneath the words being used (e.g., a raised tone of voice, quickened speech pattern, more emotive facial expressions, or more extreme hand gestures)

With sonar technology, used in submarine navigation, sonar technicians listen for "pings"—any indication of how close another object is underwater. Consider the notion of listening for emotions as your human version of using sonar (originally an acronym for SOund Navigation And Ranging), where the object of your sounding technique is to locate how close emotions are to the issue that is being discussed. The more emotions that someone is feeling regarding an issue, the more likely it is that the issue is close to something that truly matters to that individual. And the more that something truly matters to the individual, the more likely it is that he will feel the energy and want to change the situation.

We recommend following the emotions when you get close to feelings or greater energy being expressed. The emotions are likely to lead us to the heart of the matter and the true coaching issue that needs to be resolved. Emotions and feelings will lead us under the water's surface to explore the rest of the iceberg.

Let Silence Do the Heavy Lifting

In her book *Fierce Conversations*, Susan Scott offers the phrase "Let silence do the heavy lifting." We could not agree more. Feel free to use a pregnant pause as a way to prompt your coachee to continue speaking. Do not be troubled by silence, or step in to fill the gaps. Sometimes the most effective form of listening will be to allow space for the other individual to reflect more deeply and to continue her stream of thoughts.

How All of This Listening Actually Sounds in a Coaching Conversation

Let us look at how this might sound, using the example that was introduced in the previous chapter. You may recall that our coachee had an issue with her colleague, Ed—she felt that the balance between the demands on and needs from each other seemed lopsided, and she wanted to have a conversation with Ed to determine how to resolve the imbalance.

The example in Table 8-3 illustrates some key aspects of effective coaching:

1. The coach is a mirror to the coachee. The coach does not add his interpretation of what is going on but instead just reflects back to the coachee what he is hearing.
2. Included in what the coach reflects back are the emotions that the coachee is expressing—not just the descriptions or "facts" of the event.

Table 8-3

Understand the coachee's point of view.	**Coach:** So, tell me a little about what is going on. How are the requests lopsided?
	Coachee: Here's a perfect example. I would say that at least once or twice a week, Ed will e-mail me and say that he needs to find 30 minutes on my calendar *that day* to discuss something that he urgently needs, so that he can move forward on his projects. I try to jump through hoops to make those times work and to meet his requests. Yet I can't even count how many unanswered items I have, where I am still waiting on responses from him. I e-mail him and ask for information, and I would say that there is a 50/50 chance that I will *ever* get an answer from him. On some occasions, I just proceed without getting the information from him. At other times, I feel like I practically have to hound him to get him to respond. It takes a lot of effort on my part to get my needs met, but he acts as if the world will end if I don't help him on his requests the same day he makes them.
	Coach: So, not only do the requests seem lopsided—he wants his needs met immediately—but the effort you have to expend to get your needs met seems lopsided as well. I can hear the frustration in your voice as you describe this.
	Coachee: I *am* frustrated. It feels completely unfair to me. Why should I help Ed get his projects completed, when he isn't willing to help me?
	Coach: So it feels like a win/lose scenario. It seems as if Ed is always winning, and you might be losing, based on what is happening here. Is that how you would describe this?

(Continued)

Coachee: Well, *lose* is probably too strong a word. I'll still get my job done.

Coach: Hmmm. (Silence; pause)

Coachee: I just feel that I'm being taken advantage of. Why should I bend over backward to help him meet his deadlines, when he doesn't seem to be the least bit interested in helping me meet mine?

Coach: That is definitely a good question to ponder. On a 1 to 10 scale, with 1 being low and 10 being high, how much frustration are you feeling about this relationship with Ed?

Coachee: Probably a 6. Actually, this number probably moves around a bit. When I'm e-mailing back and forth with Ed, it feels like an 8. I get so angry thinking about his requests when he never responds to mine. When I'm working on my own projects, I feel like it is a 2—I keep busy and move my tasks forward. When I'm actually talking with Ed, it usually goes OK, and the number is probably a 3 or 4.

Coach: So that is interesting. When you are working alone or are in a "live" conversation with Ed, the number is fairly low. What makes the number jump up to an 8 when you are e-mailing back and forth?

Coachee: (Laughs) Probably because I make up stories about how Ed is trying to sabotage my work and expects me to set him up to be a hero.

Coach: (Laughs) Well, that could be one scenario. What else might be true here?

Coachee: Ed might just be much more clear about communicating what he needs and when he needs it. I probably just hope and assume that he will respond to my requests in a timely manner. But I never "demand" it. He is usually very clear about needing to talk to me within a certain time frame. I become resentful based on what I tell myself about the requests he makes.

Coach: So that is a great insight. You don't communicate your time frames as clearly as he does, and when he does communicate his time frames to you, you try to make those happen. While this is all going on, you are questioning his motives and starting to feel resentful.

Coachee: Yeah. That sounds silly when you put it that way. I should just be clearer in my communication.

Through the process of the coach's trying to understand the coachee's point of view, the coachee has a different insight into her own situation. In this example, she realizes that she probably has not been communicating as clearly as she could, and her own behavior in the situation may be contributing to the results she is getting—and ultimately how she is feeling.

Because the coachee now sees her situation differently, she will be much more likely to take a different action that will help her resolve the tension-causing situation. Thus, if this step of the conversation is conducted effectively, the seeds of a solution will start to become clear.

Ask Open-Ended, Nonleading Questions

If there are two sides to a coin in the skill set of coaching, one side would be listening, and the other side would be powerful questioning. As with listening, we have had a lifetime of practice in asking questions. And we have probably been practicing a form of questioning that will not necessarily lead to the most powerful coaching outcomes.

We challenge you to audiotape yourself in a dialogue with an employee or just make a mental note of the types of questions you ask. If you are like most leaders, a large percentage of the questions you ask will be closed-ended questions. Closed-ended questions (which demand a yes/no answer or a finite answer like a number or a date) are extremely useful in gaining *clarity*, but not in gaining *insight*. What is the difference?

Clarity is extremely useful in checking for understanding and/or making an obvious point obvious. For instance, our coach in the example above might have asked

- So, have you shared your frustration with Ed?
- Do you state specific timelines in your requests to Ed?
- Have you ever missed a deadline because Ed did not respond to you?

All of these questions might be useful in bringing to the surface the facts that our coachee has not yet shared her frustration with Ed, she has not been specific in her requests, and so far her work has not been compromised as a result of Ed's lack of performance.

Insight is the more useful objective at this step of the process. Some of the questions just given may, in fact, generate insight within our coachee. We do not advocate that you *never* ask closed-ended questions. Used in a timely and appropriate manner, they provide great value for the conversation. However, you will gain far greater benefit from asking more open-ended, nonleading questions.

Open-ended, nonleading questions are best used in helping to expand the conversation. If used well, they will lead to *both* clarity and insight. Our coach asked the following open-ended, nonleading questions, and promoted both clarity and insight:

- So, tell me a little about what is going on. How are the requests lopsided?
- On a 1 to 10 scale, with 1 being low and 10 being high, how much frustration are you feeling about this relationship with Ed? *(Note: this is a closed-ended question that leads to great insight for both coach and coachee.)*
- What makes the number jump up to an 8 when you are e-mailing back and forth?
- What else might be true here?

Notice that the coach does not ask questions to dive into the details of the scenario. In fact, the tactic of diving into the details of the issue can almost guarantee two things:

1. The coachee does not gain any new insight (as she is merely recounting or rehashing her version of the scenario).
2. A significant amount of time can be spent on information that does not lead to insight.

For instance, here are some questions that probably would *not* lead to greater insight in this scenario:

- What did Ed request of you?
- How did you respond?
- What requests did you make of Ed this week?
- How did he respond to your e-mail?

- How many requests did Ed make of you last week? How many did you make of Ed?
- What were your deadlines? What were his?

On the surface, all of these appear to be open, nonleading questions. However, if we remember that our primary purpose in this

This step of the coaching conversation is to help the coachee see her scenario in a new light.

step of the coaching conversation is to *help the coachee see her scenario in a new light,* we will quickly see that these questions do not provide the coachee with greater insight. They might provide us with lots of details, but details about the facts at hand—or what has already transpired—do not typically shift the way the coachee views the situation.

Exploration Guide Wanted

Your second role is that of being an exploration guide. Imagine what a true exploration guide's mission is: to help you see aspects of your surroundings that you had not seen before. I think it is helpful to conjure up the image of a guide strapping on a headlamp, with a set of binoculars in one hand or a flashlight in the other hand, and walking side by side with the coachee, with a mission to help the coachee see things that he has never seen before.

I remember going on a 13-hour park tour in Denali National Park (Alaska). At the very beginning of our day, the tour guide said, "We will probably encounter bear, fox, moose, elk, and wild birds. I don't know where or when we'll see them, so we'll all need to be on the lookout. If you even remotely think you see something—even if it ends up being just a rock—shout it out! Tell me to stop! I'll be on the lookout, too. We don't want to miss the chance to see something. If it ends up being nothing, that's OK. We've all mistaken a lot of rocks for big game. Just yesterday, I said, 'Look at that bear cub,' only to realize that it was a small brown boulder. But, better that we stopped and looked than if we missed something important. So, let's go find some wild animals!"

Imagine that *you* are that exploration guide. You do not need to ask the coachee one thousand questions regarding his background and the facts of the situation—details do not usually lead to insight. You are ready to begin looking at the here-and-now and trying to see the situation from new angles. You are hoping to see anew.

In addition to understanding the coachee's point of view, the next two steps of Understand the Current State can often lead to additional exploration and insight for the coachee:

- Determine the consequences of continuing on the current path.
- Offer your perspective, *if appropriate.*

Let us look at each of these, in turn.

Determine the Consequences of Continuing on the Current Path

Our colleague Joe Folkman often reminds us that "people won't change unless there is a felt need." We will definitely explore this concept in greater detail later. For now, suffice it to say that if people do not feel that a change will provide them with more gain than loss, they will not change. At this point in the conversation, part of the coach's role is to highlight what will happen if the coachee does nothing—the consequences of continuing on the current path. The coach and the coachee may find that the coachee can easily live with the consequences of doing nothing; this may reveal to both that the "felt need" for change is not significant.

Alternatively (and more frequently), the coachee may see more clearly that he does not want to live with the current situation for an extended period of time. This heightened awareness may provide the fuel to change his situation more readily.

Let us look at how this part of the conversation might go, using our continued example of the employee wrestling with Ed and his requests (see Table 8-4).

Table 8-4

Determine the consequences of continuing on the current path.	**Coach:** You've talked about the frustration you are feeling with this situation. What other impact is this situation having on you?

(Continued)

Table 8-4 (Continued)

Coachee: I find that I'm trying to meet Ed's requests, but I'm also dragging my feet. I guess I'm responding, but in a passive-aggressive way. So, instead of responding as soon as I see the e-mail, I might wait until the afternoon to respond. This gives both of us less time to make the requested meeting happen. On one or two occasions, we couldn't find time left in the day, because of other commitments.

Coach: So what is the overall impact on you, including those times when you can't meet Ed's needs?

Coachee: I end up feeling bad about how I am responding. I want to be a collaborative, supportive colleague, and when I feel resentful, I really don't come across that way.

Coach: So, what do you think the long-term implications are if the current situation doesn't change?

Coachee: Well, over time, I'll probably feel even more resentful. I might just stop helping Ed altogether, and I could see myself finding ways around needing to rely on him for anything. That would probably lead to a bigger breakdown in the way we work together. That scenario doesn't really work for anyone, and it certainly doesn't help the work we are trying to accomplish.

Coach: Is anyone else affected by the current situation? Colleagues? Others on the projects that either of you are working on?

Coachee: I don't think so.

Coach: Let me ask you a different question: are there any benefits of not changing the current situation? What is the payoff for continuing in this way?

Coachee: *(Sarcastically)* Well, I get to feel some glee when I get in Ed's way. Payback is only fair, you know. (Pause) But in reality, there probably aren't any real payoffs. I don't think what we have is working for either of us now. I'm sure Ed feels some tension, too. It would be hard for him not to feel tension, given the pressure he's feeling to get his work done. I'm pretty sure he is behind on his projects, so my delay in responding only adds to the pressure he's feeling.

Coach: So, it sounds as if the current situation is not sustainable, and ultimately will lead to a pretty dysfunctional—or even failed—working relationship.

By exploring the consequences of not changing, the coachee frequently realizes what is truly at stake if the situation continues in its current fashion. The coachee is likely to feel greater pressure to change the situation if the consequences of not changing are significant (as they are in the example given here).

Offer Your Perspective, *if Appropriate*

This third step of Understand the Current State gets a little tricky. Here is where your newly developed restraint muscles must be tested. We would venture to say that in many—if not most— coaching conversations, your perspective will not add a great deal of value to the situation. There are two unique times where your perspective is truly vital and critical to be shared. They are

1. Feedback conversations that you initiate. (We'll cover this in detail in Chapter 15, "When Feedback Becomes a Coaching Conversation.")
2. When the coachee is not seeing an important aspect of her situation clearly and/or when your perspective would add a different and important viewpoint.

As a manager, you may feel that we want you to abandon your point of view and rely solely on the coachee's solving his own problems. In fact, we want you to get work done in the most effective and expedient way possible. And, on occasion, that means that the coachee needs to see a critical element of the situation or its consequences that he is not currently seeing.

If you are in a coaching conversation where the coachee does not see the consequences of his contributing behavior or the impact that the situation is having on his (or others') work performance, you should definitely add your perspective.

In the scenario we are using, our coachee did not see any negative implications of her relationship with Ed for any of her colleagues or other project team members. As a manager, you might have a different view of the whole picture, since you manage some of those other team members. You may want or need to intervene by sharing your perspective—for the purpose of helping to create more of a "felt need" to change.

Table 8-5 gives an example.

Table 8-5

Offer your perspective, *if appropriate*.	**Coach:** Earlier you said that you didn't think anyone else was affected by the dynamic between you and Ed. Could I offer some other consequences to consider?
	Coachee: Sure.
	Coach: I often find that conflicts between some team members tend to "bleed over" into other relationships or even the entire team. Do you have a sense of anyone else who might see or feel the tension between you and Ed?
	Coachee: Well, I don't think it is visible to most of the team, but I have confided in Tom regarding "the Ed situation." I have been so frustrated, and Tom is on my project team. His work is also affected if Ed doesn't get us answers in time.
	Coach: How do you think confiding in Tom has affected him and his views of Ed?
	Coachee: I don't think it has.
	Coach: That may be true; Tom might be able to be a really great listener and supporter to you. But I just have to wonder whether your expressing frustration about Ed doesn't ultimately affect how Tom views Ed and how they interact with each other. What do you think? How would that work if you were in Tom's shoes and he was in yours?
	Coachee: I guess it is possible. It would be hard for me to remain neutral toward someone if a team member was having a really bad experience working with him and complained to me about him.
	Coach: Even though you think that this situation is fairly "contained" right now, I'd encourage you to consider the ripple effect of this dynamic on others on *both* your and Ed's respective teams, and on the project work itself. Would you be willing to do that?
	Coachee: Yeah. Makes sense.

While we outlined an example of how the coach might share a perspective other than the one the coachee had, you might ask yourself, "Was that really needed?" If you recall the conversation that the coach and the coachee were having, the coachee was already seeing a need to fix the situation, regardless of any impact on her colleagues. Therefore, we suggest that you use this third step of the process judiciously—only when your point of view will actually help the coachee progress toward taking better actions regarding her scenario. In this coaching conversation, the coach probably did not need to share this additional point of view with the coachee—it looked as if she was already gaining insight into the need to change.

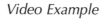

Video Example

If you would like to see examples of a coach guiding this second step of the coaching conversation, Understand the Current State, go to www.zengerfolkman.com and click on the Leadership Resource Center icon. You will find examples of a coach bringing the real issues of the coaching conversation to the surface. In the video examples that you view, pay attention to how the coach asks open-ended, nonleading questions; how the coach listens deeply to what is being said; and how the coachee gains a more complete understanding of her own situation.

Your Personal Question Treasure Trove

We encourage you to begin building a repertoire of high-impact questions that you find work very well for you. Most skilled coaches utilize a handful of select questions that lead to insight for the coachee and advance the conversation. Here are some sample questions that you might want to experiment with. If you find that they work well, consider putting them

(Continued)

into your personal question toolkit for future use. For now, place a check mark next to any questions that you believe would fit your natural style. One of our personal favorites is Question 17. This represents a scaling question and quickly gives both you and the coachee insight regarding how significant the issue at hand truly is.

1. What is the most important thing for us to be discussing right now?
2. What has happened lately that makes this an important topic?
3. Help me understand the seriousness of this to you.
4. Tell me about the business consequences of this topic.
5. How does this affect you personally?
6. How are you feeling right now about the situation?
7. Do you know anyone for whom this is not an issue? What do you think is different about their situation?
8. What makes this challenging for you?
9. What proof or evidence do you have to support that?
10. Have you checked out your perception with others? What did you learn?
11. How would others view or describe this situation?
12. If the person you are having a conflict with were here with us now, what would his point of view be?
13. Are there any outside forces that are making this continue? What are they?
14. If you could resolve this, what effect would it have on your job satisfaction? Your career success?
15. Imagine that a year has passed and nothing has changed. What would that be like for you?
16. What are the long-term implications if this situation doesn't change?
17. On a 1-to-10 scale, with 1 being "this is a small problem" and 10 being "this feels almost insurmountable," how do you feel about this issue?

18. If you could identify the three most significant factors contributing to this, what would they be? How would you rank them?
19. How have you contributed to this situation?
20. *And of course, borrowed from Dr. Phil:* So, how is that working for you?

Chapter Summary

- As you begin to Understand the Current State, remember to suspend your judgment and maintain a curious mindset.
- Your goal in this conversation phase is to help the coachee gain a different awareness of and insight into the coaching issue.
- Because awareness precedes change, helping the coachee to gain greater insight and clarity is critical. The seeds of the solution will already be present in the new awareness.
- A major challenge that prevents us from truly understanding the coachee's point of view is that we tend to fill in the gaps without even thinking.
- You have two key roles at this stage of the conversation: acting as a mirror *and* being a great exploration guide.
- Following the pings and the "emotional bunny trail" will lead you closer to the real issue and what truly matters to the coachee.
- Asking open-ended, nonleading questions allows greater insight and clarity for both you as coach and the coachee.
- Beware of asking questions that dive too deeply into the details; remember that our focus is on growing the coachee's awareness of his own situation.
- People will not change until they feel a need to change. Exploring the consequences of not changing helps to bring focus to the potential need to change the situation at hand.
- Offer your perspective when it adds to the conversation and creates greater awareness for the coachee. Just be careful here!
- Begin capturing questions that work well for you in your own personal repertoire.

Chapter 9

Explore the Desired State

Aiming for the Right Target

Getting to this next phase in the coaching conversation causes most managers to breathe a sigh of relief. The first two steps of the coaching conversation (Frame the Conversation and Understand the Current State) feel awkward because they are unfamiliar. Why? We usually rush past these and jump right into problem solving. It is as if our background processor is constantly searching for the answer to "How can we find a solution for this? What steps can we take to fix this?" And most self-confessed advice givers recognize the magnetic force that draws them to want to fix whatever "problem" they have just heard being described.

By now, we hope you see the value of spending the right amount of time on the first two steps of the conversation. By doing so, you know that you are working on the "right" issue with the coachee. The third step, Explore the Desired State, puts us back into more comfortable territory—beginning to seek solutions for the issue we have defined. Eureka! Now you can begin to directly help solve the coachee's dilemma!

A word of caution for the problem solvers and advice givers among us: coaching works best if the coachee generates the solution. Just because we are in problem-solving territory does not

Table 9-1 Explore the Desired State

Step 3: Explore the Desired State

(Identify the target and generate multiple paths to achieve the end state.)

Understand the vision for success.	• What would you like to see happen here? • What would the ideal state look like?
Set goals and performance expectations.	• What are your goals? What would you like to accomplish? • Here's how I see it: . . .
Explore alternative paths of action.	• What might be some approaches you can take? • What else might work? • Could I offer a couple of thoughts? You might want to consider . . .
Explore possible barriers or resistance.	• What are the major barriers preventing this change from happening? • Where would the biggest resistance to this change come from?

mean that *we* are the ones solving the problem. Let us review the map for this territory (Table 9-1).

DON'T LOCK AND LOAD!

Most of us love to solve problems. It gives us a sense of relief or hope. We get excited quickly at the thought of potential solutions that might alleviate the tension we are experiencing. Feeling relief and hope about moving forward with an issue is definitely a good thing.

However, we often short-circuit the value of this stage by driving too quickly toward a solution for the issue that we have identified.

We often short-circuit the value of this stage by driving too quickly toward a solution for the issue.

How does this happen? We think of a single solution that might work to address our scenario, and we "lock and load" with that one solution—never stopping to consider whether there are alternative solutions that might lead to an even better conclusion.

Imagine a coaching scenario where one of your direct reports approached you to discuss improving his "executive presence." After framing the conversation and really understanding what is at the heart of the issue for him, you discover that the coachee really feels invisible—and he wants to make sure that his accomplishments are well known to other senior leaders in the organization. He feels that this is critical if he is to be considered for other future positions.

Without utilizing all of the substeps in Explore the Desired State, the conversation might sound like this:

Coach: So, what do you think you could do to get greater visibility for your accomplishments?

Coachee: Well, I guess I could speak up more in meetings, and really highlight what we have been able to accomplish on the projects. I don't like being boastful, so I'll need to strike the right balance. I could also keep you more informed, so that you could speak about the project work in the meetings that you attend, too. I would really appreciate it if you would say a good word about my work from time to time, with your colleagues, as appropriate.

Coach: Sure. They both sound like good steps. When will you start doing those?

Now, the good news in this dialogue is that the coach is guiding the process and the coachee is generating (and owning) the solution. However, the solution could potentially be far more thoughtful and rich. By utilizing the substeps of Explore the Desired State, we will almost always generate a better solution than if we lock and load with the first few thoughts that seem to address the challenge.

Let us consider how the same conversation might go instead if we use just the first substep, understand the vision for success (see Table 9-2).

As you can see, the real vision for success is a broader target to aim for, rather than just gaining more visibility for work accomplishments. If we do a good job of understanding the coachee's vision for success (or our shared vision for success), we can create a much larger target to aim for. Then, when we begin brainstorming the alternative paths to get us there, we are likely to have an even broader assortment of viable strategies and steps to take. Would

Table 9-2

Understand the vision for success.	**Coach:** You've mentioned wanting greater visibility for your accomplishments. Let me ask you, what would you really like to see happen here? What would the ideal scenario look like for you?
	Coachee: Well, I'd like enough other senior leaders to know who I am and know my accomplishments, so that I can be considered for other positions when they open up.
	Coach: What else would be in that ideal scenario?
	Coachee: Honestly? I'd love to be considered for an international assignment. My wife and I would love to be able to work a couple of years in either Brazil, India, or China before we have kids and that option would get harder.
	Coach: What would the ideal next role look like for you? Do you have a sense of that?
	Coachee: Well, if I had a magic wand, I'd love to be leading the marketing efforts for our products in a market where we don't have a huge presence yet. And I'd like to work in a really small team, where we were all wearing a lot of hats. I think it would be fun to stretch my capabilities by having to do some tasks that I currently don't do now, just because we are so specialized.

If we do a good job of understanding the coachee's vision for success we can create a much larger target to aim for. the first few suggestions for gaining visibility still work here? Yes, *and* we would also want to create other strategies to target the greater vision of an international assignment, doing marketing work in a small team, in a market where the organization does not yet have a large presence.

THE FOUR SUBSTEPS IN EXPLORING THE DESIRED STATE

As mentioned earlier, there are four substeps to this part of the FUEL framework. These are

1. Understand the vision for success
2. Set goals and performance expectations

3. Explore alternative paths of action
4. Explore possible barriers or resistance

We will take a look at each of these substeps here.

Understand the Vision for Success: Aim for a Big Target—Don't Be Skimpy!

The first step of Exploring the Desired State is to understand the vision for success. As a coach, you want to spend as much time as necessary here, to truly elaborate on the coachee's vision.

Let us playfully illustrate a skimpy vision of success versus a bigger vision.

If I asked you if you would like a bowl of chocolate ice cream, you might say, "Sure" (assuming that you like chocolate ice cream!). How much more compelling would it be if I asked you if you would like a bowl of Ben & Jerry's New York Super Fudge Chunk ice cream with a dollop of fresh, real whipped cream on top at an outdoor table? What if I also mentioned that you could enjoy your ice cream with an ocean view at sunset, a light ocean breeze gently rustling the palm tree fronds, and your favorite music in the background? Would you be more or less likely to shout out a resounding "*Yes!*" to the second scenario? Chances are that the second choice is more compelling and enticing than the first choice of "just" chocolate ice cream.

What is the difference? The vision we painted in the second choice is far more clear, compelling, and tantalizing. It is also larger. Instead of just focusing on chocolate ice cream, we expanded the picture and presented you with the ocean setting, the perfect weather, and the music in the background. No wonder the second choice was more enticing.

When we expand and clarify the vision of our coachees, several really powerful things happen:

1. The coachee begins to see more clearly the reality that she wants to bring about.
2. The target zone expands, ultimately providing more possible options for reaching the target.

3. Details are filled in, which help to make the target more specific, as well as more compelling.
4. Excitement about creating the reality begins to grow, making the coachee's commitment to pursuing the end state more likely.

In feedback conversations, where *you* are hoping, as the leader, that a behavior is corrected, you may also have a clear point of view regarding the desired vision of success. You may be offering your thoughts on what might be possible. For instance, if you are coaching one of your employees to behave more collaboratively in team meetings, you might offer a picture of success for the coachee to consider:

> Ideally, I would like to see you be able to consider others' points of view and validate those points of view, instead of immediately deciding what won't work. For instance, if Sue says that she has thought about a process improvement that she'd like to implement, I'd love to see your first reaction be one of support for her idea—find something good in what she is saying. I'd also like to see you be able to share your point of view without sounding as if there is just one right way to tackle the issue at hand. As we both know, there are probably several different ways to skin a cat. I would imagine that both of these actions would create more good feelings between you and your coworkers, and you'd probably find the meetings more enjoyable and less conflict-ridden than they currently are.
>
> What else would you want to create, as you consider working more collaboratively with your peers?

The final question in this example reminds us that even if you, as coach, help to create the vision for success, we still need to engage the coachee to make sure that she has input into and a stake in the final outcome.

Set Goals and Performance Expectations: You Get to Have a Point of View!

The second step of Exploring the Desired State is to set goals and performance expectations. Once you and the coachee have a shared vision of success, you will begin outlining more concrete goals or performance expectations.

Occasionally, we hear from leaders that they feel that the coach's point of view is the only one that is important. Especially when they are Exploring the Desired State—what they want to see happen, and the goals that they want to accomplish—leaders express concern that the employee may not see the entire picture. As a result, his goals or desired state may not be fully reflective of what is possible or what needs to happen. We want to assure you that, as a coach, you get to have a point of view here!

Imagine having a direct report who was always late to work, took long lunch hours, and did not complete all of her assignments on time. Now imagine asking this employee what her vision of success and her desired goals are. She might say that her vision of success is to successfully complete all of her assignments in a timely fashion, while retaining flexibility in how she works. (Sounds good so far, right?) When asked what goals might help her achieve that vision, imagine that she responds, "I would love to work just three days a week, choose the days of the week that I work, and get the work done that is really most interesting to me. If I need to take longer lunches to run errands, I'd like you to just trust me that I will get the rest of my work done sometime. I'll let you know if I am running into any problems."

Now, we all might agree that this description might be a great future state—but only for her, not for us or for the organization! As a leader, you will undoubtedly have a point of view regarding the goals or performance expectations that your employees or colleagues aim for. Depending on the coaching conversation, you may choose to share your point of view or decide that doing so would not be helpful.

In a feedback conversation, where an employee's behavior *must* change, or else there will be dire consequences, you will undoubtedly need to take a more active stance in this second step of the process. Using the scenario of your direct report who wants to work selectively only three days a week, you might state your goals and performance expectations clearly:

Jane, I can appreciate your wanting to have a great deal of flexibility in your schedule; however, that won't work for your role. Your role is obviously specialized, and we have internal customers who may need your support at any time during regular working hours. Because of this, we need you to cover the standard hours during the week. That means that you need to be here Monday through Friday from 8:30 to 5:00. This doesn't mean that we can't make occasional exceptions, based on other personal needs that you have. But we will need to negotiate those in advance. Does that make sense to you?

Explore Alternative Paths of Action: "What Else? What Else?"

The third step of Exploring the Desired State is to explore alternative paths of action. The key to this step of the process is to make sure that you exhaust the possibilities before you narrow down the choices.

We earlier described what happens when people rush to find solutions: most will identify the first solution that seems reasonable to pursue, and begin action planning based on that choice.

In 1963, Norman R. F. Maier published research on the problem-solving process. Many observers still consider it the best research conducted on that topic.[1] Maier's research clearly shows that when individuals identify at least *three* possible alternatives, they end up creating a better solution than those who adopt the first plausible idea that comes to hand. How many of us pause to generate more good ideas when we have already found one that we like? We probably don't even recognize the value of generating multiple choices from which to select. We are in a hurry, and we want to begin implementing some reasonable fix.

When individuals identify at least **three** *possible alternatives, they end up creating a better solution.*

Yet, when we make a major purchase (e.g., a house or a car) most of us will consider multiple options. We then research those options and choose the one that makes the most sense, given the costs and benefits.

If we employ this same searching, evaluating, and choosing process when we coach others (or make our own decisions), we will almost always be better off.

The magical questions for you at this step in the conversation are

- What else?
- What else might work?
- What other options might get you to the desired end state?
- What else?

If your experience is anything like ours, you will be amazed at how many additional possibilities emerge when you ask these follow-up questions. Just when you thought there were no further ideas to bring to the surface, they keep coming. And the options generated later are usually the ones that are the most practical and sound. Or, some combination of the various possibilities makes the best holistic solution.

Your Advice is Welcome—with Some Caveats

As you are helping your coachee to explore alternative paths, you may find yourself in the position of recognizing that he has not identified the most obvious path to take (from your point of view, of course). You might even feel compelled to share your thoughts—because if you didn't, he might take the wrong course of action. And our message to you here is . . . feel free! This is a perfect time to share your additional good thoughts.

However, we would suggest that you offer your opinions as alternative possibilities to explore, rather than providing advice and expecting the coachee to run with it. Throw your ideas into the mix, along with the other alternatives generated by the coachee. We encourage you to exhaust the coachee's ideas, and then ask permission to add your additional thoughts: "Could I suggest a couple of other possibilities for you to consider?"

The key here is to be more tentative and less directive. We would also suggest that you not be too attached to the coachee fully embracing your good idea—even at this point. More often than not, the coachee will provide some feedback to you suggesting that the idea you have offered probably will not work here. Or, the coachee will

The ideas that are most apt to be tried and successfully implemented by the coachee come from within that person.

mutter, "Yeah, that's a good idea," while the body language behind the statement transmits an absolute indifference to what you just suggested. Don't take it personally; just recognize that (yet again) your advice may not work as well in reality as it does in the script in your mind. The ideas that are most apt to be tried and successfully implemented by the coachee come from within that person. No matter how smart or experienced you are, you will not change this fundamental dimension of human behavior.

When the Coachee Has No Ideas

When you get to this step of the conversation and ask, "What actions might you take to get to the ideal state?" the coachee might respond, "I have no idea. That is why I came to you. What do you think I should do?"

This is a very tempting trap—don't fall into it!

Remember, your primary goal in coaching is to expand the capacity of your coachee to solve her own problems—to think more critically, and to feel more confident in her ability to solve increasingly complex challenges. If you step in now and offer all of your ideas and advice, you will have short-circuited the process of development and growth for the coachee.

One manager used a device that defies logic on one dimension. Having been told by the coachee that he didn't know the answer, nor did he have any ideas, this coach would say, "If you *did* know the answer, what do you think it might be?" Amazingly, more often than not, the coachee would then come forth with insightful and reasonable ideas about how to proceed.

If you are not comfortable with that device, then step over to the coachee's side instead and *become a brainstorming partner.* Say something along the lines of, "I have a few ideas to consider, and I'm sure that you probably do, too. You are much closer to the situation than I am. What if we brainstorm some possibilities—I can throw out some ideas, and let's just bat some thoughts back and forth. Perhaps you will think of some good options in the process. How does that sound?"

Then, begin to brainstorm together. Offer one or two options for the coachee to consider, and then make sure to pause and encourage the coachee to expand on these ideas: "What else comes to mind for you? What else might work? What do those ideas trigger for you?"

Be careful not to take over the conversation and go back into advice-giving mode. Unless the coachee is truly a novice and needs more direction and advice, brainstorming is likely to jump-start her thinking and her ability to find some solutions that are not as readily apparent.

Prioritize and Choose the Path

If you have done your job well in the previous steps, you will have generated multiple possible paths that can be taken to create the desired end state. Before you drill into the specific action steps, you will want to help the coachee prioritize among the options and choose the ones that will work best.

The step of prioritizing can be a relatively simple task, if you remember to let the coachee do the work here!

Summarize and Ask for the Solution

A good place to start is by restating the various alternatives that you have heard the coachee describe (e.g., "You've mentioned four possible ways to proceed. The first is . . . ; the second is . . . ; the third is . . .").

Then ask the coachee to rank the possibilities. Doing so will help him choose among the options. Here are some possible phrases to consider:

- If you were to rank these in terms of effectiveness, what would be the best choice to start with?
- Which of these options are most feasible?
- Which of these choices do you have the most energy to pursue?
- Which of these options seems to make the best sense to start with?
- Which of these will work best to help you achieve your target?

In most cases, the coachee will choose not just one option but some combination of the various alternatives generated. You will quickly see the value of generating multiple options with the coachee, as the coachee will often select several aspects of the possibilities to implement.

Explore Barriers and Resistance

One of the more interesting and overlooked steps in any process is this final step of exploring barriers and resistance. Interestingly enough, when we are asked to determine what barriers will get in the way of our accomplishing goals, we are very accurate in predicting the problems and roadblocks.

Yet, how often do we stop to take this step? We rarely do, since we are often caught up in the excitement of implementing our new solution.

However, the real value in taking the time to identify what will get in the way is that we can then begin to anticipate and prevent the potential roadblocks that are foreseen.

For instance, if a coachee wanted to gain more visibility with senior leaders, he might articulate a detailed action plan to reach his target (monthly meetings with skip-level leaders, presenting department work at meetings where senior leaders are present, asking his immediate manager to advocate on his behalf, sharing his opinion more frequently, perfecting an "elevator" speech regarding his work, and so on). All of these steps might make sense on the surface, and the coachee may be excited to begin to take action. However, you may be missing important information—the obstacles that would prevent the coachee from successfully implementing these actions.

If you asked the coachee: "What could get in the way of your implementing these actions?" he might admit: "Well, I work in Texas, and all of my senior leaders are located in New York. Given travel restrictions, I don't have the opportunity to participate in face-to-face meetings. My old manager used to keep her boss informed regarding my accomplishments, but my new manager has been in the role for only two months and doesn't really know my work or what I have accomplished in the last year. My boss's boss has been in the Dallas office only once in the last year." These barriers represent potential challenges to implementing the previously identified actions. Additional steps may need to be put in place to prevent or minimize the potential anticipated barriers.

HOW *THIS* COACHING CONVERSATION SOUNDS

Let us return to our earlier example, where our direct report is concerned about her relationship with Ed, and the imbalance of collaboration that is taking place between the two of them. Picking up where we left off in the last chapter, we can continue the conversation with the third step of our framework. Table 9-3 shows what the entire third step of the coaching conversation might sound like.

Table 9-3

Step 3: Explore the Desired State
(Identify the target and generate multiple paths to achieve the end state.)

Understand the vision for success	**Coach:** It sounds as if you are clear about some of the dynamics that are happening between you and Ed, and what the consequences are for both of you and the work you are trying to accomplish. So, let me ask you: What would you like to see happen here? What would the ideal state look like?
	Coachee: My ideal state would look like Ed and I having a very collaborative, balanced, and "fair" relationship.
	Coach: Say more about how that might work.

(Continued)

Table 9-3 (Continued)

	Coachee: Ideally, both of us would be willing to respond to each other's requests in a timely fashion. I'd like for both of us to respond within a 24-hour window, if not sooner.
	Coach: What else would you like to see?
	Coachee: Well, if I could really create the perfect scenario, I'd love for us to be more proactive with each other—and not wait until the final hour to make requests of each other. I'd also like to feel more *willing* to respond and help Ed, instead of feeling resentful about the requests.
	Coach: Anything else you would like to create here?
	Coachee: I guess I would like to be as clear and "demanding" as Ed is when I make my requests. I think I am too soft or indirect right now. I hope that people understand the urgency in my requests. In the ideal state, I would be much clearer about what my requests truly are.
	Coach: That sounds like a really good target to aim for.
Set goals and perform-ance expectations.	**Coach:** So, are there specific goals that you would like to shoot for, regarding realigning your expectations of each other and redefining your relationship with Ed?
	Coachee: Yes—I would like to see both of us responding to each other's requests in no more than 48 hours. That would be a reasonable goal to shoot for. I'd also like to feel that we have a collaboration that feels more like 50/50 instead of 80/20 (with me giving 80 and receiving only 20). I'd settle for a 60/40 split for the time being.
	Coach: Those sound like reasonable goals to shoot for. They may not be what is ultimately possible, but they are good goals to start with.
Explore alternative paths of action.	**Coach:** So, what might be some approaches you can take to reach your desired state of being clear with your requests, being collaborative with Ed, and responding to each other's needs in a timely manner—preferably within 24 hours and certainly in no more than 48 hours?
	Coachee: I think I need to start by being really clear about my own requests. I can articulate more clearly exactly what I need and the time frame in which I need a response.

(Continued)

Coach: That sounds like a good action to take. What else might work?

Coachee: I can remind myself that when Ed asks me to support him, he is truly just trying to get his job done. Instead of feeling resentful or angry, if I can tell myself that we are both working to get our department goals accomplished, I will probably feel better about supporting him.

Coach: That makes sense. Putting yourself in Ed's shoes and knowing that he is doing his best might help you feel more accommodating of his requests. What else might be helpful?

Coachee: Something that I haven't really thought of until now would be to make sure that I am the best person to respond to Ed's requests. There are probably some times when I respond to Ed's requests when there might be someone else who is in a better position to respond. If I stop to ask myself, "Who is the best person on the team to address this?" I am guessing that I would be able to identify someone other than myself at least 25 to 30 percent of the time. Instead of jumping through hoops to do the work myself, I could let Ed know that one of our other colleagues would be in a better position to get him the information he needs. I could then step out of the loop and let Ed follow up with that person. That would probably help me feel less stressed—and resentful.

Coach: I really like that strategy—it helps both of you to work smarter, and Ed might learn of additional resources that he is not aware of. Are there any other strategies that might work?

Coachee: Um . . . I can't think of anything else.

Coach: Could I offer a couple of other possibilities?

Coachee: Sure.

Coach: You haven't mentioned actually having a conversation with Ed to discuss how you feel about the support you are giving to each other, and how you want to make sure that the relationship feels collaborative and balanced. Have you ever had a conversation like that with Ed?

Coachee: (Pause.) No . . . probably not.

(Continued)

Table 9-3 (Continued)

	Coach: What do you think of having that up-front conversation with him? Do you think something like that might help?
	Coachee: It might. But I think I'd like to try the other ideas first. It seems like confronting Ed in the middle of the work we both have going on would just cause more tension between us . . . and I don't want to take that risk right now.
	Coach: I understand. It sounds like the other options you generated might be easier to implement in the short term. You can certainly try those out, and if they don't have the impact you'd like, we can always revisit whether or not it might make sense to have a more direct conversation with Ed.
	Coachee: Yes. Let's save that until later—if the other actions don't work first.
	Coach: So let's prioritize the possible approaches that you might take. You mentioned three that seem viable to begin with:
	• First, you talked about being clearer in your requests, and including specific time frames for responding.
	• Second, you said that you could put yourself in Ed's shoes and remember that he is doing his best to get his job done.
	• Third, you said that you could really determine whether you are the right person to respond to Ed's requests.
	Of those options, which make the most sense to put into place? Are there some that would be easier to implement, or that would lead to reducing the tension you feel faster?
	Coachee: Well, I think the first and the third would actually have the biggest payoff the fastest. The second will probably be the hardest for me to implement, given how I currently feel about the situation.
Explore possible barriers or resistance.	**Coach:** So if you were to start with being more clear in your own requests, what might get in your way?
	Coachee: Time is always going to work against me. When I am in a huge hurry, I just fire off e-mail requests, without necessarily thinking about the best way to phrase my requests. When I reread the e-mails I have sent, I often see that my request is a bit fuzzy or open-ended.

(Continued)

> **Coach:** How about trying to make sure that you are the best person to respond to Ed's needs? What will get in the way there?
>
> **Coachee:** Ironically, it is probably the issue of time again.
>
> **Coach:** Why do you say "ironically"?
>
> **Coachee:** Well, when I feel pressured for time, I try to take action immediately and just get the request out of the way. If I paused before acting, I could take the time to make sure that I am the best person to respond. Ultimately, not responding immediately may buy me more time in the long run.
>
> **Coach:** So this is a great insight. When we create a specific action plan for moving forward, we might want to look at how to buy you more time before responding, so that you can implement both of these plans effectively.

Table 9-3 illustrates some key aspects of effective coaching:

- You will notice that the coach continued to let the coachee do most of the "heavy lifting" in the conversation. The coach has led the process of the conversation, while the coachee has generated the solution to her dilemma.
- The coach continued to ask a lot of open-ended, nonleading questions, while he listened intently and mirroring back what he heard.
- The coach made sure to get a complete picture of the desired state before identifying goals and brainstorming alternative action paths.
- The coach kept asking, "What else might work?" until the coachee articulated at least three possible paths to take.
- Only after the coach had exhausted the coachee's ideas did the coach offer an additional suggestion for consideration. (*You will also notice that the suggestion that the coachee speak directly to Ed was quickly dismissed—another reminder of how well-intended "advice" is often not embraced as easily as we imagine that it will be.*)
- The coach helped the coachee prioritize the possible actions that could be taken. The coachee ruled out one of the actions entirely and dismissed the coach's suggestion.

- Finally, the coach inquired about the barriers that would make either of the prioritized paths difficult. This allowed a barrier to come to the surface so that it can be now be incorporated into the action planning steps—which is the final phase of the coaching conversation.

Video Example

If you would like to see examples of a coach Exploring the Desired State, go to www.zengerfolkman.com and click on the Leadership Resource Center icon. You will find examples of a coach helping the coachee explore what she would like to make happen. Pay attention to how the coach begins with the coachee's target for success and elicits the paths of action from the coachee. Also pay attention to how and when the coach offers his opinion—and how little this influences the coachee's planned actions.

Adding to Your Question Treasure Trove

In the previous chapter, we started building a repertoire of questions. If we consider questions that are unique to this third step of the coaching conversation, we can add to your question treasure trove. Here are some possible questions to consider adding to your library:

1. What would the ideal state look like?
2. If you had a magic wand, what would you like to see happen here?
3. If you were CEO/queen/president for a day, what would you like to implement?
4. What would you realistically like to make happen, given these circumstances?
5. What would a best-case scenario look like?
6. What would you try if you knew that you could not fail?
7. What would you attempt if you had all the support and resources that you needed?

8. How would you like to see yourself behaving in this ideal situation?
9. What are some goals that you would like to aim for?
10. What would be some stretch targets to shoot for?
11. What strategies can help you realize your desired vision?
12. What are some other alternative paths to get there?
13. What else might work?
14. If you could rank-order the possible solutions in terms of effectiveness, what would be your first, second, and third best options to consider?
15. What criteria could you use to evaluate which path looks like the best one to take?
16. Which option(s) would be most feasible, or easiest to implement?
17. Which option(s) will get you closest to your goal in the time frame you would like to target?
18. What is going to get in the way?
19. What are the biggest risks or barriers to pursuing that option?
20. What might go wrong? What is the worst-case scenario?

Chapter Summary

- Do not rush into problem solving in this phase; go slow to create the ideal vision and generate more alternatives for achieving that vision.
- Resist the natural reaction to "lock and load" with the first viable option that might bring relief to the situation.
- Aim for a big target by expanding the vision of success that the coachee is trying to accomplish; do not be skimpy here!
- As a leader, you get to have a point of view! If the coachee's vision of success does not meet performance expectations, you can negotiate and influence what the minimum measures of success must include.

- If she generates at least three alternatives to consider, the coachee will end up having a more robust and effective solution in the long run.
- Feel free to offer your suggestions—after the coachee has exhausted his own ideas.
- If the coachee becomes stuck, step to his side and become a brainstorming partner. Just be careful not to take over the conversation at this point.
- Explore the possible barriers that the coachee might face in implementing the potential solution paths. We are amazingly accurate in predicting what might get in our way—when we bother to take the time to do so.
- Continue to add to your repertoire of great questions to ask. Experiment with the ones that will work best for you, and put those in your personal treasure trove of good questions.

Chapter 10

Lay Out the Success Plan

Emphasizing Accountability

You are in the home stretch of the coaching conversation. During the previous step, you outlined the desired vision of success as well as several alternatives for getting there. You prioritized the options that will work best. Now you are ready to dive into the specific detailed action steps and a follow-up plan.

Now is not the time to get lazy. When you reach this stage of the conversation, you may be tempted to ease up on the final steps that will ensure success and sustainability. After all, the coachee is clear on the desired end state and has articulated the specific actions that he intends to take. You might feel that your work is done. You might even say to yourself, "Well, the solution is obvious now. My coachee is a mature adult. He will be able to put his plan into place." Not so fast! Your role in this final step of the coaching conversation is critical—you need to be able to guide the coachee to identify and visualize the specific actions that he will take. Once your coachee becomes very clear on exactly how he will proceed, you have just increased the likelihood that he will. And, by assigning specific timelines to the most important milestones, you begin to create a natural follow-up plan and check-in opportunities.

One more word of note: research has shown that building in accountability actually helps individuals change (and therefore grow) faster than without it. Dr. James Prochaska described a great way to help mothers lose weight: providing an incentive of $10 to her children for every pound that *she* loses. You can imagine how that system works: her children become instant accountability partners. "Mom, don't eat that brownie!" "Mom, you said you were going to exercise today." "*Mom*, you can't have another helping of chicken!" Now, we aren't advocating that you become a teenage nag to your team members, but the power of accountability and sustained follow-up is profound.

> *Building in accountability actually helps individuals change (and therefore grow) faster than without it.*

In our work as coaches, we have found that approximately 85 percent of our coachees will complete their "homework assignments"— their stated commitments for actions that they will take—the *day or morning before* our next coaching conversation. We find this pattern to be an interesting and consistent reminder of how powerful accountability can be. And there is nothing wrong with waiting until the last minute—as long as they complete their actions! Think of how many times we wait until the last minute to pay bills, file tax returns, purchase airline tickets, or make plans with friends. Waiting to complete tasks is simply a function of how busy we are, how many things we are juggling, and how valuable deadlines are. Deadlines are made to ensure that we have a target to aim for.

THREE STEPS FOR TURNING UP THE HEAT ON ACCOUNTABILITY

Let's review the specific substeps of this final conversation phase (Table 10-1). There are really three key elements that you are making sure happen here:

1. Develop and agree on an action plan and timelines.
2. Enlist support from others.
3. Set milestones for follow-up and accountability.

Table 10-1

Step 4: Lay Out a Success Plan

(Create the detailed, actionable plan and follow-through that will lead to goal attainment.)

Develop and agree on an action plan and timelines.	• What specific actions will help you achieve your goal? • What will your first steps be? When will you start? • Who can help hold you accountable? • How will you stay focused on your goals and plans?
Enlist support from others.	• Who can support you in moving forward? • How can I support you? (Here's how I see my role: . . .)
Set milestones for follow-up and accountability.	• Let's review our plans: . . . • When should we touch base on this again?

Asking for Details Does *Not* Make You a Micromanager!

Consistently, leaders whom we work with express concern over getting too detailed at this phase of the conversation. In fact, you might be thinking the same thing: "I've helped my coachee determine the best action paths to take; the solution seems obvious; she just needs to get going!" One of the reasons why many leaders resist this step is that they don't want to revert to being autocratic by micromanaging their employees' actions.

We would like to offer you a slightly different perspective. Let us imagine that your coachee has determined that the best course of action to solve her problem will be to have a tough conversation with one of her peers. She needs to tell her peer that because he is missing agreed-upon deadlines, her work is falling behind, and the completion of the project is jeopardized.

Without utilizing all of the substeps in this last conversation phase, the coach might be tempted to conclude the conversation like this:

Coach: So, what will you do next? What is the best step to take now?

Coachee: Well, I just need to find the courage to have a conversation with Mike. If I don't do that, my work will continue to fall behind, and we won't hit our end goal for the project.

Coach: That makes sense, based on everything you described. I agree that this is a good next step to take. I'd love to hear how your conversation goes.

Coachee: I'll definitely let you know. This has been really helpful. Thanks.

Now, we are definitely oversimplifying one possible ending to a potentially rich dialogue that has preceded this, but at this point, many coaches and coachees are so relieved at having made progress toward solving the problem that they are eager to wrap up and begin taking action.

Asking for more details, clarity, and commitment at this stage will *not* make you a micromanager. In fact, you will add much greater value to your coachee and increase the likelihood of her actually taking action if you spend a few more moments here.

> *Asking for more details, clarity, and commitment at this stage will* not *make you a micromanager.*

Let us consider how the same conversation might go instead, by utilizing the substeps of this last conversation phase (see Table 10-2).

Table 10-2

Step 4: Lay Out a Success Plan

(Create the detailed, actionable plan and follow-through that will lead to goal attainment.)

Develop and agree on an action plan and timelines.	**Coach:** So, what will you do next? What is the best step for you to take now?
	Coachee: Well, I just need to find the courage to have a conversation with Mike. If I don't do that, my work will continue to fall behind, and we won't hit our end goal for the project.
	Coach: That makes sense, based on everything you've described. I agree that this is a good next step to take.
	When will you have that conversation?
	Coachee: Well, soon. Probably within the next week.

(Continued)

Coach: Do you have time scheduled with Mike in the next week?

Coachee: Well, no—but I can find time on my calendar.

Coach: Great. What is a good target for you to aim for?

Coachee: Well, we're scheduled to talk about our project update status next Thursday, so perhaps I could use some of that time to share my concerns about what is happening.

Coach: OK. So, if you fast-forward to next Thursday's conversation, what are the key messages that you would like to deliver to Mike?

Coachee: Um . . . well, I guess it wouldn't be helpful for me to "dump" on him and tell him how frustrated I've been. That will only make him defensive. I probably need to think more about this.

Coach: Would it be useful to role-play the conversation a little bit? I can play Mike, and you can try out your messages on me—and I'll give you feedback regarding how your message "lands." Would that help?

Coachee: It probably would, but I don't even feel ready to do that yet. I'd like to spend some time thinking through my key "asks" in the conversation and what I really want to accomplish.

Coach: That makes sense.

Enlist support from others. **Coach:** How can I help you as you move forward?

Coachee: I'd like to take a stab at what my message will be. Then, it might be really useful to practice with you, especially if I'm feeling stuck, or if I anticipate Mike's being defensive. What if I let you know?

Coach: That works for me. Is there anyone else that might be useful to enlist in your preparation process?

Coachee: Well, my husband is always a good mirror for me. He's heard me complain enough about Mike, and he is really emotionally intelligent. I can probably run my ideas by him and see what he thinks.

Coach: That sounds like a good plan, too.

(Continued)

Table 10-2 (Continued)

Set milestones for follow-up and accountability.	**Coach:** So, if your conversation with Mike is on Thursday, when would you like to touch base again?
	Coachee: How about if I let you know how I feel on Wednesday. If I feel confident, you can wish me luck. If I want more support, we can do a little role-play.
	Coach: Great. That makes sense. And then I'd love to hear how the conversation went with Mike.
	Coachee: Sounds good. I really appreciate your help. I'm feeling more confident already, just recognizing that these are all smaller steps in a larger process.

It may be useful to analyze what happened in this last dialogue. By spending just a few more moments engaged in this step of the conversation,

- The coachee articulated a deadline or target for her action (next Thursday). It would be easy to let a conversation like this float into the following week, or the week after that. Buttoning down a specific time frame brings this more into reality for the coachee.
- The coachee recognized that she probably needed to prepare a bit more to have the conversation. While she is committed to the action, she still needs to prepare. Recognizing this allowed the coach and the coachee to design some interim steps in her process—articulating the key messages prior to the conversation.
- The coach and the coachee identified some support resources and actions. The coach could role-play the conversation, and the coachee's husband might be a good sounding board. And the very process of identifying other support resources is often reassuring for the coachee.
- Identifying the specific deadline for action allowed natural milestones for follow-up to surface. The coach can check in before and/or after the conversation. Because these milestones surfaced during the conversation, if the coach were to ask the coachee on Wednesday morning, "How is your preparation for

the conversation going?" the coachee would probably not feel that the coach was micromanaging. Instead, the coachee would probably feel a sense of support and interest on the part of the coach. This continues to build the trust-based relationship between the two, and the sense that the coachee is not in this situation alone.

Interestingly enough, the coachee may not role-play the conversation with the coach, bounce ideas off her husband, or even spend a great deal of time articulating her messages in advance. Just the process of being more clear about what needs to happen by when will set her subconscious processing in motion to think through the messages that she wants to share with Mike. She'll be better able to have a productive conversation, and because she has committed to a deadline, her public declaration along with the manager's check-in is likely to spur her to go through with it.

Many people feel overwhelmed when they are faced with a complex and difficult task. One of the coach's valuable contributions is to help break that daunting task into bite-sized chunks. Doing so has been shown to greatly increase the likelihood of something effective happening.

> *One of the coach's valuable contributions is to help break that daunting task into bite-sized chunks.*

So, what happens if the coachee doesn't take action? When Friday comes along and the manager asks how the conversation with Mike went, if the coachee sheepishly replies that she didn't have it, the coach can engage in a spot conversation about what got in the way: "Would it be helpful to talk about this for a few minutes? What happened?" The coachee might indicate that it was simply a time constraint—they ran out of time for this part of the conversation, but they agreed to follow up in two days. Or the coach might discover that the coachee has an even greater barrier to overcome—her fear of Mike's reaction to her messages. Together, they can get back on the path of moving toward her desired goal and work through her resistance to having the conversation.

Video Example

If you would like to see examples of a coach guiding this final step of the coaching conversation, go to www.zengerfolkman.com and click on the Leadership Resource Center icon. You will find examples of a coach ensuring that the coachee is clear on which specific action steps to take. You will also notice how the coach determines appropriate milestones for follow-up with the coachee.

A LOVE/HATE RELATIONSHIP WITH ACCOUNTABILITY

Let us look at accountability from the coachee's perspective for a moment. If you have been coaching and guiding the conversation effectively, and your coachee has been articulating the best solution and actions to take, you would think that your coachee would appreciate your holding him accountable for his commitments. Right?

Well . . . yes and no. We all want to achieve our desired state, but most of us would like to arrive there without a great deal of effort, pressure, or timelines. I've said for years (10, to be exact) that I'd like to lose 10 pounds. Apparently, I want to do it on my own timeline— which should only take another 5 years or so! In fact, a friend of mine has suggested that she write a book, *How to Lose 5 Pounds in 10 Years*, just to address this amazing tendency that we share!

Let us outline a few more examples of why identifying specific actions and targets is so important, especially when coupled with accountability. Let us continue to consider the precarious goal of losing weight. Many, many individuals can relate to this topic, having a wish list of being 10 or more pounds thinner, and in better shape physically. In fact, if you asked someone, "What is your ideal weight? What clothes would you wear if you weighed that much? How would you be feeling then?" he would be able to articulate responses to all of those questions pretty quickly. (Try it yourself!)

What can we learn about people are who successful at losing weight? Do they

- Starve themselves?
- Become vegetarians?

- Try the latest fad, "The Bostonian's South End North Seashore All Natural Raw No Processed Food Diet"?
- Engage a personal trainer?
- Make money wagers with friends who are also dieting?

They may do some combination of a lot of different actions, but fairly consistently there is one action that tends to make a huge difference to these dieters: monitoring their calorie intake and amount of physical exercise. That's right! Keeping a food and exercise log tends to be correlated with successful weight loss.

Now, how does this work? Does keeping the diary of calories burned and consumed actually help people lose weight? Probably not—the act of writing in and of itself burns only around 80 calories per hour, so it does not make people thinner. What does? The mere fact that they are measuring their progress against their stated goals—and holding themselves accountable—by writing entries in their personal food diaries. The Weight Watchers organization, which has been perhaps more successful than any other enterprise in helping people lose weight, strongly encourages people to keep track of what they've eaten and how much they've exercised. Weight Watchers also builds another layer of accountability into the process. Every week, when dieters show up to their scheduled meetings, they have to do two things:

1. Pay their weekly fee to attend the meeting.
2. Get on a scale, where someone else is looking at the number and telling them how much they weigh, in pounds and ounces.

You might be wondering why anyone would subject himself to this punishment. In fact, years ago, I mentioned to a dear friend that I had joined Weight Watchers to help lose a few pounds. Knowing how Weight Watchers worked, he said, "Why don't you just give me the $10 a week, and I'll tell you that you're fat!" While *he* might have enjoyed that process immensely, it probably wouldn't have helped *me* too much.

The best accountability partners tend to be those who care about you and the goals you are

If you want to be a great accountability partner, don't be afraid to turn up the heat!

trying to reach, and who recognize the value of holding your feet to the fire. So, if you want to be a great accountability partner, don't be afraid to turn up the heat!

ACCOUNTABILITY CAN BE CREATIVE

We have probably all heard stories about people who have provided their own incentives for reaching certain targets or goals:

- The person who lost his goal weight and rewarded himself with a professional massage
- The person who achieved a huge accomplishment on a project and gave herself an afternoon off
- The person who got the high-avoidance task completed and treated himself to a coffee at Starbucks

It may be useful to consider how follow-up and accountability can be designed to be fun. There is no reason why you cannot build some incentives or rewards into the process.

Here's a true example, from one of the authors of this book. Kathleen and Jack had been talking about wanting to write this book for quite some time. Kathleen knew that unless she established a specific goal for herself and got serious about building accountability into the process, years might drift by with the good idea of a coaching book staying just that—a good idea. So she decided to take her own medicine. She engaged a coach, who realized that she was already fully aware of her goal and what the desired state looked like: a published book that would be really helpful to managers.

The coach helped her articulate a detailed plan of action that included specific details and timelines, starting with drafting an outline of the book and assigning writing duties by chapter. After the authors divided the chapters to write, Kathleen and her coach took a big leap and ventured into the red-hot territory of accountability.

Kathleen suggested that her coach provide incentives or rewards for every chapter that she completed by the deadline. She didn't care what the rewards were, but she wanted them to be a surprise. She even sent her coach a check to cover the rewards—$25 per chapter written. Her coach, being a wise and shrewd man, asked, "What happens if you don't hit a deadline?" Kathleen was flummoxed; she had not anticipated not making a deadline, but Lou, the coach, knew well enough that it was a possibility. He suggested that he donate the money to a charity of his choosing every time a chapter was not turned in by a deadline. Kathleen agreed. Lou continued, asking what to do if Kathleen missed more than one deadline in a row. Surely this was unthinkable, yet Lou was thinking it. Kathleen stammered a bit, and then Lou turned up the heat some more: "You send me another check for the same amount of money, and the stakes just doubled. Every deadline you reach, you'll get a double bonus, but every deadline you miss just cost you $50."

So, how did this system work? In the course of writing the book, Kathleen missed two deadlines—but never two in a row. The accountability of having someone check in, hold her accountable, and create both carrots and sticks for reaching and missing deadlines was amazingly powerful.

Now, we are not advocating that your coachees pay you to hold them accountable and to buy them treats, but we are suggesting that you think outside of the box a little. What would make achieving the goal worthwhile (beyond the goal achievement itself)? What extra nudge would make a difference in giving the coachee an incentive to take the actions that she wants to take?

This extra nudge may simply come in the form of you catching him doing something right and providing praise and positive reinforcement. We'll talk more about that in Chapter 13, "The Power of the Gold Star." But don't be afraid to think creatively here. In Kathleen's example, Lou had a great time holding her accountable and unleashing his own creative energy in the process.

Chapter Summary

- Asking for details at this step of the process does not turn you into a micromanager.
- Articulating specific action steps helps the coachee gain clarity regarding what needs to happen next, and also provides the coachee with a clearer vision of how this might go.

- In the process, the coachee may realize that more substeps need to be taken.
- Assigning actions to timelines creates fairly natural milestones for follow-up and accountability.
- Do not be afraid to turn up the heat at this point. Remember, you are helping your coachee reach her desired state. Getting more specific only helps to serve that goal.
- While the coachee may have a love/hate relationship with accountability, we know that accountability works.
- Be creative! Find unique ways to support your coachee in reaching his goals. Engage him in the process of determining what might be a good "extra nudge" on the path.

Chapter 11

Coaches Need Feedback Too

An understandable mistake that many coaches make is to believe that coaching is something that one person does to support another and that it is exclusively for the benefit of the person who is being coached. The very word *coaching* connotes that to most people. While the coaching process is normally structured with the understanding that it will largely benefit the coachee, the best coaches also recognize two important facts:

1. Coaching excels when it is a two-way street. It is a powerful indication of respect when the coach not only is open to receiving constructive feedback from the person being coached but also deliberately solicits it.

   Coaching excels when it is a two-way street.

2. Leaders improve their coaching skills when they receive feedback. The most valuable sources of that feedback, and certainly the people who can provide it most accurately and constructively, are the people who are being coached.

COACHING AS A TWO-WAY STREET

In 1964, Dr. Eric Berne published a book that had an enormous impact on the world of psychology. The book was *Games People*

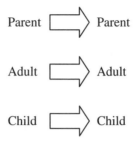

Figure 11-1 Successful Interactions

Play, and one of its central ideas was that people possessed three states of mind. The psychologist's fancier and more scholarly term was "ego states." Berne labeled these as Parent, Adult, and Child. In simple terms, the Parent ego state represented things we have all been taught, the Adult ego state represented things we have thought, and the Child state of mind represented things that we feel. The big "aha" and the practical application of Berne's work had to do with successful and unsuccessful interactions between people. His conclusion was that, in general, interactions go well when they are horizontal (see Figure 11-1).

The point is quite straightforward and simple. If two Parents are discussing how they should deal with a child who is tormenting her brother, the transaction goes well. The Parent-to-Parent discussion is a perfectly parallel dialogue about what ought to be done regarding their misbehaving daughter.

If two Adults are talking about the state of the economy, that conversation also goes well from a psychological point of view (even if they disagree about the best way to deal with the balance of trade with China or the need for health-care reform). And the reason it succeeds is because both parties see themselves as functioning adults, and that perception is mutually unchallenged. They show respect for each other. One is not talking down to the other; rather, two peers are having an intellectual discussion.

Finally, when adults are at a party where the purpose is to have fun, that interaction also goes well, just as it usually does when two young children play together in a sandbox. However, trouble can

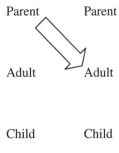

Figure 11-2 Potentially Dangerous Interactions

occur when one person takes the game too seriously and forgets that the entire purpose is to have fun.

Berne's second conclusion was that diagonal transactions normally don't go well. In general, the moment the transaction moves from being horizontal to being diagonal, things go seriously awry (see Figure 11-2).

If two adults are talking together, and person A begins to treat person B the way a parent would, it is common for sparks to fly. That is because such treatment violates B's expectations. B is thinking, "I thought this was a discussion between equals, and he's acting like a parent. He's telling me what to do and how to do it. I don't need to take that." The first person compounds it by saying and doing things that convey that he sees the other person as a helpless child. In this case, not only is one person acting parentally, but he is also signaling that his perception of the second person is someone who is quite incapable of acting independently and wisely. This becomes an even more aggravated case of a diagonal transaction between two people when one person assumed that it was to be horizontal (see Figure 11-3).

This theory helps in understanding the difficulties that often arise in business between bosses and their direct reports. The employee, who is generally a person whose self-perception is that of being an Adult, is subjected to behavior from a boss that is sending quite different signals.

It is important to note that there are times when a conversation or transaction between a Parent and a Child can go extremely well.

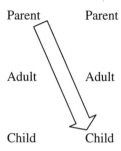

Figure 11-3 Usually Diastrous Interactions

One example is when a person who is in the Parent state of mind talks to a person who is indeed a child and is in the Child state of mind. This diagonal transaction is successful because the Parent is fulfilling an important role with another person who is willing to accept the other position. However, as we've all observed, as a child progresses into the teenage years and older, his willingness to be treated as a child usually goes down quite rapidly.

The application of this theory to the world of coaching should be obvious. Coaching relationships in business take place between two Adults. One may be younger than the other, but they are both equal as Adults. When one elects to behave as if the other person were a Child, however, you can predict that the dialogue will suffer and degenerate. Such behaviors would include a coach asking the other person to reveal challenging situations while never disclosing anything about herself. A coach who answers every question definitively is exhibiting parental behavior. Giving advice is parental, and so is withholding any information that makes you seem less than perfect.

This now brings us back to the topic of this chapter. What's the rationale for a coach opening up to feedback from his coachee? Why would the coach take the time to do that? What is to be gained?

THE VALUE OF FEEDBACK

There are countless reasons for a coach to be open to feedback. Here are a few of the most important ones.

The Quality of Coaching Is Improved

A key requirement for improving performance in any area of one's life is receiving feedback. The joy that many people derive from participating in virtually any sport comes from receiving instantaneous feedback. When playing golf, you immediately know whether your drive has gone off into the weeds, it has been shanked and narrowly missed a golfing partner, or it has landed squarely on the green. With every chip shot, you know whether you topped the ball and drove it into the turf or the club hit the ball at the wrong angle and the ball is now hopelessly lost. This instantaneous feedback is one of the elements that make participating in sports so highly enjoyable.

How would a manager who engages in coaching obtain useful feedback regarding her performance? Other than having their conversations taped and analyzed by a professional coach, there are not many practical ways for leaders to get objective information regarding their coaching performance. We strongly submit that success in this practice should be defined in the eyes of the recipient. What the coach personally thinks about the success of any given coaching conversation is not as important. Furthermore, determining what an outside expert may think about a manager's coaching skills is a luxury that few managers can access. The ultimate test of success is the reactions of the coachee and the subsequent changes that this person elects to make.

Therefore, the first test of any coach's effectiveness is whether or not the people being coached feel positive about the process. Has it been a good use of their time? Has it improved their relationship with their boss? Has it helped them to have a clearer sense of their career opportunities? Has it helped their relationships with their colleagues, as they see it? Having positive attitudes toward the coaching process is an important first step. But it is not sufficient.

Any evaluation of the coaching process must go beyond how the recipient feels. How has it changed his behavior? If his performance has improved as a consequence of one or more coaching sessions, then the coaching has been a success. If he is more enthusiastic about his work, being more creative, and working more effectively with his teammates as a consequence of coaching, then the coaching has been a success.

Greater Success for the People Being Coached

Two psychologists, Barry Duncan and Scott Miller,[1] conducted rather extensive research in an attempt to bring greater scientific rigor to the practice of counseling and psychotherapy. They have published fascinating results regarding feedback from individuals receiving counseling. There are, of course, huge differences between business coaching and the practice of therapy. Nevertheless, there may be some extremely important lessons that we can learn from these other disciplines. What Duncan and Miller found was that when counselors collected feedback from their clients at the conclusion of each session, two rather dramatic outcomes took place as a result.

1. The quality of the counseling improved by 65 percent. While this is somewhat hard to measure, the researchers collected data on a number of criteria and applied highly rigorous methods for making this evaluation.
2. The client dropout rate was cut in half. Counselors lost half as many clients by simply engaging in the process of asking for feedback.

To the degree that we all want our coaching to be more effective and also want our coachees to keep coming back for more, this research on the importance of the coach getting feedback strikes us as extremely important and practical.

Improved Relationship between the Coach and the Coachee

The coaching process will be measurably more effective when the coach solicits feedback because the relationship will be changed from Parent to Child to Adult to Adult. By being open to feedback, the coach sends the powerful signals "We are equals," "We can learn from each other," and "I value and respect you and your opinion."

HOW COACHES CAN COLLECT FEEDBACK

The researchers Duncan and Miller created a brief form that they suggested the counselor give the client at the end of each session. This questionnaire raised several issues regarding the important dimensions of the counseling experience. In applying this concept to business coaching, we have created the brief questionnaire given here.

Feedback Form

Please complete this brief evaluation form, so that I can understand what created the most value for you in this conversation. Please rate the following statements on a 1-to-5 scale, with 1 = low and 5 = high.

	Low				*High*
1. This conversation focused on the issues that are most important to me.	1	2	3	4	5
Comments:					
2. This conversation was a good use of our time.	1	2	3	4	5
Comments:					
3. The purpose and outcomes of this discussion were clarified early in our conversation.	1	2	3	4	5
Comments:					
4. The general process and flow of this conversation worked well to meet our goals.	1	2	3	4	5
Comments:					
5. I felt that you listened to me and understood my points of view.	1	2	3	4	5
Comments:					
6. I am leaving with some specific action steps to pursue.	1	2	3	4	5
Comments					

The coach who uses this or a similar brief questionnaire regularly will gather extremely valuable information. Receiving this immediate feedback will continually improve the quality of the coach's performance. Furthermore, collecting data in this way will enable the organization to compare the coaching effectiveness of all the different people within the organization who provide coaching.

A consistent feedback process also allows companies to track trends in the data over time. If the organization wished to have an objective measure of whether or not coaches were becoming more effective, this would be an ideal tool. Hopefully, the numbers you receive as a coach will be increasingly more positive over time.

Essence, Not Form: Alternative Methods for Collecting Data

While we have laid out the questions in this questionnaire in a form that could be completed by the coachee, we want to emphasize that the essence is more important than the form here. We recognize that this process may be a bit formal for some people. Managers may feel that the formality of using such a questionnaire would be unnatural, given the frequent on-the-spot coaching conversations that they hold. The immediate completion of a feedback form that is then handed directly to the coach may also be more awkward and require greater courage than many people being coached would be willing to display. The essence—asking for feedback from your coachee—is far more important than any particular form it might take. In fact, you can be creative with how you ask for feedback. So what would work instead?

The essence—asking for feedback from your coachee—is far more important than any particular form it might take.

Just Ask!

Customer service research suggests that if you verbally ask your customers for an expression of satisfaction at the end of an interaction, two important things happen for the customer:

1. The customer has time to think about the interaction, which helps solidify in his mind what worked well and whether he got his needs met.
2. The customer is able to express satisfaction—or any unresolved issues or unmet needs.

As a result, the customer feels better about his experience and the help that was provided to him. If any issues remain open, the customer service provider can continue to work with the customer to resolve them. Wilson Learning Worldwide teaches customer service providers to "ask for an expression of satisfaction" at the end of every exchange.

The same method could be used by coaches. The coach could collect data regarding the effectiveness of her coaching by simply posing several questions to the coachee at the conclusion of the session. The exact same questions provided in the questionnaire could be used, or the coach could explore other areas of interest:

- "Do you have any feedback for me—either on today's conversation, or on anything else you wish I knew?"
- "Was this a good use of our time? What would have made it better?"
- "What are you taking out of the discussion?"
- "Was there anything that you hoped we would cover, but we didn't?"
- "On a 1-to-10 scale, how helpful was this to you? What would have made this conversation a 10?"
- "How do you feel about the balance between our focus on current performance and on future development?"

By inviting this feedback at the end of the session, the coach sends a powerful message: "I want to make sure that this is of value to you. I'm interesting in getting better personally. Your feedback is important to me."

By inviting feedback, the coach sends a powerful message: "I want to make sure that this is of value to you.

E-mail

We suspect that some coaches would be more comfortable periodically sending out an e-mail to coaching participants that asks some of the questions used in the questionnaire but does not require the participants to complete the instrument on the spot and physically hand it to the coach. (We will have made huge progress when we all get more comfortable with such candor.) Some mechanism might also be arranged that would allow this feedback to be anonymous. From a host of other experiences, we know that granting anonymity to respondents goes a long way toward ensuring greater integrity and more frequent use of the outcomes.

Survey the Organization

Another method of collecting feedback would be to ask an independent party to conduct a survey of people receiving coaching in the organization. This survey could include many of the same questions as the form, but the data could be collected in such a way that the anonymity of the respondents would be guarded.

Utilize 360-Degree Feedback

Yet another approach to obtaining feedback for the coach would be to use a 360-degree feedback instrument. More than 85 percent of the Fortune 500 companies utilize such instruments to assess the leadership and management practices of their executives and managers. While many of these instruments contain a small number of items that focus on some of the leader's coaching practices, some instruments that are exclusively focused on coaching behavior now exist. We invite you to visit the Web site www.zengerfolkman.com and access the information regarding the specialized 360-degree feedback instruments on coaching.

The value of such an instrument is that it provides highly reliable data because it is derived from multiple independent individuals. The nature of the process guarantees anonymity to the respondents. This protection of the identity of the person providing the data greatly increases the likelihood that the information will be valid. We strongly encourage organizations to explore the use of such instruments as an ideal way to collect this information.

Build Feedback into Performance Review Systems

Organizations that truly want to build a coaching culture could even add a survey of the manager's coaching effectiveness to the performance review process. Direct reports could evaluate the quality of the coaching that they receive from the manager.

THE PAYOFF—FOR YOU

While asking for feedback may feel foreign and may require courage on your part, the payoff will be great. Not only will you build a strong relationship with your coachees but you will also serve as a role model to them, showing that you yourself are growing and learning. You will demonstrate that coaching is truly a two-way street and that their feedback to you is as valuable as your feedback to them. Perhaps most important, you will learn what works best for coaching your team members.

We have never *not* received value from the feedback we have requested from a coachee. Here are just a few things that our coachees have offered us, as a result of inviting feedback on our coaching effectiveness:

- Feel free to challenge me more; you can be even more direct.
- Send me an e-mail reminder in between our coaching conversations; that will help me stay focused.
- Although phone coaching works, let's make sure that some of our coaching takes place in "live" meetings.
- I like that you hold me accountable; when you say you're going to check back with me, you do. It forces me to take action.
- I need more affirmation; please point out the things that you see me doing well, even if I am just taking a risk or thinking differently about the situation.
- It would have been helpful to me to review our overarching goals more frequently instead of diving into the "issue of the day."

Feedback provides one of the few methods by which we can grow.

Feedback provides one of the few methods by which we can grow. Find the system that works best for you, and begin this process to increase your coaching effectiveness.

Application

In the space given here, identify how you will get feedback. Create the list of questions you will ask and to whom you will ask them, and establish the exact timetable that you intend to use for the collection of this information.

Who

From whom would you like to gather feedback regarding your coaching effectiveness? List specific names in the following table.

Direct Reports	Peers	Superiors	Customers
•	•	•	•
•	•	•	•
•	•	•	•

How

Which system of asking for feedback will work best for you?

❑ Handing out a brief questionnaire regarding the effectiveness of the coaching conversation
❑ Verbally asking for feedback at the end of a coaching conversation

- ❑ Sending an e-mail request for feedback at the end of a coaching conversation
- ❑ Sending a more formal feedback request periodically (quarterly, semiannually, or annually)
- ❑ Utilizing a 360-degree feedback tool to assess my coaching effectiveness
- ❑ Including a measure of coaching effectiveness in my performance goals
- ❑ An organizational survey of coaching effectiveness

What

Identify the questions that you are likely to use, or add your own.

- ❑ This conversation focused on the issues that are most important to me. (Rate from 1 to 5.)
- ❑ This conversation was a good use of our time. (Rate from 1 to 5.)
- ❑ The purpose and outcomes of this discussion were clarified early in our conversation. (Rate from 1 to 5.)
- ❑ The general process and flow of this conversation worked well to meet our goals. (Rate from 1 to 5.)
- ❑ I felt that you listened to me and understood my points of view. (Rate from 1 to 5.)
- ❑ I am leaving with some specific action steps to pursue. (Rate from 1 to 5.)
- ❑ How was this conversation for you?
- ❑ Do you have any feedback for me—either on today's conversation or on anything else you wish I knew?
- ❑ Was this a good use of our time? What would have made it better?
- ❑ What are you taking out of the discussion?
- ❑ Was there anything that you hoped that we would cover that we didn't?

(Continued)

❑ On a 1-to-10 scale, how helpful was this to you? What
would have made this conversation a 10?

❑ How do you feel about the balance between our focus on
current performance and on future development?

❑

❑

❑

When

How frequently will you request feedback from those whom
you coach? Write any specific notes regarding the type of
feedback and frequency for the different rater groups you
have identified.

Chapter Summary

- Coaches excel when they utilize a two-way-street approach and invite feedback from their coachees.
- Treating the coachee as an equal will not only serve the coaching conversation but also aid the feedback process.
- Gathering feedback not only increases the quality of coaching, but also contributes to better outcomes for the coachees.
- The act of asking for feedback improves the quality of the relationship between the coach and the coachee.
- Using a form to gather feedback allows you to track progress over time and aggregate results at an organizational level.
- The essence is more important than the form. Use a system that works for you.
- Asking for feedback helps the coachee solidify what worked well in the conversation and what he gained from the discussion.
- Perhaps most important, you will be able to grow in your own coaching effectiveness by soliciting feedback.

Chapter 12

Change Is the Yardstick

Understanding the Performance Challenge

A s we get older, most of us learn some valuable life lessons. While such lessons can be expressed in any number of ways, one lesson that seems quite universal would be something like this:

"No matter how much you want a person to do something, he isn't likely to do it until he wants to."

Yes, you can use some strong-arm tactics. Yes, you can install some powerful financial incentives. Yes, you can use your position to attempt to persuade the person

No matter how much you want a person to do something, he isn't likely to do it until he wants to.

that this is the right thing to do. All these tactics can have some effect. But in the long run, and when you aren't around to watch, the person will perform this action only if he wants to. A key issue in any coaching discussion, therefore, is whether the individual is ready to change. The change required may have to do with the person's on-the-job performance, or it may focus more on the individual's taking personal development seriously. The latter option means doing things that will improve his skills and capabilities or taking on higher-level responsibilities. Either way, let's examine what may be standing in the way of this person's changing and why this person should want to make the change initially.

WHY ISN'T THE PERSON PERFORMING?

Let's begin with the performance issue. There are numerous reasons why an individual fails to perform. When coaching an individual regarding a performance issue, it helps to have some hypothesis that explains her behavior. Let's review some of the alternatives. This fundamental approach was originally proposed by Robert F. Mager.[1] We have modified and added to that original work. What follows is a series of questions focused on uncovering precisely why the individual has not been performing as expected.

1. *Is the desired performance punishing?* In some jobs, success brings disapproval from some colleagues and contention with others. In other situations, the only reward for good performance is receiving loads of additional work. We assume that this often happens somewhat unintentionally when a supervisor or manager sees one of his people rapidly turning out high-quality work and proceeds to give that employee another large stack of tasks to accomplish. Then, as soon as that stack is completed, the manager loads on some more.

2. *Are there unintended rewards for not performing?* Suppose a salesperson has been instructed to submit to the sales manager a monthly expense report and a summary of each account's progress. If the report is late, however, the sales manager calls the salesperson. In the course of this call, the sales manager discusses each account at length and expresses enthusiasm for the progress that she is making. What the sales manager observes, however, is that this pattern persists month after month. Finally it dawns on the boss that the salesperson who submits late reports is the only one receiving such personalized attention. No one else gets to review all her accounts and receive praise for the progress being made. Upon further objective reflection, it was no surprise that the salesperson did not submit the reports on time.

3. *Are there any rewards for taking on complex tasks?* In many work situations, there are punishments for failure and few rewards for success, regardless of how difficult the assignment may be. The rewards may take many forms, including praise, visibility to higher management, official commendation, and a host of other nonmonetary payoffs. But whatever form the rewards take, if punishment for failure clearly overwhelms any and all rewards, why would a rational person take on such a task? It should be no surprise to a leader in that organization when an employee fails to willingly take on a challenging and risky assignment.

4. *Is the person unclear about precisely what is expected?* There are people who do not take the initiative to determine the end results they are to deliver. Without explicit instructions, they waste time and wander aimlessly. This is relatively easy to determine through a frank and honest discussion with them about their understanding of the end result of their work and their responsibility for accomplishing it. In Chapter 9, we explored this idea further as we discussed how the coach and coachee determine the desired future state and what goals the individual is working toward.

5. *Is the person unsure about how to perform the necessary tasks?* This obviously suggests the need for further training and development. If the coach/manager is convinced that the employee knows what to do but is uncertain or lacks the confidence needed to attempt the task, then further development is obviously warranted.

6. *Is there a lack of clarity about the reasons for a job assignment?* Some performers fail to produce an expected result largely because the reasons for the initial assignment were unclear. If you lack a clear understanding of why the task is to be performed, it becomes extremely easy to pass the assignment over. Understanding the purpose or "why" behind a task often helps individuals understand how their work contributes to the greater goals.

7. *Do serious obstacles stand in the way?* There arc many situations in which accomplishing a task is fraught with huge barriers. These are often thrown up by other departments with whom this performer needs to interact. In other cases, obstacles

come from within the team itself. There could also be a lack of adequate resources with which to accomplish the task. A variety of barriers stand in the way of accomplishing this objective.

8. *Is the person not properly motivated to do the task at hand?* It is extremely important to know whether a topic that is being discussed in my coaching conversation is a motivational question or the result of other factors. Robert Mager was well known for a classic test of motivation. The test was simple: if an employee knew that she would have a gun to her head unless she performed a task, and that employee was only *then* able to perform that task, the problem was motivation, not a competence issue.

9. *Is the individual not capable?* In this situation, the individual simply lacks the skills required to perform this task, and she is fundamentally unfit for the position that she occupies. In contrast to item 5 in this list, where the individuals require more training and time to practice new skills, this performance barrier represents someone who does not have the aptitude or capability to perform the job effectively.

It is obvious from this list (which is by no means complete) that there are a variety of reasons why someone is not performing a task. Part of the challenge in Understanding the Current State is to ensure that the coach is well aware of the true reason that a task is not being performed. It is especially important not to confuse competence issues with a lack of motivation. In an ideal world, the coach would help the individual to determine the reason for nonperformance, because only with this information is the coachee able to work toward an ideal solution.

AT WHAT STAGE OF CHANGE IS THE INDIVIDUAL?

Psychologist Dr. James Prochaska spent much of his career working with individuals who were suffering from various forms of addiction. Some were addicted to drugs, others to alcohol, and still others to gambling. Dr. Prochaska was fascinated to observe the widely different rates of success of the many professionals who worked with such patients. Some therapists had remarkably high percentages of clients who improved and stayed that way. Others had more dismal batting averages, with little positive change coming from their efforts. Why? In studying more than 6,000 such individuals, he came to one overall conclusion.

Basically, he learned that those therapists who were most effective in obtaining positive results with clients were those who recognized that change happened in a series of predictable stages rather than in one giant leap. He observed that there were six distinct phases or stages of change. By recognizing

Change happened in a series of predictable stages rather than in one giant leap.

which stage another person is in and meeting him there, you are far more likely to help him successfully implement change.

Stages of Change Model

The information in Table 12-1 is adapted from Prochaska's model and published works. The middle column highlights the behaviors you may observe in the person you are coaching. The right-hand column suggests how to be most useful in coaching the person through her their change agenda.

Table 12-1 Coaching: The Stages of Change

Stage of Change	Individual Actions or Experiences	Coaching Focus
1. Precontemplation	Not considering making a change, because of either denial, obliviousness, or resignation.	Invite the individual to begin thinking about change.
2. Contemplation	Begins weighing the benefits and costs of the behavior and the benefits and costs of the change.	Help the individual to examine the costs and benefits of the change.
3. Preparation	Actively investigates possible paths to change.	Address the barriers to full-fledged action.
4. Action	Commits to an action plan.	Help plan the action path.

(Continued)

Table 12-1 Coaching: The Stages of Change (Continued)

	Takes definitive action to change.	Provide generous praise and admiration for steps taken.
5. Maintenance	Maintains new behavior over a period of time.	Help monitor progress and hold the individual accountable.
	Follows through with ongoing milestones and measurement.	Continue to praise.
6. Relapse	Reverts to previous behavior pattern.	Promote problem solving and encouragement.
	May feel frustrated or demoralized.	Reengage efforts toward realistic goals.

So why do we cite such research? Obviously we know that there are huge differences between what a coach in the business world does and what a counselor who is working with addictive behaviors is attempting to accomplish, and we fully accept that conclusion. The severity of the problems that a therapist deals with is clearly different. Some of these addictions put a person's very life in jeopardy. That is clearly not the situation that the manager/coach encounters in most business situations.

Having said that, however, let's invoke the example of the emergency room physician and the person administering first aid. The major breakthroughs and improvements in first aid had their origins with emergency room physicians. Whether it is the use of "super glue" in place of sutures for a wound or the use of inflatable or paper splints, these are all practices that began with emergency physicians. Clearly the person administering first aid isn't doing the same thing as the emergency room physician, but valuable lessons can be transferred from one arena to another.

Another reason we cite this research is that coaching is an important tool for leaders to use to improve performance and to help people grow. But business organizations do not exist to provide coaching to their employees. Developing people is important, and coaching is a valuable tool to make that happen, but it is not an organization's reason for being. As a rule, a leader's career is not riding on his success in this specific arena. But this is the life work of many people in the helping professions. They have the luxury of being able to conduct research with hundreds and thousands of people and thus find best practices and methods that go far beyond those that we use in business. Prochaska, for example, had data on the progress of 6,000 individuals who were trying to change their behaviors. Most businesses can't imagine such an extensive research project with people being coached.

The Application to Performance Issues

We believe that the Prochaska change theory has enormous application to those who do coaching in the business world. For example, rather than expecting someone to make a dramatic change when he is underperforming or beset by some behavioral problems, Prochaska's theory would suggest that we respect the need for people to progress through several stages. This progression need not take years. Indeed, many counselors begin by agreeing with the client that if she is not seeing real progress after three or four sessions, she should seek out another counselor. A course of ten sessions is becoming more popular, in contrast to the time when people saw counselors for year upon year.

It is a logical leap to conclude that the same factors that lead to success in other professions that are attempting to bring about major changes in behavior would apply to our work as coaches. We are all engaged in a kind of "motivational interviewing" with the objective of helping the other person make positive changes in his life.

The Application to Personal Growth and Development Plans

These same principles apply to the conversations that a business coach has with someone regarding long-term career issues. Deciding on the optimum course to follow and having the discipline to implement that plan is challenging. Individuals must be given the opportunity to contemplate

Individuals must be given the opportunity to contemplate and think about the necessary changes they must make.

and think about the necessary changes they must make. They need assistance in taking the initial steps. They need understanding and support as they continue to dip their toes in the water and prepare to jump into the pool.

Remember Prochaska's major conclusion: those helpers with the least success were those who expected individuals to make a giant leap from an early stage to a fully implemented behavioral change.

A Diagram of a Leader in Change

A senior manager has an employee who has a major leadership responsibility in the financial function of the company. The subordinate manager received extremely low feedback scores from her direct reports on a number of leadership behaviors. Peers saw her as not paying any attention to the development of her people. She played favorites in terms of who received appealing assignments. She provided minimal direction and virtually no coaching, effectively ignoring the conflicts that plagued her team and the impact that this had on the group's productivity. On a 1-to-5 rating scale, where 1 represented needing significant improvement and 5 described someone in the top 10 percent of all leaders, she received mostly 1s and 2s. Her own self-scores were consistently 4s and 5s.

When the senior executive begins coaching his subordinate manager, it is not likely that she will quickly move from being totally unaware of these perceptions held by the people who report to her to being highly focused on their development and providing them with good coaching. Let us consider how this leader may move through the stages of change (see Table 12-2).

The senior executive would be unwise to expect all of these changes to occur in a sudden burst. Instead, far greater success will come if the senior executive guides her gently and firmly through the steps of becoming aware, creating a plan, taking the initial baby steps, and finally jumping into the thick of it with both feet. Greatest success will come in that fashion.

Table 12-2 A Leader's Experience through the Stages of Change

Precontemplation	Given the difference between the subordinate manager's self-perceptions and others' perceptions of her, she is likely to begin the change process in a stage of precontemplation. Prior to receiving the feedback, she may not even have recognized that a change in her leadership approach was necessary. It may take several days for the data to sink in.
Contemplation	In the process of considering the data, the leader is likely to begin weighing the consequences of not changing her leadership approach against the stated need and desire to change. The culmination of this phase is a decision to change (or not change).
Preparation	Assuming that the leader sees the benefits of changing her approach, she will need to begin to put together her own personal development plan, including how she will meet with her team to genuinely thank them for their feedback. Her plan needs to include several action steps, including a careful review of how work is currently being allocated and a plan to make that allocation more equitable.
	She may also need some support or training to learn how leaders deal with conflict within their own team. The leader will start implementing some of these early action steps and experimenting with how to lead her team differently.
Action	After successfully beginning her action plan, the leader will begin the journey of making the new behaviors into habits. This will take time, practice, and reinforcement.
Maintenance	Assuming that the leader indeed receives benefits from making her behavioral changes, and assuming that she has success for a sustained period of time (perhaps six months), we can assume that her new style of leading has "stuck." She will then move on to maintenance mode.

The worst outcome would be for the senior leader to expect his direct report to be making dramatic changes while she is still contemplating whether the change would really be worth the effort, and how she might go about leading differently.

While we naturally expect people to move forward in action, we will ultimately be far more likely to facilitate change if we recognize an individual's stage of change, meet him where he is, and help him

Recognize an individual's stage of change, meet him where he is, and help him move to the next stage. move to the next stage. Of the various stages of change, the one that seems to be frequently overlooked is the stage of contemplation. Yet this is perhaps the most critical stage. If an individual does not believe that the benefits outweigh the costs of the change, he will not be committed to moving forward.

If you have ever coached someone who has not changed in a desired manner, it is highly likely that he is not yet committed to the change. If you get the head nod and the "Sure, I'll do that" without much evidence of struggle and buy-in, you are likely to see only short-term behavior changes that are not sustainable. Coachees may go through the motions for a short time to appease you (or to get you off of their back), but the change is not likely to be long-lasting.

Knowing where someone is on the stages of change model will help us know what is possible when we begin to Explore the Desired State. Perhaps the paths we need to be exploring are not action paths but contemplation, thinking, or reflection paths.

Application

While these ideas are still fresh in your mind, try applying them to a real situation involving someone you are coaching:

1. Identify someone whom you are currently coaching.

2. If there are performance issues, what is your analysis of the real reason(s) for this performance deficiency? If you aren't certain, how could you go about making that determination as you meet with this person?

3. In your estimation, where is this person in the change
   process?
   ❑ Precontemplation (not aware, and not considering a
      change)
   ❑ Contemplation (considering but not committed to
      making a change)
   ❑ Preparation (committed to changing and beginning the
      process)
   ❑ Action (fully on board with a change agenda)
   ❑ Maintenance (continuing well-established patterns after
      six months of action)
   ❑ Relapse (he/she used to perform well, but has slipped
      into a previous habit)
          If you don't know, how might you go about discov-
   ering the answer?

4. What will your coaching focus be, relative to the stage
   of change that the person is in? How does this influence
   your expected outcomes in your upcoming coaching
   conversation(s)?

5. What do you believe to be a reasonable timetable to follow in
   helping this individual move through the change process?

Chapter Summary

- People won't change until they are ready to do so. A key issue in any coaching discussion, therefore, is the individual's readiness to change.
- There are a finite number of reasons for nonperformance. Typically these have to do with lack of clarity of expectations, lack of skills or know-how, lack of motivation, or barriers beyond the individual's control.
- Understanding the performance challenge is critical in being able to coach an individual effectively.
- Prochaska's stages of change model articulates the predictable steps that an individual will go through on her way to changing.
- Understanding the stage of change that an individual is in is critical to helping to determine the most appropriate coaching focus.
- Meeting the coachee where he is and helping him move to the next stage of change will ultimately produce greater results than expecting him to change instantly.
- Coaching someone through the change process will build commitment, not just compliance.

Chapter 13

The Power of the Gold Star

Reinforcing Feedback

If listening and questioning are the two foundation skills of coaching, providing feedback comes in a very close third. Feedback is one of the most useful elements in steering or directing progress, as it contains information that lets someone know whether he is on track or not.

And yet for most of us, the very word *feedback* probably has a slightly negative connotation. Think about the last time someone said to you, "Hey, do you have a minute? I'd like to give you some feedback." Chances are you probably winced internally, took a deep breath, and braced yourself to hear about whatever it was that you had done wrong. Many times, people say, "Can I give you some feedback?" as a way to couch the negative information that is about to come.

In this and the following two chapters, we will attempt to reframe how you view feedback and provide both motivation and guidance regarding how best to deliver feedback—both reinforcing and redirecting—to your colleagues.

WHAT GETS IN THE WAY

We will start this discussion with a quick look at what gets in the way of our providing feedback to our colleagues. Here is a list of the barriers that we most frequently hear leaders describe as roadblocks to giving feedback. Place a check mark next to any of the descriptions in this list to which you personally relate. When describing the two types of feedback, we will use *redirecting* to mean predominantly developmental feedback that is intended to change or redirect behaviors, and *reinforcing* to mean generally positive feedback that is intended to reinforce behaviors.

Barriers to Providing Redirecting Feedback

- ❑ It takes too much time.
- ❑ I do not have a good relationship with the individual.
- ❑ The person will be defensive and/or deny the feedback.
- ❑ The person will become emotional and perhaps even cry.
- ❑ I need to gather more specific evidence before I can have a conversation.
- ❑ I am afraid of the personal repercussions of providing feedback (especially to peers or superiors).
- ❑ I avoid conflict or conversations that cause tension.
- ❑ Providing feedback will have a negative impact on my relationship with the individual.
- ❑ Providing feedback will have a negative impact on the person's work on a project.
- ❑ The person won't change, so why bother?

Barriers to Providing Reinforcing Feedback

- ❑ I already provide enough positive feedback.
- ❑ The person is improving, but she is not yet at the target goal.
- ❑ He is just doing his job—nothing above and beyond what is expected.
- ❑ That is what the paycheck is for.
- ❑ The person will expect a raise at the end of the year.
- ❑ The person will get an inflated ego and stop working as hard.

It may be interesting to note that while the challenges to providing redirecting feedback seem self-evident, most leaders also experience barriers to providing reinforcing feedback. The rest of this chapter focuses on reinforcing feedback. Chapters 14 and 15 will cover redirecting feedback.

WHITE BREAD ISN'T NUTRITIOUS

If you are like most leaders we work with, you probably believe that you do a fairly decent job of providing positive, reinforcing feedback *and* that you provide your team members with enough of it. *Chances are you are actually being stingy!* If you checked any of the barriers to providing reinforcing feedback listed earlier, you are probably missing out on opportunities to bring out the best in your employees.

> *You are probably missing out on opportunities to bring out the best in your employees.*

In a large study on why people left their jobs, the third most common reason cited was that the person "did not feel their efforts were appreciated."[1] (The top two reasons cited were insufficient compensation and lack of growth/development opportunities.)

Leaders often state that they do not want to provide "too much" positive feedback because they fear that employees will have inflated expectations when the end of the year rolls around and merit increases are doled out. We want to challenge this fear. If you do an effective job of providing feedback, the effects will be positive, and you are not likely to set yourself up for these inflated expectations.

If you are providing generalizations and platitudes ("You did a fabulous job on that PowerPoint!" "You are the best salesperson I've seen come through here in years!" "You nailed that project—you handled all of the challenges superbly well!"), you may indeed be setting up false hopes on the part of your employees. We liken this type of general "attaboy" feedback to white bread—not much nutritional value and not very filling. It feels good at the moment, perhaps, but it neither reinforces behaviors (there is no specificity concerning the behaviors that you are trying to reinforce) nor seems very sincere, thoughtful, or personal.

However, if you are providing specific reinforcing feedback, you are likely to do two things:

1. Truly reinforce and extend the behaviors that help to make the employee successful—while also making the employee "consciously competent" about what works well.
2. Provide much-needed personalized appreciation and acknowledgment of a job well done, which in turn will provide motivation to do an even better job in the future.

SATISFIERS AND MOTIVATORS

Frederick Herzberg is often cited for his research on motivational theory—what truly motivates employees. He coined the term *hygiene factors*, which you may recognize, to indicate that some factors (e.g., safe working conditions, fair pay, and fringe benefits) are expected as conditions of employment. They do not motivate employees *per se*, but the absence of them creates dissatisfaction. In addition to identifying these dissatisfiers, Herzberg clearly points to two satisfiers or motivators.[2]

According to Herzberg, the number one motivator is achievement itself—accomplishing something beyond what one achieved yesterday. Other research supports this idea; in fact, it has been said that a great way to increase one's self-esteem as an adult is to learn a new skill (which represents a new achievement). As a leader, you can certainly facilitate this motivational factor with your employees. Provide them with "stretch" assignments that encourage them to reach beyond their comfort zone or tap into new skills or behaviors.

The second motivational factor that Herzberg identified for employees is personalized, specific recognition and feedback from their managers. When the manager provides specific, personalized feedback, the employee feels that the manager is paying attention, notices, and cares about the employee's efforts.

Now, the beauty of these two top motivators is this: if an employee achieves more and her manager reinforces her performance, the employee is likely to strive harder and reach increasingly higher levels of performance. This dynamic creates a positive spiral of ever-increasing motivation and performance.

What does it take to achieve this momentum? Coaching, in and of itself, can help to create such an opportunity. If you encourage your employees to find their own solutions for complex problems and support them by holding them accountable, they will undoubtedly feel better about their achievements and progress toward goals.

THREE GUIDELINES FOR PROVIDING PERSONALIZED FEEDBACK

Let's focus on the second motivational factor, providing specific, positive, personalized feedback and recognition. Reinforcing feedback is a wonderful tool for creating greater engagement, it is *completely* within your control, and it does not require a great deal of planning! Of course, you still need to do this right—no "white bread" attaboys will do here. So, here are three guidelines, and we will devote the rest of this chapter to diving into these and offering examples of their application.

1. *Reinforce the behaviors and actions* that you want the employee to continue and extend (not just the end results that were achieved).
2. *Be specific, focusing on what the individual did or said and its impact* on you, on others, and on results.
3. *Provide at least three times as much positive, reinforcing feedback as redirecting feedback.* This 3-to-1 ratio seems to be the secret to creating good feelings and improved results.

Reinforce the Behaviors and Actions That You Want to Extend

Too often, we praise and recognize people for getting the job done—for meeting a big goal. While it is important to acknowledge the attainment of the end result, if that is all we do, we miss the opportunity to truly reinforce the behaviors that made the individual successful. Likewise, an individual might perform all of the right actions and follow best-practice processes but not achieve the final desired result. It is important to remember what you are trying to do with positive feedback: reinforce and extend behaviors that you wish to encourage.

When Means Justify Imperfect Ends

Early in my career as a training and development specialist in a large health-care system, I taught a performance management process class. This class was required for all managers to train them on how to conduct annual performance appraisals. It was soon apparent that there were plenty of "prisoners" in the class—managers who had to be there but who would rather have been in a dozen other places. My relatively new boss decided to observe the session, to watch me in action and to provide me with feedback at the end of the session. Needless to say, my tension started to climb upon hearing this news.

From my point of view, the workshop was a disaster: I could not get the managers to participate, they would not answer the questions I posed, they were checking their watches frequently, and they seemed to delight in arguing against any of the policies and processes that I was reviewing with them. (Fortunately, this was years ago, before PDAs and smartphones were the electronic toys of distraction that they are today!) I was horrified that my manager was sitting in the room, observing *this* particular session. After the workshop ended and the participants left their evaluations at the door, my manager asked if we could review how the session went. I was practically shaking, waiting for her to say the inevitable words, "I don't think you are a good fit with the company—please consider this your notice of termination."

Instead, what she said absolutely took me by surprise. Instead of focusing on the *results* of the classroom evaluations, she spent 15 minutes talking about actions and behaviors that I demonstrated that she wanted to reinforce. What did I do well? She observed that I was

- Being clear about purpose, process, and payoff of the class; I laid out a clear road map for learning
- Encouraging class participation through questions, affirmation, and validation of contributions

- Using humor appropriately to break the ice and lighten the seriousness of the subject matter
- Using real-world examples and encouraging application of the concepts to real scenarios

The list went on as Lisa used specific examples, reciting actual phrases that I had said and actions I had taken. And during this 15-minute feedback discussion, something amazing happened: I was clear on what I had done well and which behaviors I should continue performing in the future. I felt better about my efforts, in spite of what I had perceived to be a lackluster session. I could sense my manager's support as well as her objective focus and positive intent to help. I was also far more ready and willing to hear what I could have done differently, and how I might have contributed to the experience in the classroom. You can bet that the next time Lisa wanted to sit in on a session that I was leading, I looked forward to it. And I definitely repeated all of the behaviors that she had noticed and reinforced through that powerful feedback discussion. What struck me the most, though, was that she recognized that my good efforts did not necessarily guarantee good results, and she still wanted to reinforce what I was doing right.

Take another example—someone who actually achieved his goal and hit the target that he was shooting for. Several years ago, the organization I worked for hired a new account executive. In his second year with the organization, he sold over $2 million worth of services—a goal that most experienced salespeople in that organization never attained. Of course, his manager was thrilled at his success, but instead of merely applauding Ken for reaching what Jim Collins has labeled a "big, hairy audacious goal," his manager made it very clear exactly what Ken had done that had contributed to his success:

- He created a stakeholder map for his client organizations and used this information to create a strategy for penetrating the accounts.
- He developed a truly consultative relationship with customers, and he was not afraid to tell the truth or deliver the tough messages.

- He utilized the more experienced resources in the organization in appropriate ways to support his sales efforts.
- He set monthly and weekly subgoals that supported his overall targets. Every week, he reviewed his priorities and did not quit until he had met his weekly targets.

While the rest of the company waited to see if Ken was a one-hit wonder, his manager was busy ensuring that Ken would have a repeat performance his next year on the job by reinforcing the behaviors that would lead to good results. (Ken did end up hitting a $2+ million goal the next year, as well.)

In both of these examples, the manager focused on the behaviors that he or she wanted to reinforce and extend. We absolutely want to celebrate the big wins and successes, but sometimes the employee is performing in the right ways but not necessarily achieving the results because of extenuating circumstances. By taking the time to focus on the behaviors that you want to extend in your employees, you help them become more consciously competent at what they are doing right, so that they can continue to employ those behaviors in the future.

By taking the time to focus on the behaviors that you want to extend, you help them become more consciously competent.

Video Example

For a video highlighting real people in a real feedback conversation, we invite you to watch Jack provide positive feedback to Kelly in a short video clip. Go to the Web site www.zengerfolkman.com and click on the Leadership Resource Center icon. As you view this video, answer the following questions:

- What behaviors was Jack reinforcing? Which behaviors is Kelly likely to repeat as a result of this conversation?
- How is Kelly likely to be feeling at the end of this conversation?
- Was Kelly doing anything above and beyond the call of duty in his role as a salesperson?

In the examples given earlier and in the video vignette, managers provided reinforcing feedback to individuals who were not necessarily going above and beyond job expectations. In my personal example, I was just doing my job. In the second example, Ken was just doing his job (and achieving superior results). And in the example in the video, Kelly was just doing his job.

One of the great errors that managers make regarding giving positive feedback is that they wait until their employees or colleagues do something that is above and beyond the call of normal duty. We absolutely want to celebrate these exceptional performance moments. But if that is all we reinforce, we are missing countless opportunities to provide the second most important motivational factor.

What We Can Learn From Shamu

Years ago, I lived in Orlando and was exposed to the training techniques used by the animal trainers at SeaWorld. Many of you will be familiar with Shamu—the name given to the killer whale that jumps out of the water, to the delight of eager onlookers. The trainers use behavioral shaping techniques to train each new Shamu how to jump on command.

How does it work? Put fairly simply, the trainers provide only positive reinforcement (fish to eat) when the whale does something right (swims over a training target); they provide absolutely no negative reinforcement or punishment when the whale fails to perform.

Now, imagine a brand new whale in a tank or pool at SeaWorld. Early in the training process, the animal trainers place a stick on the bottom of the pool. During training hours, when the whale swims over the stick, it gets a fish. (Note: It is absolutely *impossible* for the whale to swim *under* the stick at this point.) If the whale swims around the pool without going over the stick, it does not get punished or whapped on its nose. The whale merely gets no positive reinforcement, or fish.

Progressively, the trainers bring the stick to increasingly higher levels in the water. The reinforcement system remains the same, however. If the whale swims over the stick, it gets fish. If the whale is playing or goofing off, it gets nothing. Over time, by using behavior shaping alone, these masterful animal trainers teach whales, dolphins, and other animals to perform seemingly miraculous feats on cue.

So, how does this apply to you as leaders and managers? We invite you to consider all the ways in which you could be shaping your employees' behavior gradually over time, praising and reinforcing all of the incremental gains that your employees are making. Too often, we wait until the desired target is reached—when the employee reaches the final goal. By doing so, we miss the opportunity to shape behavior more quickly and build positive recognition and feelings along the way.

For instance, let us imagine that you have an employee who is consistently tardy. Three days out of any five, she is 10 or more minutes late for work. While this would not be a problem in some roles, she is a representative in a call center, which must have telephone support and coverage at exact times of day. You have talked with this employee and set performance expectations: she needs to be at work and ready to take calls exactly at 8:00 a.m., Monday through Friday. She agrees.

Now, imagine that the next week, she is still late—but this time, she is late only two days during the week. Are you thinking to yourself, "This is progress!"? Or are you thinking, "She still doesn't get it!" Do you feel like congratulating her for the progress or whapping her on the nose (figuratively speaking, of course) and chastising her for missing the target? If you are like most leaders we work with, you are probably thinking the latter.

What would Shamu's trainers do? They would give her a fish. What if—instead of giving your employee a fish—you said:

> Andrea, I notice that you are making progress toward the goal of being on time this week. I appreciate your making the effort to be on time three days this week; that is an improvement over where we have been. And, let us aim for five on-time days out of five next week.

This statement accomplishes three important things:

1. It positively reinforces the progress that Andrea is making.
2. It reiterates the end goal (we do not want to stop in the middle of our path, of course). Praising incremental gains while still focusing on the end state sends two strong messages.
3. The message (and the timeliness of the message) demonstrates clearly to Andrea that you are paying attention and noticing her performance in this area. Too often, when managers set expectations for changes in an employee's behavior, they fail to reward the behavior when it happens—especially when the behavior falls short of the final destination. If Andrea does not think that you are paying attention, she may revert to her normal pattern of behavior or comfort zone.

Be Specific, Focusing on the Actions and the Impact

You probably already know that the best feedback is specific, based on data and focused on objective reality: what the employee said, did, or accomplished. The examples listed earlier highlighted the behaviors that the manager wanted to reinforce. In any feedback conversation, the more that you can *The best feedback also provides information on the impact that the actions had.* point to specific behaviors or actions that the employee demonstrated, the more likely it is that you will reinforce the right behaviors in the future. However, the best feedback does more than just describe what the employee did or said that worked well; it also provides information on the impact that the actions had.

Compare the following examples:

> Statement 1: Terry, I appreciate how responsive you are in following up on the e-mails I send you. You almost always return my e-mails the same day that I send them to you.
>
> Statement 2: Terry, I appreciate how responsive you are in following up on the e-mails I send you. You almost always return my e-mails the same day that I send them to you. As

a result, I know that I will not have to track the requests I have made to you. I don't have to set reminders to myself or worry that I will need to follow up with you if I have not heard back from you. This makes my job a lot easier, and I want you to know that I really appreciate your diligence and follow-through.

You can see that the first statement is specific and focused on Terry's behavior (returning e-mail messages the same day). However, adding the impact statement to the behavior we want to reinforce helps Terry see how her responsiveness makes a big difference to this particular colleague. Understanding the consequences of our actions often provides the reinforcement or motivation that we need if we are to continue (or change) the highlighted behaviors.

In their book *How the Way We Talk Can Change the Way We Work*, Robert Kegan and Lisa Laskow Lahey emphasize the power of making statements that do not characterize another's attributes but rather describe the speaker's experience.[3] If we were to say to Terry, "Terry, you are so responsive and consistent with your follow-through," but Terry doesn't see herself that way, she is likely to discount or debate the message. When you describe instead the personal impact of Terry's actions, using "I" statements, Terry will probably not resist the message.

Your Turn: Application

In Table 13-1 or on a separate sheet of paper, select an employee to whom you would like to provide reinforcing feedback. And we challenge you to pick an employee who is not a superstar but rather someone who is a good overall performer and meets job expectations. (It is easy to provide positive feedback to high performers who frequently exceed our expectations; we invite you to provide positive feedback to a person whose steady, ongoing contributions you might otherwise overlook.)

Table 13-1

Name of Employee	Specific Behaviors/ Actions That You Want to Recognize and Reinforce	Impact of the Behaviors or Actions (on You, on Others, and/or on Results)

Now that you've created your own example, let's run it by a few tests:

• Did you pick an employee who is meeting (but not exceeding) performance expectations?
• Are the behaviors and actions that you observed (directly or indirectly) specific and objective? (If others viewed the same events, would they be able to describe them in the same way?)
• Is the impact related to your personal experience of the individual's actions (versus statements about his/her attributes in general)?

Provide Three Times as Much Positive, Reinforcing Feedback as Redirecting Feedback

OK, there is one last critical point that we want to make about providing reinforcing feedback to your colleagues: *stop being stingy!* We have asked thousands of individuals over several years, "How many of you are getting too much positive feedback?" Only two individuals have ever raised their hands. When we probed them further (being incredulous at this possibility), we found that the feedback that they were receiving was neither specific nor sincere.

One gentleman said, "My boss always praises everyone in superlative statements—'Josh, you are the absolute best! That was a fabulous job!' He does this with everyone, so I just stopped believing him." (Note that the failing of this boss was providing white bread feedback, lacking specificity of behaviors and the subsequent impact.)

The other individual said, "I know when I do things right. Hearing my boss tell me that doesn't help me. The only way I can grow is by knowing what I am doing wrong." After probing this person a bit further, we learned a very similar story: the boss was not providing reinforcing feedback regarding the actions and behavior to repeat. Instead, the boss was praising the end results garnered by this individual.

There have been many research studies conducted by individuals (Barbara L. Fredrickson, Marcial S. Losada, Emily Heaphy, John M. Gottman, and others) that illustrate the power of creating a lopsided positive-to-negative environment for those around you. Positive contributions include expressing gratitude, appreciation, or support, while negative contributions include expressing dislike or disapproval, sarcasm, or cynicism.

In work settings, Fredrickson and Losada[4] statistically proved that for individuals to flourish, they needed to receive *three times as much positive reinforcement*, feel-

> *For individuals to flourish, they needed to receive three times as much positive reinforcement as negative.*

ings, and experiences as negative. Their description of the results to be gained by inducing more "positivity" resembles what we are aspiring to create by coaching more effectively. Studies show that increased positivity, which generates good feelings,

- Widens the scope of attention
- Broadens behavioral repertoires
- Increases intuition
- Increases creativity
- Increases resilience to adversity
- Increases happiness
- Contributes to psychological growth
- Contributes to physical health and longevity

Multiple studies have indicated this need for a 3-to-1 ratio of positive to negative interactions. Gottman's work with married couples indicates an even higher ratio: a 5-to-1 ratio is indicative of the health of a marriage. Of course, the positive interactions must continue to be genuine and grounded in the situation rather than forced, insincere, or trivial.

How Stingy Are You?

So, how are you doing with this ratio? Let us find out. Review your day yesterday (assuming that it was a workday and you were in part of a fairly normal routine). In the left column in Table 13-2, make a mark indicating how many people you explicitly and genuinely appreciated, praised, or supported. Indicate the name or the initials of the person(s) you positively influenced. In the right-hand column, indicate how many interactions you had with colleagues (or customers) where you expressed negative emotions or were critical. Please feel free to include the name or initials of the people with whom you interacted. Keep yourself honest here by putting yourself in the shoes of the people you are thinking of. What would they say about your interactions with them? Which column would *they* put you in?

Table 13-2

Positive Interactions (Name/Initials)	Negative Interactions (Name/Initials)

(*Continued*)

How did you do? Chances are, you have far fewer marks in the left-hand column than would be possible if you were *really* on the lookout to share your praise, appreciation, and reinforcement. Challenge yourself—how can you increase the amount of appreciation and support you provide your team members? Can you increase this by 10 percent each week? By 20 percent? We hope we hear from your employees someday that *you* were the manager that provided too much sincere, specific, reinforcing feedback. (Oh, let us all wish for that!)

SOMETIMES THE MEDIUM *IS* THE MESSAGE

Sometimes the medium *is* the message. How does this relate to providing positive, reinforcing feedback? As we have mentioned earlier in some of the examples, the mere act of providing reinforcing feedback becomes worthy of doing in and of itself.

The mere act of providing reinforcing feedback becomes worthy of doing in and of itself.

When you praise and provide specific reinforcement, you are building strong bonds of trust with your colleagues. You are demonstrating that you care and are paying attention. And you are showing your colleagues that you care enough to offer your feedback and your time.

Power of the Gold Star

Sometimes the very act of providing feedback can be something that creates value for employees. We were working with a client organization that truly represented the best-in-class for its industry. The client was in the financial services sector, and the timing was immediately after the mortgage crisis and subprime lending meltdown of 2007–2008. We heard a great story about a powerful leader who endeared himself to people and motivated everyone around him. Curiously enough, he did so by handing out gold stars. We are talking about the little sticky gold stars that children used to receive from teachers when they completed an assignment well—the little gold stars that were fastened to submissions in the top right corner.

This leader did not fasten the gold stars to papers, though. He would literally walk over and place them on people's foreheads in the middle of meetings. After applying the gold star to an employee's forehead, the leader would announce, "Larry did something really great this week," and go on to explain Larry's contribution and the difference that it made.

Soon, the medium became the message. People would look forward to—and even compete for—the opportunity to get a little sticky gold star stuck to their forehead. The stars became a badge of honor of sorts. Now, before you think that this practice was sophomoric, we will tell you that the leaders who vied for these coveted symbols of recognition were mostly senior leaders (directors or vice presidents) who were successful and who earned a very healthy paycheck. The fascinating phenomenon that this leader created really underscored the value of—and desire for—receiving praise and appreciation from our leaders.

While we do not recommend that you begin applying sticky stars to your colleagues' foreheads, we do encourage you to consider how the act of expressing positive feedback can be a powerful medium for driving performance. When you provide genuinely positive feedback that is focused on specific behaviors and the resulting impact, you create a motivating culture in which people want to excel.

Chapter Summary

- Giving feedback is the third critical coaching skill set to master, in addition to questioning and listening.
- Most leaders are resistant to giving too much positive feedback, fearing that employees will slack off or expect a large raise at the end of the year.
- Herzberg's motivational theory outlines the two most motivating factors: achievement (accomplishing more) and personalized, specific reinforcement from the manager.

- Reinforcing feedback not only underlines the specific behaviors that you want to extend but also helps employees be more consciously competent with the behaviors that will lead to success.
- Remember to reinforce the specific behaviors and actions that you want the employee to continue and extend (not just the end results that have been achieved).
- Be specific, focusing on what the individual did or said and the impact (on you, on others, or on the results).
- Stop being stingy! Provide three times as much positive feedback as negative feedback (or three times as many positive interactions as negative interactions).
- Remember that sometimes the medium is the message. Pay attention to what your colleagues are doing well. Notice those behaviors and call attention to them. The very act of providing feedback can help to build strong relationships.

Chapter 14

Sometimes It Just Comes Down to the Numbers

Redirecting Feedback

L et us now turn to the subject of redirecting feedback. In the previous chapter, we outlined the typical and even understandable barriers that might keep us from providing feedback that could truly be useful in helping our colleagues change. Many of those barriers have to do with our own discomfort in offering information that may upset our colleagues or make them angry at us.

Later in this chapter, we will distinguish between feedback that can be delivered in an on-the-spot conversation and feedback that might best be delivered in a coaching conversation, utilizing the Coaching Conversation Guide that we discussed earlier.

However, before we make this distinction, let us review what feedback truly is. Feedback is merely information that helps us (or our team members) know whether our actions are "on track"— whether we are moving closer to or farther away from our target. We might view feedback in a similar manner to the children's game

"Hot or Cold," where players use temperature-related words to direct the blindfolded seeker as he moves closer to or farther away from the target.

PAPER-WHACKING

Years ago, we often led managers through a fun interactive exercise called "paper-whacking." The sole purpose of this exercise was to demonstrate that a combination of both reinforcing and redirecting feedback would work to change behaviors faster than either reinforcing or redirecting feedback alone. Using negative feedback alone, we would demonstrate that you could get an individual to perform a targeted task. Similarly, we could also get an individual to perform a targeted task using positive feedback alone—and usually a little faster than with just negative feedback. But if we provided both types of feedback in concert, the individual would perform even more complex tasks more quickly. The individual received the feedback as information that allowed her to know whether or not she was on course. As a result, she could quickly correct her course. Here is how the exercise went.

Round One: Chase the Cheering Crowds!

A participant in the group was identified as the "employee" who had a task to perform. The rest of the group would agree on a task, unbeknownst to the employee—usually a set of physical actions, like walking around the room in a circle, picking up a designated pen, and writing something on a specific piece of flipchart paper. Another participant was then assigned to be the employee's "manager" and was directed to cheer, clap, and praise the employee whenever she was performing the "right" task. When the employee was going off course, the manager was directed to be silent. The manager was also directed to clap and cheer more loudly when the employee got "closer" to the target.

This is almost identical to the approach used by Shamu's trainers, described in the previous chapter. When the employee did something right, the manager gave her "fish." The more "right" the employee was, the bigger the fish. When the employee went off course, the manager was silent; no punishment ensued.

The end result: invariably, the employee learned to perform the task, without any guidance, direction, or verbal cues other than the praise and cheering from the manager. How did the employee feel as a result? She felt supported by the manager, even though she lacked direction in what she was supposed to do (lack of clear goal expectations). Typically, the volunteer employees during this first round said that they could have been much more efficient if the goal had been clearly outlined to them; they would have been able to get the job done far faster. But they felt supported and appreciated the positive reinforcement and information that let them know that they were on track.

Of course, it may be interesting to consider how any of these dynamics might be at play in your own work environment. Do employees receive positive feedback when they perform well but the targets and goals are not clearly defined up front? How much more efficient would your team members be if they were moving toward well-defined targets? Do they stray too far off course without knowing it or receiving any information to that effect?

Round Two: Bad Dog!

Next, a new "employee" and "manager" were selected from the group, and a new task was identified for the employee to perform (again without the employee knowing what the task was). The manager was provided with a piece of rolled-up flipchart paper, which was then folded in half. The manager was instructed to use the folded paper "fan" to "whack" the employee whenever the employee was moving *away* from his target. However, when the employee was doing the "right thing"—as defined by the group—*nothing* would happen. This negative feedback was the exact opposite of the training offered to Shamu.

For fun, we would often build a second layer of management into this round—a "senior manager" who was also given a rolled-up sheet of flipchart paper. This senior manager was instructed to whack his direct report—the manager—when the manager was not performing his duty. The senior manager was also told to keep an eye directly on the employee and to reach around the manager, if needed, and whack the employee directly. You can imagine this dynamic—there were times when the manager was not whacking the employee (and thus the employee thought he was moving in the right direction) but the senior manager was. The employee was confused, as was the direct manager, who was wondering why the senior manager was getting involved.

Pause for a moment and predict the end result under these circumstances. Again, employees typically were able to complete the task at hand, with no guidance other than the negative feedback. How did the employee feel as a result? You can imagine that the employee's morale was low, to say the least. Employees in this second round would often report feeling helpless or completely disheartened, feeling that nothing that they did was right. Some of these round two participants would report severe frustration or anger. On occasion, the employees would literally "quit." They stopped moving and refused to go further, stating that they were tired of being punished, seemingly without regard for the direction in which they turned.

You may have seen or heard of dogs who have lived under abusive hands, who have known mostly punishment from their masters. The dog may do what the master wants the dog to do, but his heart and soul have been diminished. By only punishing the employees, we created our own virtual "Bad Dog" phenomenon in the workshop setting. We still got the employee to do what was needed, but his enthusiasm was greatly diminished.

Again, consider how these dynamics might be in play at your own work setting. Do employees hear from their managers only when they make mistakes or veer off course? Do they even know what the target is that they are aiming for, or do they learn along the way as the punishment is doled out? Do senior leaders jump in and provide feedback that is not completely aligned with the direct managers' feedback and input?

Round Three: Yeahs *and* Boos

During the third round, one more volunteer "employee" was selected, and a task was designed for this person—one that was usually far more complex than the earlier tasks defined in rounds one and two. Instead of feedback coming from just one person, this time it came from everyone in the room.

If the employee performed the assigned (but still unknown) task, the crowd would cheer and applaud. If the employee veered off course, the crowd would yell, "Boo!" As you can imagine, not everyone saw the same thing at the same time. Therefore, some of the feedback was out of sync and confusing to the employee. But the vast majority of feedback coming to the employee was quick and accurate. If the employee began to take a half step in the wrong direction, one or more onlookers would quickly yell, "Boo!" In a heartbeat, the employee would change direction, and almost instantaneously one or more people would see the progress and shout, "Yeah!" There was no shortage of feedback, given that everyone in the room was granted permission to provide data to the employee.

The result of this third round? *The employee was usually able to complete a far more complex task in less time.* How did the employee feel? Because feedback was plentiful and immediate, the employee could use the information very quickly to direct the best course of action. And, because the negative feedback was balanced with positive feedback, it no longer felt like punishment but merely like information.

CARROTS AND STICKS BOTH WORK

So what can we learn from the paper-whacking exercise?

- We can conclude that carrots and sticks—positive reinforcement and negative reinforcement—both work to shape behavior. In fact, in a relatively short period of time, you can demonstrate the efficacy of either positive feedback alone or negative feedback alone.

- While both positive and negative reinforcement will shape behavior, the experience of the individual in those two circumstances is significantly different.
- When feedback is frequent, timely, and balanced, the individual is more likely to interpret the feedback as useful *information* that helps direct a course of action.
- We want to reemphasize here, however, that "balanced" does not necessarily mean a 1-to-1 ratio between positive and negative feedback. As mentioned in the previous chapter, it is important to aim for a 3-to-1 positive-to-negative ratio. And other studies have encouraged a 5-to-1 ratio as the ideal.

When feedback is frequent, timely, and balanced, the individual is more likely to interpret the feedback as useful information.

So here is a perplexing question: if feedback is truly just data or information to help direct a course of action, why do most of us not view feedback as helpful information?

IT IS JUST A NUMBER

It may be useful to identify where we already use feedback as information, helping to shape our course of action. If we agree that information is inherently neutral and can help direct our course of action, we should all welcome as much data and information as we can get. Right?

Table 14-1 has a list of types of data (information or feedback) in the left-hand column. In the column headed "Your Reaction," please indicate whether you feel neutral (0), negative (−), or positive (+) about each of the data sources.

Chances are that the first two data items (fuel gauge and speedometer) garnered a primarily neutral reaction, and that the strength of your feelings (either positive or negative) grew in intensity as you moved down the list. In fact, even though each item in the left column is really "just a number," those numbers get woven into a story about the worth of that number very quickly.

Table 14-1

Data Source	Your Reaction (0, +, or −)
Fuel gauge	
Car speedometer	
Weight on a bathroom scale	
Customer satisfaction ratings	
Progress against your year-to-date sales quota	
Employee satisfaction ratings	
Annual salary increase	
Annual bonus	
Number of times per day your children say, "I love you"	
Number of times per year your children say, "I hate you!"	

Our weight comes to be equated with our overall fitness and attractiveness, our annual merit increase or bonus becomes tied to our value and performance for the company, and our children's utterances reflect our worthiness as parents. How does this happen? Well, one reason is that we are "meaning-making machines." We rarely can view information without assigning meaning to it or interpreting it. While this ability to instantaneously and subconsciously process vast quantities of data ultimately helps us to function and be efficient in the world, it can lead to a slippery slope for giving *and* receiving feedback. Not only do people giving feedback typically assign meaning and inferences to the data that they assess but so do the people receiving that feedback.

Is 15 Pounds Just a Number?

Take a simple, nonwork example: you have gained 15 pounds, and your spouse has noticed. Out of concern and caring for you, your partner says, "Sweetie, it looks like you are gaining weight; in fact, I would say you look about 15 pounds heavier than you did at this time last year. Your belly is a bit flabbier, your face is a bit more pudgy, and your pants seem a bit too tight around the waist. What is going on?"

We do not know too many people who would react kindly to that data stream and say, "Thank you for noticing. In fact, my bathroom scale confirmed that I have gained 15.5 pounds, and I have had to loosen my belt notch by one hole. You are accurate in your assessment." Instead, we leap to a different and deeper (and often inaccurate) meaning: "My partner must think I am fat . . . even unattractive . . . perhaps disgusting."

On the other side of the conversation, your partner is probably also assigning meaning to the data at hand, "Gosh, my sweetie has gained weight. She/he must be under too much stress at work and is not able to find time in the schedule to exercise. Poor baby. I wonder what I could do to help."

STAY AT THE BOTTOM RUNG OF THE LADDER

We cannot control how someone might interpret and react to the feedback that we share. Thus, all we can do as feedback givers is to present information as neutrally and objectively as possible—truly reflecting the objective data in the world.

All we can do as feedback givers is to present information as neutrally and objectively as possible.

Perhaps the most useful framework we have run across to help us remember to do this is Chris Argyris's Ladder of Inference model. Argyris created this useful concept years ago, and it was later popularized by Peter Senge in the book *The Fifth Discipline*.

Picture a ladder standing on the ground and leaning against a tall wall. Where is the safest place on the ladder to stand?

If you are an engineer, you might answer, "On the ground." Otherwise, the first thought you probably formulated was "on the bottom rung." We would agree. The higher you climb on the ladder, the more potentially dangerous and tenuous your footing becomes until you reach the top step of the ladder, which is very unstable and unsafe.

In the world of observing data and providing feedback, consider the ground at the base of the ladder to represent all of the information that can be observed. This pool of data represents objective reality—all of the facts and information that can be seen, heard, or otherwise observed.

Of course, as humans, we naturally tune in or tune out certain information. Therefore, we take the first step up the ladder by observing only what we see for ourselves. However, our first data input is still objective reality—what we observe directly. These are the facts of the situation—what someone says or does, or the results that she is able to achieve. If three people were to observe the same scenario, they would all see the same objective reality.

An Example

For instance, if someone forcefully slammed his fist on a table, three onlookers could all potentially see the same reality—an individual forcefully slammed his fist on the table. What happens next and naturally for us is that we quickly climb one or more steps up the Ladder of Inference (see Figure 14-1).

We assign meaning to what we have observed and draw conclusions. We reinforce our own beliefs and tend to act based on that thought pattern and belief choice.

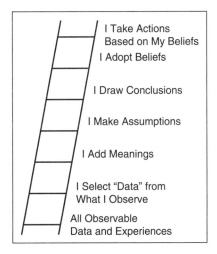

Figure 14-1 Ladder of Interference

Table 14-2 Three Different Ladders

	Observed Data	Add Meaning	Draw Conclusion	Reinforce Beliefs	Take Actions
Person 1	Scott slammed his fist on the table during the monthly team meeting.	"He must be mad about the sales numbers again."	"He is wound too tightly. They are just numbers, after all. There is more to life than meeting quota."	"We should all keep our work in perspective; this is a good reminder for me not to take this month's numbers too seriously."	Dismiss Scott's frustration; make sure to get to yoga practice tonight.
Person 2	Scott slammed his fist on the table during the monthly team meeting.	"Scott seems to do that every time Jodie talks."	"I don't think Scott and Jodie get along. There is always tension between the two of them. Scott must be chauvinistic; he acts this way with all his female colleagues."	"This work environment minimizes all of the great contributions made by women. This just reinforces that."	Stop speaking up in meetings; start looking for another job.
Person 3	Scott slammed his fist on the table during the monthly team meeting.	"Scott is usually so calm. I bet there was a bug on the table."	"Since Scott is a practicing Buddhist, I am surprised that he would actually kill a bug, instead of capturing it in a cup and taking it outside."	"Bugs are people too, you know. Just because it wandered into the wrong place at the wrong time does not mean that it should be killed."	Tell Scott that he should not harm any living creatures that happen to find themselves where they would not want to be anyway.

Table 14-2 shows how three different people observing the same objective reality might climb three ladders—all leading in different directions.

Now let us assume that Scott's fist-slamming behavior disrupted the meeting, causing tension and disrupting the conversation. If you were going to share feedback (information) with Scott, the safest place to stand on the ladder would be the bottom rung: what you observed.

And, to reiterate one of the key feedback guidelines we mentioned in the previous chapter, you would want to *be specific, focusing on what the individual did or said and its impact* (on you, on the results, or on others).

> *Be specific, focusing on what the individual did or said and its impact.*

Table 14-3 shows how a feedback conversation might sound if someone (you!) stayed at the bottom rung of the ladder when offering feedback to Scott rather than climbing up a step or two, as Persons 1, 2, and 3 unwittingly did.

Table 14-3

Message Is Based On	*How the Feedback Might Sound*
Action (Person 3)	"I cannot believe that you just killed a bug that just happened to wander into the wrong territory. He cannot help what happened to him, but you certainly could have. Poor little creature."
Belief (Person 1)	"Scott, *dude*, you need to put all of this into perspective. There is a lot more to life than missing our target for the quarter. Calm down, man."
Conclusion (Person 2)	"You just cannot stand it when Jodie—or any other woman, for that matter—has a good idea to contribute, can you? I mean, the tension between you two is palpable. Everyone notices it, too."
Meaning (Person 1)	"Well, this is predictable. There you are, getting uptight about the sales numbers again. I can almost predict the point in the meeting when you are going to blow a gasket."
Bottom rung (you)	"Scott, I noticed you slammed your fist down. I was personally startled, and I must say that it was hard for me to concentrate on what you were saying after that happened."

Imagine that you were Scott, on the receiving end of any of these statements. As you can imagine, because Scott is also a meaning-making machine, he will ascribe his own meanings and draw his own conclusions based on what he hears. However, you can almost predict that the only message that might not lead to a quick defensive reaction on his part is the bottom-rung message. He still may not like the data—just like I do not like the number on my bathroom scale most mornings—but he will be more likely to be able to receive it in the way that it was intended: as feedback that might help him correct his course.

While the sample statements in Table 14-3 are a bit exaggerated, we have been absolutely shocked by the feedback that some managers actually do share with their employees. Sometimes the manager seems to be teetering on the top step of the ladder, standing on tiptoe, with only one foot on the step. Here are some classic top-of-the-ladder statements that we have heard managers say to their employees or colleagues:

- "You have a bad attitude. Every time someone else says something in a meeting, you have to rain on his parade. Your attitude is spoiling the meetings for everyone." *(Danger! Careening on the top step! Can you objectively observe an attitude?)*
- "I don't think you are motivated to do what it takes to succeed around here. This is obviously a poor fit for you, and it probably is not going to work out. You just do not have what it takes to succeed." *(Warning! Foregone conclusion apparently reached!)*
- "Do you know what your problem is? You do not care about what is going to make the most sense for the company; you are just trying to tell the customers what they want to hear. That is no way to run a business—not a profitable one, anyway." *(Even the lead-in to this statement is guaranteed to garner resistance.)*

Now, if you happen to be squirming a little bit, do not worry. You are in good company. And, between the rest of this chapter and the next one, which is also about redirecting feedback, you will be well equipped to have better redirecting feedback conversations than you have had in the past.

Do You Open Your Mouth? Or Keep It Closed?

So, when do you share what you have observed with another person? Each of us is constantly observing a multitude of data points every day, assigning meaning and inferences, drawing conclusions, and taking action.

When do *you* decide to stop and provide feedback to someone else? What criteria do you use? Record your own criteria in the space given here.

Compare your criteria to those in the Fast Feedback Test (Table 14-4).

The Fast Feedback Test

Now that you've really thought about the way you give feedback, Table 14-4 gives some useful questions to ponder that might help you ascertain whether or not you choose to speak up and offer your observations to another individual.

Table 14-4 The Fast Feedback Test

1. Will the information be useful to the recipient?	Yes ❏	No ❏
2. Do you have a trust-based relationship in place that will support the conversation?	Yes ❏	No ❏
3. Is the behavior change critical for the individual's success?	Yes ❏	No ❏
4. Will the feedback be new or surprising to hear? Will the data fall into a blind spot for the individual and perhaps be shocking to him?	Yes ❏	No ❏

(Continued)

Table 14-4 The Fast Feedback Test (Continued)

5. Will the behavior change take significant time, effort, or support?	Yes ☐ No ☐
6. Are you personally invested in the behavior change?	Yes ☐ No ☐

We have drawn a line after the first two statements. If you answer both of those with a "yes," we would encourage you to share the information you have observed with the individual.

Your answers to the other questions will help you determine whether you can simply share the data on the spot or need to hold a coaching conversation.

Let us look at some examples to highlight how these questions might be useful as criteria (see Table 14-5).

Table 14-5 Examples for the Fast Feedback Test

Example A	A direct report has broccoli in his teeth right before he is about to make an important presentation.
Example B	A peer tends to interrupt you and other colleagues in meetings, jumping in before they can complete their sentences.
Example C	Your skip-level leader presented upcoming news about an impending organizational change with great candor and transparency.

If we were to apply the previous criteria to any of these feedback opportunities, we would probably note the following:

1. Will the information be useful to the recipient?	Yes ☑ No ☐

The information is likely to be useful to—or appreciated by—the recipient.

2. Do you have a trust-based relationship in place that will support the conversation?	Yes ☑ No ☐

You have a good working relationship with all of these coworkers, and they would welcome the feedback from you.

3. Is the behavior change critical for the individual's success?	Yes ☐ No ☑

These behaviors are probably not critical for any of the individuals' success. Whether they sustain those behaviors for the future or change them is not likely to have an impact on their performance to a significant degree.

4. Will the feedback be new or surprising to hear? Will the data fall into a blind spot for the individual and perhaps be shocking to him?	Yes ☐ No ☑

While the feedback may in fact be new information (and perhaps a bit of a surprise, in the case of the stuck broccoli), the receiver is not likely to be too anxious upon hearing the news. The sustained shock factor is likely to be relatively minor.

5. Will the behavior change take significant time, effort, or support?	Yes ☐ No ☑

As a behavior change, checking one's teeth in the mirror requires virtually no time, effort, or support. Stopping interrupting colleagues might take a little longer, especially if the behavior is in a blind spot for the direct report. However, making a change (assuming that the individual wants to do so) will probably not require a great deal of time, effort, or support—merely a little feedback whenever the behavior occurs. In the third example, providing positive feedback to the senior leader, the behavior of transparency does not need changing—just reinforcing.

6. Are you personally invested in the behavior change?	Yes ☐ No ☑

It is highly likely that you, as the feedback giver, are not personally invested in most of the behavior changes.

If your answers to questions 1 and 2 are "yes," but your responses to questions 3 through 6 are mostly "no," you do not necessarily need to carve out the time for a full and rich coaching conversation. The feedback you offer may be simply shared on the spot, using the Fast Feedback Guidelines that follow.

Obviously, for many of these questions, there is a continuum between a simple "yes" and a simple "no" answer. There are shades of gray. If your peer consistently interrupts colleagues, and as a result they stop wanting to work with her, it would be more important to change the behavior. Your personal investment may increase as your peer's behavior starts causing you or other team members to perform less effectively. Likewise, if the behavior is a longstanding pattern or habit that has generated some positive consequences for the individual, it may in fact take more effort or support before the individual could change.

If, however, you answer "yes" to the first two questions *and* to more than one of the questions between 3 and 6, you will probably want to carve out time for a coaching conversation, where your feedback is the issue on which you focus.

Fast Feedback Guidelines

If you are ready to share your feedback on the spot, without a longer coaching conversation, you can utilize the Fast Feedback Guidelines given here. By using the word *fast*, we are truly implying two things:

- Your timing for the feedback can probably be immediate, quickly following the observation of data.
- You do not need to spend a great deal of time engaged in the feedback conversation.

Here are the two key guidelines that we would offer you for these Fast Feedback conversations.

1. Ask permission to share the feedback.
2. Be specific, focusing on what the individual did or said and its impact (on you, on others, and on the results).

Let us look at how one or two of the previous examples might sound, using these Fast Feedback Guidelines (see Table 14-6).

Table 14-6

Broccoli in the teeth	**You:** "Hey, Sally, do you have a second? Could I share something you might want to know before you take the stage? You have a piece of broccoli between your two front teeth."
	Sally: "Thanks." (Rubs her tongue over her teeth.) "Is it gone now?"
	You: "Looks good."
Your peer interrupts you and other colleagues in meetings	**You:** "Pat, could I share something with you? I noticed in this last meeting that when I was speaking about my department's monthly accomplishments, you interrupted me three different times."
	Pat: "I did? I was not aware of that."
	You: "I didn't think you were, and I certainly didn't think you were doing it on purpose."
	Pat: "I'm sorry."
	You: "That's OK. I know that I am sensitive about wanting to make sure that my team gets credit for all of the great work they are doing, and when you interrupted me, the conversation typically went in another direction. As a result, I was not able to showcase the accomplishments I am really proud of and that others in the group can benefit from."
	Pat: "I totally get it. I will make sure to wait for my turn next time! Tell me if I do it again. You can interrupt my interruption!"
	You: "Thanks. I really appreciate it."
Your skip-level leader presented upcoming news about an impending organizational change with great candor and transparency	**You:** "John, could I offer some positive feedback based on the meeting you just led? I appreciated your candor and transparency, especially when you said that we should all be expecting a 5 percent downsizing as a result of the new reorganization."
	John: "Thanks. I was trying to be honest about what is coming."
	You: "I really valued your directness in letting us know that some groups would not lose any employees, while others would be losing up to 10 percent of their team members. I know this is not an easy message to communicate, but I personally prefer to hear it 'straight' rather than being surprised later. Thank you for being so open with what you disclosed to the team."
	John: "Thanks for your feedback. I appreciate hearing it."

As you can see, the feedback giver did not need to explore the consequences of the broccoli-in-the-teeth situation. The consequences are obvious. However, in both the other examples, the feedback giver shared both the specific behaviors observed and the impact of the behaviors.

Your Turn

Consider feedback that you would like to deliver to a colleague. Run it by the Fast Feedback Test to determine whether it's a fast feedback conversation or whether it deserves a longer coaching conversation. Use Table 14-7 to consider how to proceed.

Table 14-7

Name of individual	*What you have observed*

Fast Feedback Test

1. Will the information be useful to the recipient?   Yes ❑   No ❑

2. Do you have a trust-based relationship in place that   Yes ❑   No ❑
   will support the conversation?

3. Is the behavior change critical for the individual's   Yes ❑   No ❑
   success?

4. Will the feedback be new or surprising to hear? Will   Yes ❑   No ❑
   the data fall into a blind spot for the individual and
   perhaps be shocking to him?

5. Will the behavior change take significant time,   Yes ❑   No ❑
   effort, or support?

6. Are you personally invested in the behavior change?   Yes ❑   No ❑

What will you do next?

❑ Fast feedback conversation	❑ Coaching conversation	❑ Nothing
("Yes" on 1 and 2)	*("Yes" on 3, 5, and 6)*	*("No" on 2)*

In Your Own Words

Fast Feedback Preparation

1. Ask permission to share the feedback.

2. Be specific, focusing on what the
   individual did or said and its impact
   (on you, on others, or on the results).

Chapter Summary

- Feedback is simply information that helps us know whether our actions are on target.
- Positive feedback alone can change someone's behavior.
- Negative feedback alone can change someone's behavior; however, the person's experience of this treatment is not necessarily positive, and the change is not necessarily sustainable.
- Using a combination of reinforcing and redirecting feedback can change behavior faster.
- When feedback is frequent, timely, and balanced, the individual is more likely to interpret the feedback as useful *information* that helps direct a course of action.
- Feedback feels so emotionally charged because humans are meaning-making machines. Both the receiver and the giver of feedback tend to interpret the information through their own filters and beliefs.
- Use Chris Argyris's Ladder of Inference as a reminder to stay on the bottom rung when delivering feedback.
- Be specific, focusing on what the individual did or said and its impact (on you, on the results, or on others).
- Use the Fast Feedback Test to determine whether or not you should share what you have observed.
- If the behavior change is not significant or vitally important to either you or the recipient, perhaps the fast feedback conversation will fit the bill.
- If, however, the feedback is more important and changing the behavior will take greater effort, you will probably want to have a coaching conversation. In this conversation, the feedback topic is the heart of the issue to be discussed.

Chapter 15

When Feedback Becomes a Coaching Conversation

Before we investigate how redirecting feedback is best delivered through a coaching conversation, let us suggest a few guidelines for providing tough feedback:

- Coach with backbone and heart.
- Stay on the bottom rung of the ladder; keep your feedback focused on objective reality.
- Drip irrigation works best; do not pummel your colleagues with data.
- Ask before you tell; make sure that your employee is doing most of the talking.
- Follow the Coaching Conversation Guide.

COACH WITH BACKBONE AND HEART

Mary Beth O'Neill wrote *Executive Coaching with Backbone and Heart,* a book with an important message. One of the key themes in her book is that the tougher the message is to deliver, the more you should deliver it with heart. We could not agree more with O'Neill's message. Too often, when leaders feel uncomfortable with the message they are about to deliver, they tend to want to distance themselves in the conversation and from the person—perhaps believing that "this is just business, and so I must remain objective and dispassionate."

When leaders take this cool, objective stance, they often fail to realize that the person on the other end of the conversation needs reassurance and warmth in order to best hear the tough message that is being delivered.

Consider the following hypothetical situation.

What if your style of interacting with colleagues irritates almost everyone you work with? Your manager knows this, and your colleagues experience it. As a result, they do their best to keep you from being brought into projects. In fact, most of your colleagues find creative ways to avoid working with you. You have technical knowledge and capability, but the way you interact with others creates tension in almost everyone around you. Your manager is about to sit down with you and provide you with feedback that is certainly in your blind spot. You are not even remotely aware that your behavior creates problems for others.

Here is the question we would like you to reflect on:

What could your manager do or say that would help you to best hear the feedback? Take time to really consider your response before reading further. Your response may provide you with insight into how others around you would prefer to receive tough feedback.

If you are like many leaders we work with, you might have noted many of the following in your own list of what a manager should ideally do:

- Set the context for the conversation.
- Be direct.
- Share specific examples to support her point of view.
- Be willing to hear my side of the story.
- Give me the benefit of the doubt.
- Let me know that she supports me and is on my side.
- Give me time to digest a difficult message.
- Do not expect instant change.

You will notice that you probably have a desire for both back-bone *and* heart if you are truly doing something that is getting in your way. You want to know the truth, backed up by evidence and data (the backbone), but you also want to know that your manager is on your side and will hear your side of the story (the heart).

Therefore, remember that tough conversations are tough for both you and the other individual. It is important that you be open and transparent about this fact. Set the proper tone for the conversation by letting your colleague know that you care about his well-being and success. Consider the following heart statements for your redirecting feedback conversations:

"I would like to share some feedback with you. It may be hard for you to hear, and it is also hard for me to deliver."

"You have a lot to contribute to our team and this organization. I want you to be successful, and I have some feedback to provide you. My intention in sharing this with you is to help you to . . ."

"I know that this feedback may be a surprise to you. I want to make sure you know that I am on your side, and that we can work through this together."

Do not be afraid to acknowledge the emotional component in the conversation. You and the feedback receiver are human, and, as noted

When we connect to emotions, we are generally able to effect greater change.

earlier, when we connect to emotions, we are generally able to effect greater change than if we do not connect to the other person's emotions.

DRIP IRRIGATION WORKS BEST

If you are like many leaders we have worked with, you have learned to come to the tough redirecting feedback conversations well prepared—with lots of evidence and data pointing to the specific ways in which the employee's behaviors have created performance issues. Now, let us assume that redirecting feedback conversations are not necessarily conversations that you look forward to with joy and glee. Chances are that you face these conversations with anxiety, dread, and frequent procrastination. You are worried about your colleague's reaction, your own ability to deliver a calm and neutral message that will make a difference, and the probability that the individual's behaviors will change as a result.

Put these two elements together—a bushel of supporting data and high levels of anxiety and procrastination—and you might just have a "perfect storm" on your hands. There is a high likelihood that any of the following behaviors or feelings may occur. (Please check off those that you personally have experienced or typically anticipate feeling before delivering tough feedback to a colleague.)

❑ You delay having the conversation until you are fully prepared and/or you cannot wait any longer to deliver the message.

❑ You are thoroughly prepared to defend your position, using data and evidence that you have amassed.

❑ You want to get the conversation over with as quickly as possible. As a result, you cut to the chase and move quickly.

❑ You are completely convinced that your point of view is right, given all of the evidence you have to support it.

❑ You feel compelled to "convince" the feedback receiver of the evidence you have collected.

❑ It is hard for you to hear another point of view, especially if it conflicts with your own. (After all, you have gathered a ton of supporting data!)

❏ You hope that the receiver will accept the feedback calmly, without having an emotional reaction.

❏ You hope that the receiver will see your point of view quickly and move forward with an action plan to solve the problem, without debating the feedback that you are sharing.

One of our colleagues lives in Phoenix, Arizona. In desert areas like Phoenix, drip irrigation is the preferred (and even necessary) method for watering landscapes. If you use a spray method for watering plants in the desert, most of the water evaporates before it soaks into the ground, where it is needed. Drip irrigation ensures that the water penetrates to the intended plants. Here is how it works: irrigating in very small quantities close to the intended plants enables the dry earth to absorb the needed water. Water is not wasted, and it does not evaporate. Drip irrigation is a very efficient method of providing the necessary moisture to plants.

So, what does drip irrigation have to do with providing redirecting feedback? The connection is twofold:

1. Dispense the bottom-rung data that you have collected in small quantities. A little goes a long way, and you want to hear how your colleague views the information that you are sharing. As we have already explored, negative information stings more than positive information; therefore, small doses are often potent.

2. Let the information "soak in" before providing more. Test the information you are sharing for its "fit" with your colleague before sharing additional data. Does your colleague have a sense of what you are saying? Does it ring true for her? If the first example does not soak in or make sense, adding more evidence does not necessarily accomplish anything more. Chances are that the additional evidence will evaporate or run off because it has not had a chance to soak into the ground and be received.

ASK BEFORE YOU TELL

A corollary behavior to providing drip irrigation feedback is to ensure that the message is received. In order for you to make sure

Table 15-1 Observed Behavior and Resulting Impact

Behavior	Impact
• Terry shows up 10 minutes late to 80 percent of team meetings.	• Coworkers are forced to wait to begin the meeting, since the team is small and Terry is critical to the dialogue. • Coworkers perceive that Terry does not respect or value their time.
• Terry will accept phone calls or check incoming e-mail messages on a cell phone during team meetings.	• Colleagues perceive that Terry gives almost any other project or person priority over the team objectives and the current meeting agenda.

that the message soaks in, you have to leave some space in the conversation for the recipient to react. The best way to do this is to involve the feedback recipient in the conversation. For each piece of data you deliver, ask for the recipient's point of view and thoughts before you deliver any more information. *Ask before you tell.*

Involve the feedback recipient in the conversation; ask before you tell.

How does this work? Imagine that you have gathered data on a direct report's interactions with other team members and internal customers. You have noticed or collected evidence regarding the behaviors given in Table 15-1 and their impact.

While you (as Terry's manager) have not observed all of these behaviors directly, you have carefully tried to accumulate data regarding the observed behaviors and the impact of those behaviors. You are committed to staying at the bottom rung of the ladder when offering your insights.

Here are two vastly different ways that the conversation might go.

Conversation 1: Keep Talking; Dump the Bucket of Data

You: Terry, do you have a minute? I'd like to share some feedback with you regarding your participation in our team meetings and how your teammates are reacting to it. Here are some behaviors I've observed and heard about and the resulting impact on your colleagues.

You show up 10 minutes late to most team meetings. Last week, you were late to the team meeting, the beta test meeting, and the project debriefing meeting for the lost RFP bid. As a result, your peers and I feel that you don't really value our time. We end up waiting for you, because your point of view is critical to our meeting agenda. But, because we are waiting, we all feel that we are wasting time needlessly. I assume that there are reasons for your coming late to most of these meetings, but your tardiness is starting to cause tension for your team members. Three individuals have asked me if we should just start our meeting 10 minutes later, to make sure that we are all there when we begin.

I have also noticed that you frequently take phone calls or check your cell phone in the middle of our meetings. In the team meeting this week, you answered a phone call in the middle of Karl's presentation. I appreciate that you took the call outside, but Karl was visibly upset—and while you were out of the room, we discussed whether or not to wait for you. We agreed that we would wait, but when you didn't come back within five minutes, we moved on. We have all agreed on the ground rules to turn off our phones during meetings—to check them only during breaks. When you choose to answer your cell phone, I'm personally frustrated, and I know that others are too. I think this sends a signal that you are "above" following the rules that we have all agreed to. I don't believe that is your intention, but others have said as much to me.

Now, imagine Terry's reaction to this feedback. What do you think it might be?

- Thankful that you (Terry's manager) have taken the time to provide this valuable feedback
- Eager to hear more data that illustrate how he has been negatively contributing to team meetings and team members' reactions

- Committed to changing his behavior so that it will have a different impact
- Defensive and wanting to provide evidence to the contrary
- Shut down; not listening
- Willing to say anything to end this conversation quickly

Chances are that at this point, Terry is leaning back, becoming defensive, and using coping mechanisms to get through the rest of this conversation. Why? You decided to dump your entire bucket of data on Terry, sharing enough evidence to convince him of your point of view.

Conversation 2: Ask Before You Tell—Utilizing Drip Irrigation

Table 15-2 shows a very different way that the conversation might have gone. Notice the two key differences between this conversation and the prior one: the conversation is framed, so that Terry understands what you want to discuss, and drip irrigation is used, allowing Terry to describe his own awareness and sense of the issue.

Table 15-2 Conversation 2

Step 1: Frame the Conversation
(Set the context and focus for the conversation.)

Identify the behavior or issue to discuss.	**You:** Terry, do you have a minute? I'd like to share some feedback about your behaviors during our team meetings, and how others perceive your actions. Is this a good time to talk?
	Terry: Sure.
Determine the purpose or outcomes of the conversation. Agree on the process for the conversation.	**You:** I really just want to share some observations I've made about some team ground rules that seem to be being broken, and I want to hear your point of view on the situation, to find out what is working and what we might need to do differently. How does that sound?
	Terry: OK. What's up?

(Continued)

Step 2: Understand the Current State

(Explore the individual's point of view before sharing your own.)

Understand the coachee's point of view.	**You:** Well, as you know, we established a goal of starting meetings on time. Over the last month, I've noticed that you tend to show up at most team meetings around 10 minutes late. *(Ask before you tell.)* Are you aware of that?
	Terry: Well, I know that I usually have meetings stacked back-to-back. I guess it is possible that I've been late before, given the travel time between offices and buildings. Yeah, that wouldn't surprise me.
Determine the consequences of continuing on the current path.	**You:** *(Ask before you tell.)* How do you think your lateness is affecting the team meetings and your colleagues?
	Terry: I guess I haven't thought about it. I know I'm not the only one who is late to our meetings. Are you saying that I am the worst offender?
	You: Well, you are right in noticing that you are not the only one who is ever late. And, I think you might also be right in saying that you are the worst offender, to borrow your words! The pattern seems to be pretty consistent, and most of the other team members manage to show up on time every week.
	Terry: So, what are you saying? I need to schedule more time in my agenda?
	You: Well, I am saying that we need you at the team meetings, because of your insightful contributions and your knowledge about the projects we are working on. And when you are late, we end up waiting for you because we do not want you to miss what we are talking about—and we do not want to miss hearing what you might have to say. But because we end up waiting for you, it does feel like a waste of time to show up promptly and expect to get started right away. That is how it feels to me personally, and I think others may feel the same way.
	Terry: Yeah, I understand. I hate showing up at meetings on time and having to kill time waiting for someone who isn't there yet. It seems as if whatever else people are working on is more important than getting to our meeting on time.

(Continued)

Table 15-2 Conversation 2 (Continued)

	You: *(Drip.)* The other thing I have noticed in the last few meetings is that you seem to check your iPhone pretty frequently once you do arrive. We established a "No Electronic Toys" rule at the beginning of the year. *(Ask before you tell.)* I'm just wondering how you think the rule is working, especially for you personally.
	Terry: I know, I know. I'm guilty. I just have all of these critical deadlines, and I need to be able to get through my e-mails before the day ends; I have clients waiting for responses from me.
Offer your perspective, *if appropriate.*	**You:** I appreciate your concern for making sure that we meet our clients' expectations. That is why our customers trust you and want to work with you. I'm just wondering if the unintended consequence of prioritizing e-mail responses to customers is failing to meet our agreed-upon ground rules regarding how we will operate as a team. *(Ask before you tell.)* What do you think?
	Terry: I guess it is not fair to my peers, and I need to figure out a different way to either schedule my meetings or block time to make sure that I can meet customer needs without carrying that work into my other meetings.

Now imagine Terry's reaction to this second feedback conversation. Chances are that he may still be squirming a bit, as he understands the impact that his behaviors are having on others, but he is also likely to feel that you are open to hearing his point of view.

FOLLOW THE COACHING CONVERSATION GUIDE

If your redirecting feedback really belongs in a coaching conversation (rather than just being information to be shared), you will have more success when you utilize the full coaching conversation process.

You probably noticed that the second example in the previous section included a better setup for the conversation, as the conversation was framed more appropriately than the first example. Most of the feedback descriptions and Terry's reactions fall into the second conversation step, Understanding the Current State.

At the point where we left off the conversation with Terry, we are really ready to move into the third step of the coaching conversation: Explore the Desired State (see Table 15-3).

Table 15-3 Conversation 2, Continued

Step 3: Explore the Desired State
(Identify the target and generate multiple paths to achieve the end state)

Understand the vision for success.	**You:** So what would you like to see happen here?
	Terry: Well, I guess I would like to do a better job of abiding by the ground rules we set up for the team meetings, and to show up as a more respectful participant. I don't want to be late all the time or distracted by other things.
	You: Is there anything else that you would like to make happen?
	Terry: Well, I really do want to contribute to the meetings and know what is going on.
	You: Great. I'd like those things, too.
Set goals and performance expectations.	**You:** What would be some reasonable goals to set regarding your punctuality and being fully present when you are there?
	Terry: I can't promise I'll make it to every meeting on time, but I should be able to make most of them.
	You: What would be a good target?
	Terry: I think 80 percent of the time. And, I should be able to minimize my "electronic toy" usage. Unless I have an emergency or a deadline, I will put my iPhone away. Better yet, if I can leave it at my desk, I will.
	You: Sounds good. That would be a good goal for all of us.
Explore alternative paths of action.	**You:** You also mentioned that you really want to make a contribution and know what is going on with the team. Is there anything else that will help you do that, in addition to being on time and less distracted?
	Terry: I could make sure that I express my opinions when I have them. I'm sure I sometimes miss the chance, especially if I'm distracted with other things.
	You: What else might work?
	Terry: I have been meaning to connect with Maria and Josh to find out how their latest project is going. I should make time to meet with them offline.

(Continued)

Table 15-3 Conversation 2, Continued (Continued)

	You: Anything else?
	Terry: That sounds like enough to me!
Explore possible barriers or resistance.	**You:** All of that sounds really good. And those are pretty ambitious goals, given where we are today. Is there anything that will get in the way of your making this happen?
	Terry: Well, my next three weeks of meetings are already scheduled, and some of those are back to back. That will make it difficult for me to show up on time for my next meetings.
	You: That makes sense. What could help there?
	Terry: I guess I could make it clear that I need to leave five minutes before the hour to get to my next meeting on time. I'm sure others would benefit from that as well. Most of us are rushing to our next meetings, anyway. Maybe we could make some of our meetings 55 minutes long, instead of a full hour.
	You: I like that idea. I'd be willing to limit our meetings to 55 minutes, too, if we could start on time.

Step 4: Lay Out a Success Plan

(Create the detailed, actionable plan and follow-through that will lead to goal attainment.)

Develop and agree on an action plan and timelines.	**You:** So, what are your next steps going to be?
	Terry: I'll start tomorrow—by letting folks know that I will have to wrap up at five minutes before the hour. For future scheduling, I will try to leave at least one hour in the middle of the day to check incoming e-mails and voice mails and create a window to respond to any urgent customer needs.
	You: And what are your plans for our next team meeting, next Tuesday?
	Terry: On time, with iPhone off. I promise.
Enlist support from others.	**You:** I really want to support your being fully present for our meetings. I think it will make a positive difference for our team meetings, let alone other meetings you attend. So, how can I support you?
	Terry: Well, I know you will be paying attention and making sure that I'm on time and not distracted. Just knowing that you are watching will help keep me honest. I think that is good enough.

(Continued)

You: Who else might support you?

Terry: If I involve my other team leads in helping to manage our meetings, that will make a big difference. I need to enroll them in this idea of starting on time and ending in 55 minutes. And I guess it wouldn't hurt to review our ground rules at our next team meeting. If we all focus on the ground rules, we can all hold each other accountable to them.

You: I think you are right. That is a great suggestion.

Set milestones for follow-up and accountability.

You: So, let's review the plan. What happens now?

Terry: Starting tomorrow, I'm going to start reshaping how meetings are conducted in this company forevermore! Starting on time and lasting only 55 minutes! *(Laughs.)* No, seriously, I'm starting tomorrow. And I guarantee you will see me on time next Tuesday. With my iPhone off before I walk into the room.

You: Great. I can work to keep our meetings to 55 minutes. I'll also review the ground rules at our next meeting. I think that all of these steps will help all of us maximize our time and ensure that we are all contributing as we can. And I will experiment with leaving my phone at my desk too. That should be interesting! Terry, thanks for being willing to listen to me today and for brainstorming some good solutions to the current situation. And thanks for the positive way you reacted to this conversation. Is there anything you'd like to add?

Terry: Nothing to add. I appreciate your bringing these items to my attention. Thanks for hearing me out, too.

You can see from the example in Table 15-3 that Terry realizes that he is late and being distracted and owns up to these problems. He is also engaged in creating the solution moving forward. Terry shares some of his reasons for being late and distracted. That does not make Terry's behavior OK, but his reasons for his actions may be useful for his manager to hear—if the manager is open to considering the reasons behind the performance. It obviously helps in the process of finding solutions that will succeed.

Terry has a far greater likelihood of changing his behavior because he was engaged in the conversation and not just "punished" for his inappropriate behavior. Because Terry was engaged in the solution, the manager will be able to hold him accountable if he does not live up to his own commitments.

AN IMPERFECT WORLD

While you may think that Terry is the ideal employee, and far too willing to problem-solve, we would like to share with you a real-life example of a feedback conversation involving real-life characters. One of the characters is Kathleen Stinnett, the coauthor of this book. She engaged her colleague, Sue, in a feedback dialogue shortly after a thorny client situation was resolved.

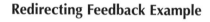 **Redirecting Feedback Example**

Kathleen and Sue videotaped their conversation so that others can see how feedback might sound in the context of a collaborative discussion. Visit www.zengerfolkman. com to watch this taped segment. This was not rehearsed or scripted—it was a real conversation based on real events. We make no claim that this conversation is perfect, only that the conversation models a productive, healthy, collaborative feedback discussion.

As you watch the video, follow the Coaching Conversation Guide to see how the conversation unfolds.

Application

In this application, we would encourage you to think about feedback that you would like to deliver to a colleague. First, run this feedback past the Fast Feedback Guidelines to determine whether or not this qualifies for a coaching conversation.

If the feedback you have to share warrants a coaching conversation, use Table 15-4 to prepare for a redirecting feedback conversation. Prepare how you will open the conversation, what specific examples you might share, and how you will get the feedback recipient's point of view throughout your conversation.

Table 15-4 Your Redirecting Feedback Conversation

Name of individual	What you have observed/impact of behaviors and actions

Fast Feedback Test

1. Will the information be useful to the recipient?   Yes ❑   No ❑

2. Do you have a trust-based relationship in place that will support the conversation?   Yes ❑   No ❑

3. Is the behavior change critical for the individual's success?   Yes ❑   No ❑

4. Will the feedback be new or surprising to hear? Will the data fall into a blind spot for the individual and perhaps be shocking to him?   Yes ❑   No ❑

5. Will the behavior change take significant time, effort, or support?   Yes ❑   No ❑

6. Are you personally invested in the behavior change?   Yes ❑   No ❑

What will you do next?

❑ Fast feedback conversation	❑ Coaching conversation	❑ Nothing
("Yes" on 1 and 2)	*("Yes" on 3, 5, and 6)*	*("No" on 2)*

Step 1: Frame the Conversation
(Set the context and focus for the conversation.)

Identify the behavior or issue to discuss.	*How will you begin the conversation?*

(Continued)

Determine the purpose or outcomes of   *What's in it for your colleague*
the conversation.   *to listen and discuss this par-*
                                          ticular topic? How can you
                                          show some "heart" early in the
                                          conversation?

Agree on the process for the   *What structure for the conversa-*
conversation.   *tion will you propose?*

Step 2: Understand the Current State
(Explore the individual's point of view before sharing your own.)

Understand the coachee's point of   *What questions can you ask that*
view.   *will help you better understand*
                                          the coachee's point of view?

Determine the consequences of   *What have you observed,*
continuing on the current path.   *specifically? What is the impact*
                                          of the coachee's behaviors and
                                          actions? What is the coachee's
                                          point of view regarding that
                                          impact? What questions will you
                                          ask to ensure that the coachee is
                                          actively engaged in this part of
                                          the dialogue?

Offer your perspective, *if appropriate.*

Step 3: Explore the Desired State
(Identify the target and generate multiple paths to achieve the end state.)

Understand the vision for success.	*What questions can you ask to elicit this from the coachee's point of view?*
	What is your vision of success?
Set goals and performance expectations.	*What performance standards are nonnegotiable?*
Explore alternative paths of action.	*Remember to ask for multiple alternatives before sharing your own ideas. What ideas do you have for solutions?*
Explore possible barriers or resistance.	

Step 4: Lay Out a Success Plan
(Create the detailed, actionable plan and follow-through that will lead to goal attainment.)

Develop and agree on an action plan and timelines.	
Enlist support from others.	*What are you willing to offer, in terms of support?*
Set milestones for follow-up and accountability.	

Chapter Summary

- Coach with both backbone and heart. The tougher your message, the more heart you need in the conversation.
- If the message will be tough for you to deliver and for the coachee to hear, be open and transparent about this.
- Stay on the bottom rung of the ladder; keep your feedback focused on objective reality.
- Drip irrigation works best; do not pummel your colleagues with data.
- Ask before you tell; make sure that your employee is doing most of the talking and sharing her point of view regarding what you are describing or noticing.
- Follow the Coaching Conversation Guide when feedback is more than information and when you have a vested interest in helping your colleagues change.

Chapter 16

Signaling the Lane Change

Managing Expectations

By now, we hope that you have picked up several useful ideas for changing the way you currently coach your employees. If you are like most leaders we work with, you

- Realize that you tend to give more advice than you should
- Recognize the value of Framing the Conversation—setting the stage and being clear on the expected outcomes
- See the value of asking more nonleading questions
- See the wisdom of creating at least three alternatives before narrowing down the path of action

In any case, you plan to change your way of approaching coaching conversations.

When we work with leaders after they have learned all of these skills and frameworks, we often hear statements like these:

- "If I actually coach like this, my employees will wonder what has happened to me."
- "Some of my direct reports will think an alien has abducted me if I start coaching like this."

- "I see the value in all of this, but my employees will just think that I've read some book on coaching and I'm trying out some new techniques on them. It won't seem genuine."

If any of these thoughts or similar ones are on your mind, just know that you are in good company.

TELL THEM YOU ARE CHANGING!

There is great value in letting your colleagues know the changes you intend to make. One of our peers uses the expression "signaling the lane change" to help people understand that a change is coming and that the change is completely intentional. If you are driving down a busy highway, you are counting on your fellow drivers to behave in particular ways. You count on their signaling changes that they are making, so that you can make adjustments accordingly. If cars suddenly veer into your lane without signaling, well . . . we all know the consequences there. At a minimum, when a car swerves into your lane, you are likely to be a bit miffed. In the worst-case scenario, it disrupts traffic and can lead to accidents.

When you think about changing your coaching conversations, one approach might be to just make the changes and hope that everyone else notices. This is the approach that many leaders think makes sense: changing lanes without signaling. They want to make the changes to their coaching skills and trust that their employees will see the improvements over a sustained period of time. However, we can accurately predict several likely responses to this approach:

1. People will not see the complete change the leader is making.
2. If they notice the change, they will ascribe some meaning to why the leader is changing—which may not reflect the true reason for the change.
3. The leader will not receive positive feedback that the direct reports are noticing her efforts—which in turn ensures that the leader is less likely to continue the behavior change.
4. Direct reports may not believe that the change will last and/or they will be suspicious of the leader's motives or intentions.

Sad, but True: The Case of Andy

One of our clients is a perfect case in point. Andy was a senior leader overseeing a small but highly profitable division of an insurance company. We were providing 360-degree feedback to all of the senior leaders of this organization for the purpose of helping them improve their overall effectiveness. We were all a little surprised when Andy received his feedback: the scores on his leadership competencies were very low, and Andy's direct reports clearly thought that many aspects of his leadership needed a major overhaul.

Andy was a classic autocratic leader. It truly was "his way or the highway," and people were crystal clear on which path pointed in which direction. Andy also belittled people. He took satisfaction in catching people doing something wrong and immediately rubbing their nose in it. No one could recall him rewarding anyone when he did the right things.

I (Kathleen) was subsequently asked to engage in a six-month coaching relationship with Andy, for the purpose of helping him become a better leader. The company wanted to invest in Andy, as it knew that his business contribution and bottom-line results were worth keeping him around. After getting Andy's agreement to engage in a coaching relationship, our first task was to identify the few development areas that would make the biggest difference in his overall effectiveness. We identified three significant changes to implement:

1. *Stop being so autocratic.* Andy needed to do more to empower his leaders to make decisions and provide more coaching and mentoring instead of dictating the path forward.
2. *Begin building more personal relationships with the members of his team.* Andy almost never discussed issues that did not pertain to work, and as a result, the members of his team found him to be cold and distant.
3. *Improve communication regarding decisions.* Coming from a military background, Andy had adopted the principle of sharing information on a "need to know" basis. As a result, most team members never had the full picture of what was happening in their division, let alone why certain decisions were being made.

After building a plan of action, I strongly encouraged Andy to let his entire team know what he was working on and how he would be changing his behavior. Specifically, I wanted Andy to share the three key development areas that he would be focusing on, so that his team members would understand and be able to support his change. Andy resisted, insisting that his people would see the change without any announcements. After we discussed the benefits of signaling the lane change, he agreed that it made sense to discuss his plans with his direct reports. We scheduled our next coaching conversation and parted ways.

Of course, a good coach keeps coachees accountable for their commitments. So, I naturally asked Andy at the next meeting if he had communicated his plans to his team members. He said, "No, but . . ." and provided me with a halfhearted reason why he had not taken this step. We reviewed the benefits of taking this step, and he agreed to let folks know what he was up to. Again.

During each conversation, I would ask Andy whether he had shared his plans with those around him, and each month Andy provided a new reason for not having found the time. This little dance continued for the first four months of our coaching relationship. In the fifth month, I reminded Andy that we were going to interview all of his direct reports and ask for their feedback regarding his progress. Earlier in the process, we had agreed that we would do a six-month check-in and find out from his direct reports if he had improved in the areas that he was committed to. We worked together to articulate the questions that Andy would ask his direct reports so that we could assess his progress, cycling back to the three big buckets of improvements on which we had focused our five months of coaching.

One by one, I scheduled time with Andy's direct reports, letting them know that, as Andy's coach, we had been trying to improve in three areas. Then I asked whether they had seen improvement in Andy's behaviors. To his credit, some people *had* seen changes in Andy's behavior. However, none of the individuals knew that he was working with a coach or even that he was trying to improve his leadership skills. They did not know that Andy had taken the 360-degree feedback seriously or that he was trying to make a shift. Instead, here is what they said:

- "He's been a bit more relaxed and distant—he wasn't hounding me so much on my work. I thought he was probably out looking for another job. Is he staying with the company?"
- "He's been giving me more freedom to manage my projects, but I think he is just setting me up for a fall. I've come to him with issues and asked him what his point of view was, and he said, 'You're leading this area; I trust you to make good decisions.' I'm sure he is just letting me take the rope—get far enough out, and then just hang myself."
- "He's been acting strange. He has been talking about his personal life more and asking me about mine. I wondered if he had cancer." (Yes! One person was pretty sure that Andy was *dying* of cancer, because this was be the only reasonable explanation she could think of for why he was acting differently!)

After the interviews, I shared the good and bad news with Andy. The good news: everyone saw a change in his behavior. The bad news: no one thought that Andy had changed as a result of good intentions or positive goals. His key learning from this: when you start making changes, you have to let people know what you are doing and that it is completely premeditated and intentional. Equally as important, people need to understand why you are doing this, lest they assume totally incorrect motives or reasons for the behavior change.

> *When you start making changes, you have to let people know what you are doing.*

If Andy had in fact shared his intentions for his development with his team members, they would probably have had a very different experience with and reaction to Andy. Instead of thinking that he was quitting the company, setting people up to fail, or dying of cancer, they would probably have had an extremely positive reaction to the changes. We would predict that Andy's subordinates would have:

- Appreciated that Andy was taking the 360-degree feedback process seriously

- Felt relieved to know that Andy was going to change the way he was leading
- Noticed and understood the changes in behavior that they were seeing
- Acknowledged the positive changes and provided Andy with reinforcing feedback
- Felt emboldened to let Andy know whenever he fell down on his commitments

PEOPLE SEE WHAT THEY ARE LOOKING FOR

Marshall Goldsmith, a well-known executive coach and author, has conducted compelling research that shows the value of leaders informing those around them of what they are working on and asking for ongoing feedback. One of Goldsmith's studies focused on leaders who participated in a 360-degree feedback process and how colleagues around those leaders perceived the change in them over time.

The expectations placed upon the leaders who embarked on this development process were that they would do the following:

- Review their 360-degree feedback with an internal or external consultant.
- Identify one to three areas for improvement.
- Discuss their areas for improvement with key coworkers.
- Ask colleagues for suggestions on how to increase their effectiveness in selected areas for change.
- Follow up with coworkers to get ideas for improvement.
- Have coworker respondents complete a confidential custom-designed "mini-survey" 3 to 15 months after the start of their programs.

Goldsmith found that if leaders did not follow up with their colleagues after receiving the 360-degree feedback, almost half of the colleagues saw no improvement (or even perceived a decline in performance). Using a scale of -3 (indicating a significant decline in behavior) to $+3$ (indicating a significant improvement), Figure 16-1 depicts the percentage of colleagues indicating the degree of change that they observed in the leader.

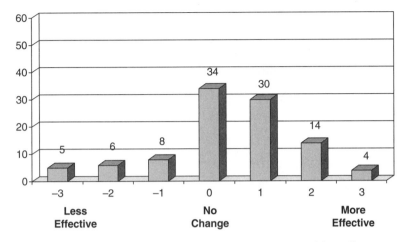

Figure 16-1 What Happens When There Is No Observable Follow-Up?

As you can see, a full third of the leader's colleagues saw no change. Why? Perhaps the leader did not change as a result of the feedback. Or perhaps the leader did change her behavior, but no one saw the change because no one was looking for anything different.

However, when leaders informed their colleagues of their development priorities and plans, and then engaged in consistent follow-up (checking in with others to see if the others saw a behavior change and inviting ongoing feedback), the vast majority of the leaders' colleagues saw a great deal of improvement (see Figure 16-2).

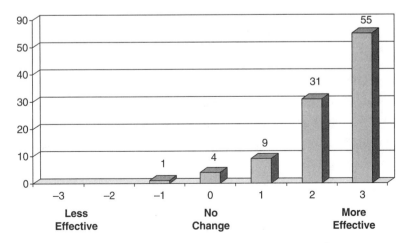

Figure 16-2 What Happens When There Is Consistent Follow-Up?

So, what is going on here? We believe that when leaders tell people what they are working on, two important things happen.

1. The leader is "signaling a lane change" and letting those around him know that he will be changing his behavior. When others experience a different approach from that leader, they will not think it strange and will be able to better assimilate the leader's new behaviors into their expectations and framework.

2. Letting others know that you will be changing your behaviors opens the door for them to give you feedback on the skill changes you are striving for. If you invite and welcome feedback on your new behaviors, you are far more likely to accelerate your own development process and skill enhancement. Leaders who genuinely welcome feedback on their changed behaviors will create a cycle of reinforcement and learning for themselves.

> *If you invite and welcome feedback on your new behaviors, you are far more likely to accelerate your own development process.*

Indeed, simply having ongoing contact between the leader and her team members is so powerful that Goldsmith and Howard Morgan report that some organizations have seen great success merely through doing that, without any full-scale leadership development effort. This was the driving force for the title they gave to the article reporting their research: "Leadership Is a Contact Sport."

SIGNALING A LANE CHANGE

So once you know that you are going to be signaling a lane change, where do you start? A helpful place to begin is by making a quick inventory of the aspects of your coaching style and approach that you plan on changing.

From/To

If you recall the systems model that we presented in Chapter 2, you will remember that systems tend to be self-reinforcing. You have a pattern of behavior that you have established, and your employees and colleagues have their response to that pattern. Successfully changing your pattern of behavior will require the entire system to change with you. If you stop giving advice and start asking more questions, the people you are coaching will need to stop waiting to take direction and participate more fully in creating the solution. This underscores the need to help them understand that your side of the system is going to be changing!

Table 16-1 lists some of the aspects of coaching that you might be shifting "from" and "to." As you read the list, identify any shifts that you intend to make personally. Then we will explore how to have this conversation to signal the lane change.

Table 16-1 A Shift in Coaching Approach

From	*To*
• Having no structured process for the conversation	• Having a process for the conversation (FUEL)
• Jumping into problem solving	• Framing the conversation first
• Giving advice	• Asking the coachee for his thoughts first
• Asking leading questions	• Asking nonleading questions
• Listening for information to support your point of view	• Listening to truly understand the coachee's point of view and story
• Talking more as you are solving people's problems	• Getting the coachee to talk more as she solves her own problems
• Expecting that people are ready for action	• Identifying someone's stage of change
• Listening for and responding to only facts and information	• Listening for the emotions underneath what is being discussed
• Going with the first solution that comes to mind	• Identifying at least three different alternatives before action planning
• Trusting that change will happen	• Following up and holding people accountable
• Focusing on project or task status updates	• Focusing on development and growth
• Talking about development and career opportunities once a year	• Targeting regular discussions focused on career development

Messages to Share

Once you have identified the ways in which you will be shifting, consider how you will let those around you know. Most leaders find it easy to share this information in one-on-one meetings with employees or at regularly scheduled staff meetings. We would encourage you to Frame the Conversation that you want to have by targeting the key messages that you want to be sending.

Here are some possible messages that you might want to share with your team members. Check any of these that might be relevant to your planned change, or articulate your own unique phrases.

❑ You want to shift from spending the majority of the time in one-on-one meetings focusing on status or project updates to having a significant portion of the time devoted to what is on the employee's mind.

❑ Your concern goes beyond immediate performance to the coachee's career and personal growth.

❑ Your desire is to discuss topics that are of interest to the coachee. You will sometimes introduce topics, but you will also want the coachee to identify subjects of interest for exploration.

❑ You want to learn and grow yourself, and you view these coaching discussions as "two-way," not "one-way."

❑ The coachee is often closer to the issue and therefore will be in a better position to determine the best solution or resolution. Instead of quickly offering your point of view and advice, you will ask more questions to help the coachee determine the best solution.

❑ At the end of each coaching conversation, you will ask for some feedback about how the discussion was from the coachee's perspective. The purpose of this is to help you improve and to ensure that sessions stay focused on issues that are important and of interest to the coachee.

❑ You would like to improve your ability to coach effectively by specifically targeting a coaching skill (name the skill that you want to improve). At the end of a coaching conversation, you would also like feedback on how you are progressing with your own skill development.

What else would you add? Take a moment to write in the space given here any additional messages that you might want to communicate with your team.

Example: Sharing the Message

Here is an example of how this might sound. One of our clients shared this message with his team of direct reports at a monthly staff meeting.

> As you all know, we've just completed our development planning for the year—everyone had to articulate business goals and development goals to target. I wanted to share one of my new goals with all of you, because you are all going to be affected by this—hopefully, in a positive way.
>
> I have a tremendous amount of respect for each of you, and I believe that you are a truly talented team of contributors. I also think that my style of coaching and leading has probably

gotten in your way from time to time. Because I move quickly, I know that I am quick to offer advice and solutions when you talk to me about challenges that you are struggling with on your various projects. While that might be helpful—and I want to emphasize the word *might*—I can see that providing you with my thoughts does not necessarily help promote your thinking about these issues.

At the end of the day, I want to be a people grower—and I want you to be stretched in your own learning and contributions to the business. So, I am going to make a concerted effort to ask you for your opinion more often—and *before* I offer mine. You are much closer to the issues, you've thought about them, and 9 times out of 10 you will be in a better position than I will to figure out the best answer to any given problem. I'll still be here to help work through the issues, but I'd like to be more of a thinking partner than a fixer.

So, that is what I will be working on: asking more questions and providing less direction. I promise I won't leave you hanging, but I'll be asking you for the alternatives that you think will work best. Together we can weigh the pros and cons, and we'll probably come up with better solutions.

And I'll also need your help to change what comes very naturally for me—to be that problem solver and advice giver. So, from time to time, I'll ask you for feedback. I'd genuinely like to know if I am getting better (and not reverting back to giving direction automatically) and if you feel that I am tapping into your good thinking to solve the challenges at hand.

This leader chose to share a specific area of change—from not giving as much advice to asking the coachee for his own solution. Other leaders have shared the entire conversation process and model with their team, saying, "Here's what you can expect!" Some leaders have had one-on-one discussions, tailoring the message to each individual employee, while others have shared their change messages with their entire team. There is no one right way to do this, but the important step is that you do it.

Remembering back to the systems model, whenever one half changes, it automatically creates a ripple effect on the other half. If you begin changing without letting folks know that you are doing so, they are likely to wonder what is happening and work extra hard to keep you in your own "lane," or pattern. So, signal the lane change; your fellow commuters will appreciate the advance notice!

> *Whenever one half changes, it automatically creates a ripple effect on the other half.*

Chapter Summary

- When you change your approach to coaching, you may feel some anxiety or tension regarding how your employees might react. This is natural and to be expected.
- By signaling the "lane change" you are trying to make in your coaching skills, you will let others know what to expect.
- If you do not signal the lane change, others either will not notice the behavior change or will attribute it to other (not necessarily helpful) motives.
- By letting others know what you are working on, you will be more likely to invite their support and ongoing feedback.
- People see what they are looking for, so help them know where to look and what to look for.

Chapter 17

"Send in the Coach"

Finding More Coaching Opportunities

W e are all familiar with the scenario of the player on the bench who is constantly looking at the coach and often blurting out, "Send me in, coach." If we reverse that idea and apply it to organizational life, we might ask, "When do you send in the coach?" How much playing time should the coach have?

INCREASING THE AMOUNT OF COACHING

While we are clearly sold on the value of coaching, let's begin by stating the obvious: not every conversation is, nor should it be, a coaching conversation. There are important discussions that occur during a day at work that have extremely different purposes.

Not every conversation is, nor should it be, a coaching conversation.

Some are designed to

- Seek or deliver information
- Solve a technical problem
- Obtain an approval
- Coordinate activities
- Build relationships

The list goes on and on. Simply put, lots of conversations have little to do with coaching, and we believe that this is quite appropriate.

Let's not lose sight of some important facts, however. We have presented data that show that coaching has a high payoff for the organization. Furthermore, whenever employees are asked if they are receiving as much coaching as they desire, the answer is amazingly consistent: "no." People want more coaching than they are receiving. Think of your personal situation. Are *you* receiving as much coaching as you would like or could benefit from?

So how do we achieve an increase in coaching? Two practical approaches provide the obvious solution:

1. Schedule more frequent sessions that are specifically identified as coaching times.
2. Transform casual and informal dialogue into coaching opportunities.

Scheduling More Frequent Formal Coaching Sessions

An interesting phenomenon occurs when surveys on performance appraisal practices are conducted: the percentage of managers who indicate that they've conducted a performance appraisal is significantly higher than the percentage of subordinates who report that they have received a performance appraisal. What could explain the difference? One possibility is that the managers are stretching the truth a bit and are worried about looking bad in the eyes of their senior leaders. The other explanation is that, in the boss's mind, the conversation that occurred over lunch at the boss's favorite restaurant was a performance review, and, in the subordinate's perception, it was a discussion about how things were going on the job. To prevent this misalignment from happening, many organizations insist that the employee sign an official performance appraisal document.

If this problem of widely differing perceptions of the same event is true for performance appraisal, think how much more true it is for coaching discussions. Therefore, it is valuable to make some coaching discussions more formal. Having a scheduled time labeled "coaching sessions" on a calendar gives more definition and focus to these discussions. We have suggested some techniques that ask the coach to seek out topics that the coachee would like to discuss, and some other techniques for collecting feedback. Using such devices magnifies the seriousness of the entire process and elevates it to a new level of professionalism. It also lets the employee know that coaching is happening.

Transforming Casual and Informal Dialogue into Coaching Opportunities

Imagine two very different scenarios that start out in exactly the same way:

> *Scenario 1.* Your direct report, Bill, pokes his head into your office and says, "We need to get a technical manual prepared for the new Tridex product. Who do you think we should put on that task, or should we subcontract it outside?"
>
> It happens that you have an enormous amount of experience in overseeing the creation of technical manuals. You know the good technical writers inside the organization, and you also have lots of contacts on the outside with excellent technical writing firms. It is extremely easy (and tempting) for you to reply:
>
> "I think we should go outside. The best outside group for this project is Grenny and Lombard. Do you have their number?"

What is nice about this reply is that it is quick. Bill will get what he apparently wants, but it may not be what he really needs. There are times when such a dialogue may be exactly the right outcome.

As we explored earlier, when risks are high and time is of the essence, giving advice may be the best solution.

But let us examine the outcomes of this. We suggest that Bill will have learned very little, certainly far less than he could have learned. The situation also reinforces the idea that you, the boss, are there to give answers and solve problems that really belong to him. And aside from the opportunity that Bill is missing, if the manual is not finished on time, he has *you* to blame because the chosen firm was your recommendation.

There are numerous unintended consequences of this kind of dialogue. They happen with enormous frequency in every organization we know.

> *Scenario 2.* Your direct report, Bill, pokes his head into your office and says, "We need to get a technical manual prepared for the new Tridex product. Who do you think we should put on that task, or should we subcontract it outside?" You reply, "Come in for a minute and let's talk about that." Taking the time to talk allows the conversation to evolve into a useful coaching dialogue.
>
> You ask, "So what are *your* thoughts about this project? What have *you* been thinking?" This question shows respect for Bill's ideas and gives you insight into his thoughts on this subject.
>
> You continue, "What do you see as the pros and cons of staying inside versus going outside? What process are you using to go about making this decision?"

After hearing Bill's point of view and being assured that Bill has considered both options with reasonably clear thinking, you could ask, "What criteria are you using to make your final selection?" If Bill admits that he has not thought about using any specific criteria to make the selection, you might decide that there are some things you have learned that could be useful to Bill.

> "Bill, would it help you if I explained how I go about making these kinds of decisions?" Assuming that Bill says "yes,"

you continue to explain. "When I was in your role, I tried to determine the two or three most important issues about each project. Sometimes it was completion on time. In other cases it was cost. I can think of some cases where our potential liability on a product was so high that the big issue was having absolute accuracy in the manual. I can also recall some cases where the issue was minimizing the time required for our engineers to provide information to the technical writers. I'd write the three major decision criteria up on the board in order of importance. I also did a couple of other things. I had an informal chat with the one or two internal people who I thought could handle the project, just to feel out their current schedules and also to get some idea about their level of interest. I was careful not to offer them anything in a formal way, but to explain that I was just getting the lay of the land.

"Anyway, for what it's worth, those were some things I learned to do. I stirred all those facts together and then made a decision. You should know that I did make some bad decisions, but hopefully over time I made a few more good ones than bad.

"So, I'll be looking forward to what you decide in this case. I'm confident that you will make a decision that has been well thought through. You know, that's all that we can ask in making tough calls like this—that there's some good rationale for your having decided to go in any particular direction."

In this second scenario, it is clear that the boss was using this situation as an opportunity to get Bill's thinking. The boss asked questions that were designed to expand Bill's analysis of the issues. The boss then shared the process that he used in making such decisions and carefully passed it back to Bill to make the final call. If it had become clear in the early part of the discussion that Bill had already thought about the criteria for this project and that he had some good insights into the availability of internal people and their level of interest in such a project, then the leader would obviously not have initiated that part of the dialogue.

"What do you think we should do?"

It should be apparent that there are dozens of opportunities every day for a leader to use a question or a request from an employee to initiate a meaningful coaching dialogue. Very often, all it takes is the simple, "What do you think we should do?"

The big challenge for most of us boils down to a couple of fairly simple questions: Do I enjoy answering questions and making decisions more than I enjoy developing people? Or do I have a deeply ingrained belief that giving answers and making decisions is what managers are supposed to do? And if I naturally gravitate toward being the expert, and I love solving problems and making decisions, has the time come for me to reflect and ask myself whether I am really doing the best thing for my employees by doing what I personally prefer to do rather than what, perhaps, I should be doing?

THE COACHING MINDSET

We propose one mindset that we think would help leaders everywhere to do more and better coaching:

What could I say or do in this situation that would help this person succeed and grow?

My job is basically one of developing people, not solving problems. What could I say or do in this situation that would help this person succeed and grow in the long run?

Think of how that mindset would play out in the everyday conversations you have with all of your colleagues—not only your subordinates but your peers as well. If we constantly keep asking ourselves how we can help others succeed, it will make an enormous difference in the quantity and quality of the coaching that we provide.

It means offering suggestions if we see someone doing something that we know will get him in trouble. It means offering a newcomer some tips about how best to adapt to your organization's unwritten rules and culture. It means speaking up if you see someone about to make a serious mistake. Finally, it means wanting to help others be perceived in the most positive light by their peers, superiors, and employees. If you see a way to make that happen, it is a great coaching opportunity.

As we have noted earlier in this book, the people that we interview in organizations indicate that more than 80 percent of all meetings with managers are basically project reviews. Seldom is there any discussion of "What did you learn?" or "How could we do this better next time?"

Career Discussions

The other conversational piece that many employees claim to be wanting more of is the leader overtly discussing the career issues facing a direct report. Questions like

- "How do you feel about the progress you are making in your career?"
- "Have your thoughts changed at all about where you would like to go or what you would like to ultimately be doing?"
- "What could I do to help you better meet your career goals?"

Such discussions obviously don't occur every week. But they also should not occur only every few years—or never. By periodically expanding the conversation beyond a typical project status review or report on operational problems, the boss sends an important, two-pronged message. First, it says, "My boss cares about me as a person. I am valued for more than just getting the job done. My boss is interested in my career ambitions and desires." Second, it says, "My boss cares about my future. It is a great feeling to know that someone is looking out for me and my future." We know of no specific research that links such conversations to employee retention statistics, but we strongly believe that such conversations have a strong impact on an employee's long-term commitment to staying with an organization.

Such conversations need not be lengthy, and the payoffs from the leader's expression of interest in the career progress of the person being coached are nearly impossible to calculate.

TWO POTENTIAL MISTAKES THAT COACHES CAN MAKE

One mistake that coaches can make is giving way too much coaching and spending far more time doing so than is really warranted. The second mistake is at the opposite end of that scale: giving far too little coaching and leaving your people desiring far more. So which error do you think most leaders commit? Imagine asking a large group of employees, "Please raise your hand if you think you are getting more feedback and coaching from your boss than you would like and is helpful to you." We doubt that one person in a thousand would say, "She takes far more time coaching than we'd like. She should cut back and focus more time on the project plans and the financial side of things."

On the other hand, we have heard innumerable people lament the lack of coaching that they receive. As leaders, we need to be more engaged in coaching than we normally are. Most leaders say too little, wait too long, and hold back when they should have stepped in.

Most leaders say too little, wait too long, and hold back when they should have stepped in.

If you are canceling your coaching conversations with your team members on a regular basis, you are sending your team members a message regarding the importance of these conversations—and of their time and development. Unfortunately, we hear frequent reports of leaders canceling their periodic one-on-one meetings with their employees. Direct reports tend to draw negative conclusions about their leaders when these sessions are canceled with great regularity.

One manager in an organization we work with was so unreliable that the entire work team snickered and laughed about his inconsistency. Team members would say things like, "Well, you know . . . he must have had another emergency." The direct reports would chortle and roll their eyes, then someone might remark: "If it's important to him, he'll be there. I guess this isn't important."

While employees snickered about this publicly, the underlying message clearly was that the employees felt devalued and ignored.

Let us contrast that example with the best leaders we have worked with. Unless there was an emergency that could not be avoided, these leaders would not cancel coaching appointments. In fact, one exceptional leader we worked with at Microsoft sought out coaching conversations whenever *he* was having a bad day. He knew that by coaching an employee, he would be able to reset his own priorities and focus. He would also feel better about his day by being able to support a colleague in solving his or her struggles and challenges.

Reflection

Complete the following self-reflection questions to determine where you may have additional opportunities to coach your team members and peers.

1. How frequently (on average) do you currently coach each of your direct reports?
2. Of the time you spend in those coaching conversations, what percentage of your time is allocated to each of the following focus areas?
   ____% Project or task updates
   ____% Resolving task or people conflicts
   ____% Increasing performance and skills
   ____% Career growth/development for the future
   ____% Other: _____
3. What percentage of the time do you cancel these one-on-one meetings with your team members? How often has this been your pattern?

(Continued)

❑ Less than 5 percent: almost never; only emergencies get in the way.

❑ 5 to 15 percent: infrequently, but it does happen.

❑ 16 to 30 percent: more often than I'd like to admit, but I always have good reasons.

❑ 31 to 50 percent: the odds are close to even regarding whether or not I will keep this commitment.

❑ More than 50 percent: I'm completely unpredictable, sometimes even to myself.

4. How frequently do you engage in career-focused conversations with your employees?

5. How frequently do you provide your peers with feedback regarding their effectiveness and performance?

6. Which conversations are you not having now that would make the biggest difference to the organization?

Chapter Summary

- Not every conversation is, or should be, a coaching conversation.

- The evidence is in: people want more coaching than they receive.

- Scheduling more frequent sessions that are specifically identified as coaching sessions can increase the focus and awareness of the coaching that is occurring.

- Look to transform informal and casual interactions into coaching opportunities. A simple way to do so is by asking, "What do you think we should do?"

- The coaching mindset will help you coach more frequently and better. If you believe that your job is one of developing people, not solving problems, you will lean more toward coaching more often.

- Spend the time to make some conversations that are explicitly focused on career discussions; the payback will be enormous.

- While you may err on the side of providing too much coaching, most leaders err on the other end of the continuum—providing too little too late.

Chapter 18

Growing Your Skills as a Coach

The experienced race car driver is thoroughly attuned to the unique capabilities of the car he is driving. He knows how the car takes corners and how it responds to a tap on the brake or pushing the accelerator to the floorboard. Experience has taught him how fast he can take corners before the car fishtails or spins out of control. The car is the vehicle of the driver's success or failure in both meanings of that word.

The instrument that coaches use to succeed is themselves, including their worldview, their attitude toward people, their view of what motivates people at work, their models of human behavior, their own idiosyncrasies, and their overall *persona*.

THE NEED FOR SELF-AWARENESS

We are not advocating that coaches spend years in psychotherapy or that they spend long periods in self-contemplation and meditation. While there may be some personal benefits from such practices, they are not necessary in order to be a good coach. However, having some grasp of your own beliefs, biases, agendas, and mental models will be of enormous help.

Here are a couple of examples:

- One senior executive had strong feelings about people who were overweight. He saw it as a mark of weakness and irresponsibility. Yes, he had read the evidence indicating that there could well be a strong hereditary element to obesity, and a powerful impact of body chemistry on one's metabolism. Despite that, he continued to look down on people who were overweight. He acknowledged that it would be hard for him to be an effective coach to a seriously overweight subordinate.

- Another executive believed deeply in the idea of "servant leadership." This concept that the leader's role was to serve others was the driving force behind most of her views of good leadership and the appropriate behavior of people in the organization. She was highly intolerant of those who held the view that people should and did act out of self-interest. She disagreed with those who presented projects to their team with a "WIIFM" (What's In It For Me) approach. For her to be a good coach to a person with that approach to life would be extremely challenging and would clearly require a certain level of self-awareness regarding the way her own beliefs would color many of their conversations.

Our counsel is rather simple: be aware of any strong biases that you have. Take note of those areas where it becomes obvious that your views diverge from those of others. Be aware of powerful beliefs that strongly set you apart from many others in your organization. As Peter Senge stated, "The structures of which we are unaware hold us prisoner."

The structures of which we are unaware hold us prisoner.

Most managers we know lead extremely busy lives. They are caught up in a swirl of activity, much of it not of their making. The Russian spiritual leader and physician Anthony Bloom presents an interesting way to view our lives. He cites the passage in Dickens's *Pickwick Papers* that describes how Pickwick hires a carriage to take him to his club. On the way, Pickwick asks the driver a string of questions. One of them is, "Tell me, how is it possible that such a mean and miserable horse can drive such a big and heavy carriage?" The driver answers, "It is not a question of the horse, Sir, it's a question of the wheels." Mr. Pickwick replies, "What do you mean?" The driver answers, "You see, we have a magnificent pair of wheels which are so well oiled that it is enough for the horse to stir a little for the wheels to begin to turn and then the poor horse must run for its life."

In today's organizational life, managers are often running to keep ahead of the forces that are constantly pounding upon them. So much energy is expended in this quest to keep ahead of so many other forces that many of the high-value activities are pushed aside.

BEING FULLY PRESENT

One area of growth for many coaches is the practice of being fully present with the person who is being coached.

> A long-time colleague, Larry Senn, tells the story of flying a kite on the beach in Hawaii with his six-year-old son. Larry had lots on his mind, but he knew that he should spend time with the boy during this family vacation. Finally, after he had been in this distracted state of mind for some period of time, the boy walked over to Larry, pulled on his jacket, looked up at him, and said, "Would you *really* play with me for a while?"

Chances are that every parent can identify with the boy's plea. It is easy to be with someone physically but not have any genuine mental or emotional connection with him. What's really unnerving about that fact is how quickly and accurately the other person senses it.

In a similar way, the person being coached senses acutely whether or not you are really paying attention. She can sense that you are thinking of other things and not putting your full focus on this discussion.

The best coaches have learned to put away all the things on their desk that would distract them. They have learned to take a deep breath and use their "psychological eraser" to clean the whiteboard in their mind so that nothing will distract them from this important conversation. To be fully attuned to the ideas and the emotions coming from the other person requires such focus.

THE CHALLENGE OF IMPROVING THE COACHING PROCESS

Once you have the self-awareness to recognize where your coaching may need some improvement, it is up to you to take it to the next level. Here is an example of how a different kind of coach approaches his craft.

A friend decided to learn to play the banjo. He is not exactly a spring chicken, given that he is 62 years of age. He hired a teacher, from whom he takes a lesson once a week. He performs, and the teacher gives him some tips on how to play each song or instrumental piece more effectively. He records himself playing and then listens to the recordings. It is reasonably easy for him to pick out things that need improving. He also belongs to a group whose members are also learning the banjo, the mandolin, or a similar instrument. They coach one another and learn new methods and techniques from watching and listening to one another. The point is that when learning some skills, there are lots of obvious approaches for acquiring those skills and then for constantly advancing.

Coaching, on the other hand, normally takes place behind closed doors. In most cases, only two people are present. There is often an element of confidentiality built into the activity, so it is uncommon to audiotape or videotape the conversation. Because many people view the process as simply one more chat with another person, it is easy to assume that any half-decent manager should already possess that skill. The unique qualities of coaching discussions are not readily apparent.

All these elements combine to make it difficult to utilize the more usual methods for improving a skill in dealing with the coaching process. This may explain in large part why managers often get stuck in a rut in terms of showing any improvement in their coaching skills. Combine that with the fact that coaching is a highly discretionary, voluntary act on the part of the manager, and it becomes clear why formalizing the process and working to improve the leader's skill in coaching are so important.

Use Assessment Tools

Despite all the admonitions to "know thyself," the simple truth is that most of us do not. Indeed, the evidence is clear. While some people say and believe that they know both their strengths and their weaknesses, the harsh reality is that people who actually do so are extremely rare. In

Despite all the admonitions to "know thyself," the simple truth is that most of us do not.

our extensive work with the 360-degree feedback process, we are able to look at the relationship between someone's total score, her self-score, her manager's evaluation of her, her peers' scores, and the scores of those who report directly to her. So which of these correlates most accurately with the total, and which is least accurate?

You guessed it: the lowest correlation for virtually every data set we have examined is the self-score versus the total score. It is not unusual to see reports in which individuals have scored themselves a "5" on a 5-point scale on virtually everything, and everyone else has scored them a "1" or a "2." Even more frequently, we see the converse situation, in which self-scores are quite low and everyone else's scores are significantly higher.

We strongly advocate the value of obtaining objective feedback regarding your coaching skills. Having accurate, objective feedback is an extremely helpful first step in the creation of a personal plan of development to which you will be highly committed. Zenger Folkman has created a specialized 360-degree feedback instrument that focuses exclusively on coaching skills. It examines 14 competencies of coaching, identified by studying the most highly effective leader-coaches. The instrument is simple to complete and includes 46 items describing coaching behaviors and an 8-item employee commitment index that is completed only by those who are direct reports. If you are interested in obtaining accurate multirater feedback regarding your current coaching skills, contact us at www.zengerfolkman.com and go to the Products and Services link.

Coaching Competencies

Results from the 360-degree assessment are clustered in four categories. The 14 coaching competencies are contained in these four broader categories. Having accurate data on your current behavior in each of these areas allows you to identify those in which you have reasonable strengths and that lend themselves to further development. It also enables you to see any major deficiencies that would curtail your effectiveness going forward. Armed with that information, you are now able to construct a personal plan of development that will enable you to go forward to even greater heights.

Builds a Strong Relationship

1. Personally supports the development of others
2. Generates trust
3. Builds relationships
4. Encourages collaboration

Communicates Effectively

5. Listens actively
6. Asks powerful questions
7. Values diversity
8. Provides feedback
9. Welcomes feedback

Facilitates Action and Results

10. Helps others to set goals and performance expectations
11. Inspires others to change
12. Fosters innovation

Provides Ongoing Support

13. Gives recognition
14. Provides follow-up and accountability

Self-Assessment

If you'd like to assess your own skills as a coach, you can go to the Zenger Folkman Web site and complete a self-assessment. You will see how your self-assessment scores compare to those of others. We would remind you, however, as we noted earlier, that we believe that these self-assessments have limited value relative to that of a true 360-degree assessment. Self-assessments have modest validity because it is difficult, if not impossible, to be objective when it comes to evaluating oneself. Go to Products and Services and then to The Extraordinary Coach section to access the self-assessment.

360-Degree Feedback

For a fee, you can participate in a full-fledged multirater feedback process. In this case, you identify several people with whom you work, including your boss, several peers, and the people who report directly to you. To that we add your self-appraisal. The combination enables you to have a comprehensive analysis of your coaching skills. The process is quite simple. You are given a message to send to all the people whom you select to participate in your personal feedback process. The message tells them that you would like them to provide feedback to you, and that it will be completely anonymous. You will not know exactly which people respond, and there is no way for you to know how each respondent scored you or the written comments that they provide. The entire process takes place online. We strongly recommend such a process for all people who coach others in their organization.

For further details of how to complete this process, go to www.zengerfolkman.com, click on the Contact Us tab and indicate your interest.

Getting Frequent Feedback from Those You Coach

In Chapter 11, we described a brief questionnaire that could be used to collect information from those you coach. We are sufficiently realistic to know that leaders will not use this in every coaching session that they conduct. However, we submit that it would be extremely helpful to use a more formal and objective process periodically to obtain information from those who are being coached. This information is designed to let you know whether the person being coached sees your coaching as relevant and useful. It also lets you know if these coachees are leaving discussions with you with some actionable steps that they believe they can take. We noted earlier that when professionals in other "helping" fields collected this information, it greatly increased their success and more than cut in half the number of people who quit getting help. We are convinced that similar results can be found in business coaching.

Table 18-1 gives the feedback form.

Feedback Form

Please complete this brief evaluation form, so that I can understand what created the most value for you in this conversation. Please rate the following statements on a 1-to-5 scale, with 1 = low and 5 = high.

Table 18-1

	Low				High
1. This conversation focused on the issues that are most important to me.	1	2	3	4	5
Comments:					
2. This conversation was a good use of our time.	1	2	3	4	5
Comments:					
3. The purpose and outcomes of this discussion were clarified early in our conversation.	1	2	3	4	5
Comments:					
4. The general process and flow of this conversation worked well to meet our goals.	1	2	3	4	5
Comments:					
5. I felt that you listened to me and understood my points of view.	1	2	3	4	5
Comments:					
6. I am leaving with some specific action steps to pursue.	1	2	3	4	5
Comments:					

CONDUCTING POSTMORTEMS ON COACHING CONVERSATIONS

Every coaching conversation affords an opportunity for reflection and determining ways in which it could have been better. We begin with the premise that very few conversations are so flawless that they could not possibly have been improved. Therefore, pausing to review what happened is a useful exercise. As believers in the value of a positive approach, we recommend beginning by analyzing what went well and the positive outcomes that you saw coming from the discussion. That logically paves the way for you to ask, "What could have gone even better?" An honest look will usually unearth something that could have been executed even more effectively.

Recording the conversation (with the permission of the person being coached) is an extremely valuable exercise. It affords you the ability to listen one more time to the dialogue that occurred. The huge advantage of this review is that you can devote 100 percent of your attention to listening to what was said, without any pressure to devise the next question or make an appropriate response to what was said. We promise that you will be pleasantly surprised with what you can learn by doing this.

Invariably you will hear messages and feelings that were not so obvious when you were in the thick of it. You will also notice your own effectiveness (or ineffectiveness) in clarifying the purpose of the conversation, asking open-ended questions, and summarizing what you've heard. You can also assess your success at avoiding the pitfalls and traps of giving advice and shifting the conversation to focus on you.

One valuable approach is to begin every coaching session with your own self-improvement goal in mind. For example, in one session, you may focus on improving the clarity of expectations that you and your coachee have for each other. This has often been described as "contracting," and it identifies the expectations that the coachee has regarding you and your role. In another session, *Begin every coaching session with your own self-improvement goal in mind.*

you may elect to emphasize obtaining clearer agreements regarding the next steps and ensuring that the coachee creates a detailed plan for implementation.

Alternatively, you may decide that you want to improve your ability to ask questions that help individuals see their world in a new light. Good questions cause people to see their world more clearly and crisply. This often helps them to make greater progress in their career. Therefore, as you review a given coaching discussion, you can reflect on the quantity and quality of the questions that were asked and whether they had the hoped-for impact on the person who was being coached.

CONCLUSION

It is relatively easy to reach a given skill level and stay there. The recreational skier often gets to the point of skiing the blue intermediate slopes comfortably but never ventures onto a black diamond run. Ski seasons come and go, and the skier stays at exactly the same level. Golfers reach a certain score and stay there—often for years. Getting better requires tenacious determination. It may entail hiring an instructor or joining a class. Deliberate effort is necessary to break out of the rut and to get better. The same holds true for the skill of coaching. Staying at the same skill level is extremely easy. Getting better is the challenge.

Chapter Summary

- Being self-aware is critical for being able to coach others effectively. Know your own biases, agendas, and underlying belief systems and models that define how you think and act.
- Be fully present. Know how to remove distractions—real distractions and psychological distractions—so that you can fully attend to the coachee in the conversation.
- Intentionally focusing on the art of improving one's coaching skills takes discipline. Without such intentions, coaches will often repeat patterns of behavior without displaying real improvement.

- Our self-assessment is often not aligned with the way others view us; therefore, getting others' feedback about our strengths and weaknesses is important in the development process.
- Tools like 360-degree feedback instruments can provide insights into how our behaviors affect others.
- Asking for informal feedback and conducting postmortems are also critical in helping us become more consciously competent about the skills we are using.
- Have a coaching focus for your own coaching conversations: be clear on what skills you want to use and improve.
- Improving requires both intention *and* action.

Chapter 19

Each Individual
Is a Whole Person
(Not Just a Worker)

You have probably heard many stories over the years about Henry Ford, the founder of the famous American car company. One of our personal favorites was the description of Henry Ford's being perplexed by the workers he was hiring and how they did not just neatly show up to work on the assembly line. He thought he was hiring mere employees, but whole people showed up instead.

While we cannot confirm if this story is fact or fiction, we believe that this realization often occurs to coaches and leaders. We imagine that we are leading employees—individuals who are hired to do their jobs and who leave their personal lives at home. However, we must recognize that employees are always bringing all of their humanity into the work environment. Leaders do the same thing, too. We can all work to stay within certain boundaries, but our wholeness never goes away.

ALREADY IN PROCESS

In his book *Coaching: Evoking Excellence in Others*, James Flaherty astutely writes, "Each individual is in a life that is already in process."

The meaning behind this statement is significant. The individuals with whom we interact have a lifetime of experience that has shaped their beliefs and actions. Each individual has dreams, goals, and hopes, as well as unique motivations and interests. Each is enmeshed in a full life that is replete with a multitude of roles and systems. Work is just one role, and completing job tasks is just one activity in which individuals invest themselves. We will go over what some of these other roles are in more detail later in this chapter.

As leaders, we are often walking the same path as our employees and colleagues for just a short period of time before they go on to the next phase of their lives. We were not present to witness everything that occurred before our working relationships began, and we probably will not be there after our working relationships end. Therefore, we must remind ourselves that we cannot know everything about our employees and what the wholeness of their lives looks like, even though our working relationships with them may seem very full and complete for the period of time that we work with them.

DON'T GO THERE! (OR SHOULD WE?)

When coaching, leaders often express concern about hearing too much information related to an individual's private life. They do not want to either explore the emotions that an individual is feeling or delve into any context beyond work itself. We often hear leaders say, "I do not want to learn more about their emotions or personal lives—that feels like therapy." One concern stems from not wanting to intrude on someone else's privacy. Another concern is about getting too close and losing what they believe to be their professional distance.

We absolutely agree that coaching is not counseling, and we do not recommend that a leader help an individual *solve* every problem in her personal life. However, we also know that it is often useful to remember that the individual is a whole person and that her entire life influences who she is and how she performs at work.

Exploring the broader context of a person's life often lends a richness and a better understanding of the "performer" who shows up at work. We expect human "doings" to show up at work, and we must remember that it is usually human "beings" who show up. We think that we hire workers—people who will show

> *Exploring the broader context of a person's life often lends a richness and a better understanding of the "performer."*

up and simply complete their assigned tasks. However, each individual we hire brings an entire history and unique background and life with him. As leaders, if we can balance how to treat the human doing and the human being within the individual, we will all be better served.

Susan's Fiftieth Birthday

I (Kathleen) was recently coaching a senior leader who had a very demanding role at a Fortune 100 organization. Our coaching work began when she was trying to understand how her colleagues viewed her performance; we started a 10-hour series of conversations, with the first two conversations focused on interpreting her 360-degree feedback results. From the beginning, it was clear that my coachee was a star performer and a tremendously effective leader. Within the context of the conversation, we began exploring her goals for the year and how she could leverage her strengths to maximize her work output and team leadership.

By the third conversation, I learned that Susan was on the verge of turning 50 and was in the middle of planning her fiftieth birthday party. This was very useful for me to know. Why? Because many adults tend to enter a relatively significant reflection process whenever they approach a decade-year birthday. The big "50" tends to be a time when even more adults question where they are in their lives—whether or not their lives have purpose—and they may begin to sense that there is less time remaining before them than they have already logged in this world. Therefore, the transition to 50 often ends up being fairly significant.

By noticing Susan's emotions and energy in the coaching conversation, I could sense that she had less interest in focusing on how she was going to achieve her goals for the remainder of the year. Because she was an exceptional leader, she would easily finish what she had set out to accomplish, and she could easily incorporate some of the feedback to leverage her leadership strengths.

By the time we reached the fourth coaching conversation, the range of topics had moved to a deeper level. As she turned 50, Susan felt that she was feeling burned out with work and was questioning whether she really wanted to continue to climb the corporate ladder. She began wondering if she was living a purposeful life, and whether all the hours she invested in work were making a difference in a way that was meaningful to her. Her manager had approached her about taking his role when he retired and had given her his vote of confidence. Instead of feeling elated about the possibility, Susan understandably was wondering whether she wanted to take on the mantle of a larger—and more demanding—leadership role. Rather than seeking out ways to ensure that the next position was hers, Susan was longing instead to cancel her business trips, stay at home, and reconnect with her life outside of work. She was craving time with friends, time with her pets, and time in her home.

In our coaching work, we changed our focus, based on where Susan was in the grander scheme of her life. It made less sense to ensure that Susan was gunning for her annual targets (which it seemed that she would meet anyway) and more sense to help Susan manage her demanding workload while feeling overwhelmed and burned out. We started crafting strategies that would enable her to protect her discretionary time and energy; we began identifying tasks that could be delegated to others and meetings that could be attended by her employees instead of her. The end result? Her employees had an opportunity to grow and be challenged, while Susan was able to manage her job within the context of her whole life. Her introspective, "burned-out" phase passed, and Susan ultimately returned to her role with renewed energy and strategies to sustain that energy for the long haul.

I admit that there are probably some differences in my coaching work with Susan because I was playing the role of an external coach. If I were Susan's manager, it may be unlikely that I would even listen for any cues that would suggest that Susan was not fully engaged in her work, nor would Susan be likely to volunteer such information. However, Susan would still be in the same place—burned out and wondering how to reengage in her work with a sense of purpose.

We are not suggesting that good leaders never engage in these dialogues. Some of the best leaders we partner with are courageous enough and emotionally intelligent enough to know that if they ignore these deeper conversations, they will not know what their employees are really thinking and feeling. And if they do not, the leaders will be less likely to be able to help employees navigate through tough spots with greater intention.

THE HATS WE WEAR

None of us lives outside of a diverse set of systems and roles. In every aspect of our lives, we probably find ourselves in a multitude of roles. Drawing from the work of the Hudson Institute of Santa Barbara, the most common roles we live in are listed in the left-hand column of Table 19-1. We have added the core activities that an individual might engage in for each role.

Please note: some of the activities listed in Table 19-1 may overlap with other roles, depending on how any individual chooses to negotiate his life and how his roles overlap.

Table 19-1 Roles and Activities

Role	Activities in This Role May Include
Personal Role The time we spend with ourselves, tending to ourselves, or being in the world by ourselves alone	• Caring for oneself: grooming, exercise, meditation practices, prayer • Entertaining oneself: reading, playing solitary games, surfing the Internet • Learning: education, attending classes, studying, practicing, mastering an activity • Managing the home: chores, shopping, home maintenance, lawn and yard maintenance

(Continued)

Table 19-1 Roles and Activities (Continued)

Couple Role The time we spend with a significant other—a romantic partner	• Spending time together • Managing the home together • Entertaining together • Assisting each other through hardships
Family Role The time we spend in any combination of family relationships, whether with children, siblings, parents, or extended/combination families	• Caring for children • Helping with schoolwork • Caring for elderly parents • Visiting with extended family members • Negotiating combination family relationships (stepparenting and so on) • Recreation with other family members • Holidays
Work Role The time we spend on behalf of our work commitments	• Traveling to and from work • Traveling for work engagements • Performing job responsibilities • Learning new job responsibilities as organizational needs shift or career opportunities appear • Entertaining colleagues and clients
Friends Role The time we spend with friends—those individuals who nurture us and support us	• Spending time together • Entertaining together • Assisting each other through hardships
Community Role The time we spend with a larger group of which we feel a part	Types of community groups include: • Religious communities • Neighborhood or town/city communities • Book clubs • Sports clubs • Choral (singing) groups • Active political affiliations

Why is it helpful to recognize all of the roles and systems in which individuals live? To recognize the multiple and competing demands and interests that individuals have, and to be aware that the work role must be engaging to individuals if they are to bring their best selves to the workplace. The work role also represents just one role that individuals play in the greater context of their lives.

One leader whom I coached shared with me the agony of having to lay off more than 80 employees at his prior employer organization. While the layoff was absolutely necessary if the business was to survive, the leader's heartache came from the process of firing employees and hearing them pour out their personal stories, one by one. An employee whose performance had gradually decreased over time—and who was being let go—finally shared that his wife had brain cancer, and that without insurance, he would not be able to continue to afford her treatments. Another employee was financially supporting her elderly mother, who had been diagnosed with Alzheimer's. Without a job, this employee did not know how she would manage to care for her mother in the same assisted manner.

What shocked my client (the leader) the most was that he had been unaware of the personal stories and challenges with which many of his employees had been silently wrestling. While the leader acknowledged that the layoff was necessary, he admitted that he might have made different choices if he had known of some of his employees' struggles. Had he known that his declining performer's wife had brain cancer, he admitted that he might have tried to work out a temporary solution or have been more tolerant of the employee's performance during the most challenging cancer treatment phases.

You have undoubtedly experienced many instances when your own colleagues or employees were struggling with personal challenges: dealing with divorce, sick children, or spouses who were being laid off or relocated.

Every Human Doing Has a Human Being

You have every right to expect that your employees will continue to meet your performance expectations and fulfill their job duties. However, if you can acknowledge that the work role sits within a larger context for most people, you may be able to generate a more supportive work *A human being accompanies the human doing into the office.* environment when employees do encounter challenges outside of the office walls. As leader-coaches, we will be well served by recognizing that a human *being* accompanies the human *doing* into the office. And both sides of the person need our support and caring.

If the challenges and issues that arise are beyond your capability to address, or if you are unsure about the boundaries that you may be crossing, we encourage you to consult your human resources department. Many organizations offer resources (either an HR representative or an external employee assistance program) that can provide a great deal of useful information for managing these unique situations. For extremely serious personal issues, it is usually best to encourage the person to work with the external employee assistance program.

However, there may be many challenges that your employees are struggling with for which you can lend support and understanding. Lending support and understanding does not mean that you stop expecting satisfactory work performance. Being supportive may mean that you work creatively with the employee to both meet his work obligations and also deal with his struggles outside of the workplace.

HOW YOU CAN HELP

It is certainly possible to notice signals that might indicate that an employee needs support. If you begin to hear or see signs of the following, consider inviting a conversation that allows the employee to explore and explain what is happening:

- A decline in performance, especially when the individual has been a consistent and strong performer
- Complaining more than usual about work situations
- Contributing less frequently in meetings
- Appearing less optimistic or joyful than usual
- Criticizing organizational initiatives more and supporting them less than is typical

What can you do in such situations? Initiate a coaching conversation, with the goal being to understand if there is anything that may be contributing adversely to the employee's work performance. Remember to stay on the bottom rung of the ladder when sharing the observations that triggered you to initiate the conversation. Here is how this conversation might begin.

You: Ruben, I'm wondering if you have a few minutes to talk.

Ruben: Sure.

You: I've noticed that you have been fairly quiet in our recent team meetings, which is not your typical behavior. Usually you are very participative, and I can count on you to share your point of view at almost all our meetings. I'm curious to know if anything is happening that may be influencing your quietness.

Ruben: Well—I don't know. Not really.

You: Are you sure? I want you to know that I am interested in hearing anything you have to say, and I promise that it will stay between you and me. My interest is in making sure that if there is something that we can address, I would like to do so.

Ruben: I guess I'm just contemplating the direction the company is going in. We are all hearing rumors, and I know that you have promised that you will share information with us when you know it, but that doesn't stop the rumor mill. And our rumor mill is usually pretty darn accurate.

You: So which rumors are bothering you the most—especially if your statement is true and our rumor mill is usually accurate?

Ruben: Well, if I join all the dots here, it looks as if we are heading into a downsizing. No one is saying so, but I cannot believe that we can continue without laying people off. And, my wife just lost her job last quarter. So, the whole situation feels pretty precarious to me. I have one kid in college and another graduating from high school this year. It will be hard enough to manage for a few months without two incomes. I guess I've been quiet lately so that I don't catch anyone's attention—in the wrong way. I can be pretty opinionated.

You: Would you like to talk a little more about this? Perhaps we can figure out how to navigate these times—from the perspective of both managing the uncertainty and continuing to work effectively. I'd also like to hear more about your wife's situation—perhaps there are some contacts in other organizations that I can give you to help her with her job search. Would that be useful?

Ruben: Actually, it probably would be.

Now, you may read this passage and think to yourself, "I would not be comfortable having that conversation with an employee." You are certainly not alone in being apprehensive about venturing into this territory. Consider, however, the consequences of *not* having that conversation with the employee. Chances are that the following are probably happening now or may happen in the future:

- Ruben is probably spending time worrying out loud with other coworkers; this adds to their concerns and the ongoing rumor mill.
- Ruben is spending more discretionary energy than he needs to, worrying about the rumored potential layoff.
- Because Ruben is choosing to "lie low" and stay out of the spotlight, he is limiting his contributions in meetings.
- As a result of all these things, Ruben's performance is not as high as it could be or usually is.
- Ruben is bringing his added tension home, which is affecting how he interacts with his wife and family.

Now, clearly this situation is contained primarily within the scope of the work environment—Ruben's key stated concern is a potential layoff at the organization. However, this news certainly bleeds over into Ruben's home life and affects how he will manage the rest of his role commitments—as husband, father, and financial contributor. When this is coupled with his wife's job loss, Ruben is undoubtedly feeling great pressure and potential anxiety.

So what can you do as Ruben's manager?

Sometimes the Medium Is the Message

Sometimes the medium *is* the message. As we previously mentioned, sometimes the very act of engaging in a coaching conversation— hearing an employee's point of view and determining whether there is a desired end state that you can move toward—is enough. In Ruben's situation, it is not likely that the leader can "fix" Ruben's predicament: the leader cannot guarantee that Ruben will have a job or that no layoffs will ensue, nor can the leader ensure that Ruben's wife will find a job or that work will resume as usual. However, by being willing to engage in the conversation, the leader sends a powerful message to Ruben:

- I understand your concerns and am willing to listen to them.
- If we can figure out anything about the nature of the situation, I am willing to do so—*with* you.
- I care about you, your performance, and your family.
- I am on your side.

These are useful and powerful messages to convey—even if you, as a leader, cannot "solve" your employee's dilemma. Too often, leaders feel that the best way to add value is to be a problem solver. In reality, sometimes the only problem that can be solved is that the employee knows that she is not alone—that her leader is truly on her side.

Many times after we have coached individuals, we have asked for feedback at the end of the coaching conversation. Often, what coachees share with us are sentiments such as

- Just having someone to talk with about these things is helpful.
- Talking through this situation has helped me see it in a different light.
- I trust that you are not going to judge me, but really try to support me.
- I know what I need to do now.

While coaches often help individuals solve their problems, coaching, in and of itself, is useful for those who are being coached. As a leader, you hold a powerful and influential role. Both you and your colleagues will hope and even expect that you can help them solve dilemmas that arise in the workplace. We hope you remember that sometimes, just being willing to engage in the coaching conversation is the best gift that you can offer those around you. Sometimes the medium *is* the message.

> *Being willing to engage in the coaching conversation is the best gift that you can offer.*

For the past several decades, there has been a debate regarding the ideal relationship between leaders and those reporting to them. Many people have suggested that the most effective leaders maintain a distance between themselves and their teams. They believe that this separation brings respect and allows the leader to be more objective in her appraisals of subordinates, and these are both logical arguments.

We recently had the occasion to conduct some research with leaders who scored at the 99th or 100th percentile on a number of leadership competencies. Simply put, they were extraordinary leaders. We interviewed them, and we also engaged their direct reports, their peers, and their managers in telephone conversations. On these calls, we probed everyone on what these leaders did that caused them to be so highly effective.

One of the striking conclusions that all the researchers observed with the approximately 150 people we interviewed was the warm, close relationship that existed between the leaders and their direct reports. It was illustrated by the remark of one leader who was the head of a large and important activity for the firm; at the end of the call, she remarked: "I just want you all to know how much I love working with you." It was said with total sincerity. Everyone on the call knew that she genuinely meant it. In none of our interviews did we ever hear evidence that these outstanding leaders worked to maintain distance between themselves and their subordinates. It was totally the opposite. Becoming too close with subordinates seemed to be the last thing they would worry about.

Chapter Summary

- We do not hire workers; we hire whole human beings who bring all of their humanity into the workplace.
- Each individual lives within a multitude of systems, and he is already a work in progress by the time we meet him in the workplace.
- Exploring the broader backdrop of a person's life helps us to understand the worker in the context of the rest of her life.

- While we hope that human "doings" show up to work, we must remember that they also bring their human "being" side with them.
- As a result of living in a multitude of roles and systems, individuals are constantly pulled by the various competing demands and expectations. Work is just one of these, although it is a very important one.
- While you have every right to expect employees to fulfill their work commitments, understanding the larger context will help you to be more supportive.
- Engage the appropriate human resources personnel or resources to assist employees in solving their problems outside of the workplace.
- Be willing to engage in a coaching conversation when you see evidence that an employee's performance or engagement is declining.
- Sometimes the medium is the message—just the act of engaging in a coaching dialogue will convey to the employee that you are on his side.
- According to our research, the most effective leaders consistently build warm, close relationships with their colleagues.

Conclusion

As we reflect on the major contribution that this book makes to the art and science of coaching, we submit that it is to provide you with a framework or checklist for every coaching discussion. We have provided a track for you to run on that has been proven to work. It guides you to apply the best techniques and principles. Some people may think that this is too simplistic, arguing that frameworks or checklists are way beneath their dignity. We understand this point of view, but we strongly beg to differ.

Our experience working with thousands of managers over the years confirms that practical job aids that summarize the ideal steps to take in difficult situations can be extremely valuable. We have talked to managers who went through a training program 20 years earlier in which they received a card that summarized the key action steps that were useful to follow in handling a termination interview or in discussing a behavior problem. These managers kept these cards in the top drawer of their desk and referred to them just before a key event.

In the book *The Checklist Manifesto*[1], the surgeon Atul Gawande makes a strong case for the use of a checklist as a way to improve the performance of even the most highly trained professionals, such as surgeons. This fundamental idea was adopted from a practice that is very common among pilots, in which the pilot and copilot follow a detailed list of steps that must be executed in the proper sequence during takeoff and landing.

For example, a common procedure in hospitals is the insertion of a catheter into a major vein for the purpose of administering medication or supplying some nutrient. These are referred to as central line catheters, and in one prestigious hospital, one out of every nine insertions became infected. This resulted in a prolonged illness with an accompanying extended hospital stay or additional surgery, and these infections sometimes caused death. A Johns Hopkins physician, Dr. Peter Pronovost, decided to conduct an experiment. He wrote down five things that doctors needed to do when performing such a procedure. These were steps that had long been taught to surgeons. They were seemingly simple and straightforward, but one-third of the time, one of the steps was omitted. The steps were

1. Wash hands with soap.
2. Clean the patient's skin with chlorohexidine antiseptic.
3. Cover the patient's entire body with sterile drapes.
4. Wear a mask, hat, sterile gown, and gloves.
5. Put a sterile dressing over the insertion site once the catheter is in.

After this checklist was implemented at Johns Hopkins, the central line infection rate in the Hopkins Intensive Care Unit dropped from 11 percent to zero. Two years after the checklist was introduced, Dr. Pronovost calculated, it had prevented 43 infections, avoided 8 deaths, and saved the hospital approximately $2 million. When the state of Michigan began using this checklist, its infection rate dropped 66 percent in three months. Soon its ICUs were outperforming those of 90 percent of all hospitals nationwide. The state estimated that in 18 months it had saved $175 million and 1,500 lives.

In an interview broadcast on National Public Radio, Dr. Gawande described how he introduced the concept of checklists to a large group of surgeons. After using this job aid for a period of time, they were asked if they planned to continue doing so. He reported that 80 percent said that they would. That meant, of course, that 20 percent felt that they did not need such a crutch. But the telling conclusion came when he asked the 20 percent this follow-on question: "If you were going into surgery as a patient, would you want the surgeon operating on you to follow a checklist?" In answer to this question, 94 percent said, "Yes."

THE VALUE OF A TEMPLATE TO FOLLOW

In the book *Getting Things Done*[2], David Allen argues that the human brain does only one thing at a time well. Despite all the talk of multitasking, it is clear that doing more than one thing at a time causes serious degradation of performance. A checklist allows the individual to focus on the immediate action and not divert his attention to what is coming next.

Having a guide to follow reduces stress and anxiety. It increases your confidence that nothing important will be forgotten.

OUR HOPE

You may be a highly experienced manager. We hope that you are extremely comfortable having conversations with people regarding performance issues. And we hope that discussing people's careers is something that you enjoy. However, no matter how good you currently are, just like the surgeons described here, we know that following a proven template or checklist will make you even better. Consider the Coaching Conversation Guide as a checklist to support your coaching conversations. We want to reduce the stress involved in such discussions as much as is humanly possible. Most of us tend to do those things that are pleasurable and fun or those things for which we see a substantial payoff. If we have helped your coaching experiences to be more pleasurable and to produce highly rewarding outcomes for you and those whom you coach, then our efforts will have succeeded.

Appendix

Powerful Coaching Questions

The best coaches we know tend to have a small stable of powerful questions that they know expand the coaching conversation and deliver great value to their coachees. We have listed here some of our favorite questions, categorized by the potential step in the FUEL coaching conversation where you might best utilize them.

FRAME THE CONVERSATION
Identify the Behavior or Issue to Discuss

- What is the most important thing for us to focus on?
- Of all the things that we could talk about, what will give you the most value?
- Tell me why you chose that topic to focus on today.
- What has happened lately that makes this an important topic?
- Help me understand the seriousness of this to you.

Determine the Purpose or Outcomes of the Conversation

- What would you like to accomplish in this conversation?
- How might I help you with this issue?
- What would you like to leave this conversation with?

Agree on the Process for the Conversation

- How should we proceed?
- Where should we start?
- What might be an agenda for this conversation?
- What do we need to cover to reach our end goal?

UNDERSTAND THE CURRENT STATE
Understand the Coachee's Point of View

- How do you see this situation? What is happening?
- What is working well?
- What makes this challenging?
- How might you have contributed to this situation?
- How might others see the situation?
- How are you feeling right now about the situation?
- Do you know anyone for whom this is not an issue? What do you think is different about their situation?
- What proof or evidence do you have to support that?
- Have you checked out your perception with others? What did you learn?
- If the person you are having a conflict with were here with us now, what would his or her point of view be?
- Are there any forces that are pushing to make this continue? What are they?
- On a 1-to-10 scale, with 1 being "this is a small problem" and 10 being "this feels almost insurmountable," how do you feel about this issue?
- If you could identify the three most significant factors contributing to this issue, what would they be? (How would you rank them?)

Determine the Consequences of Continuing on the Current Path

- What impact is this having on you? On others?
- What are the consequences if the situation doesn't change?
- How does this influence your goals and what you are trying to accomplish?
- Tell me about the business consequences of this issue.
- How does this affect you personally?
- If you could resolve this, what effect would it have on your job satisfaction? On your career success?
- Imagine that a year has passed and nothing has changed. What would that be like for you?
- What are the long-term implications if this situation doesn't change?

Offer Your Perspective, *If Appropriate*

- Could I share some observations I have made?
- Could I offer some other consequences to consider?

EXPLORE THE DESIRED STATE

Understand the Vision for Success

- What would you like to see happen here?
- What would the ideal state look like?
- What opportunities can you see in this situation?
- What is possible here?
- If you could be the best version of yourself in this situation, what would that look like?
- If you had a magic wand, what would you like to see happen here?
- If you were CEO/queen/president for a day, what would you like to implement?
- What would you realistically like to make happen, given these circumstances?
- What would a best-case scenario look like?
- What would you try, if you knew you could not fail?
- What would you attempt, if you had all of the support and resources that you needed here?
- What bold steps would you take, if you could guarantee success?
- How would you like to see yourself behaving in this ideal situation?

Set Goals and Performance Expectations

- What are your goals? What would you like to accomplish?
- What would be some stretch targets to shoot for?
- How will you measure your success?
- How could you quantify what you are hoping to achieve?
- What "stake in the ground" would you like to make around this vision?
- What are you committed to achieving? What would a goal for that be?

Explore Alternative Paths of Action

- What might be some approaches you can take?
- What strategies can help you realize your desired vision?
- What else might work? What else?
- Could I offer a couple of additional possibilities to consider?
- If you could rank-order the possible solutions in terms of effectiveness, what would be your first, second, and third best option to consider?
- What criteria could you use to evaluate which path looks like the best one to take?
- Which option(s) would be most feasible or easiest to implement?
- Which option(s) will get you closest to your goal in the time frame you would like to target?

Explore Possible Barriers or Resistance

- What are the major barriers preventing this change from happening?
- Where would the biggest resistance to this change come from?
- What is going to get in the way?
- What are the biggest risks or barriers to pursuing that option?
- What might go wrong? What is the worst-case scenario?

LAY OUT A SUCCESS PLAN

Develop and Agree on an Action Plan and Timelines

- What specific actions will help you achieve your goal?
- What will your first steps be? When will you start?
- How will you stay focused on your goals and plans?

Enlist Support from Others

- Who can support you in moving forward?
- Who can help hold you accountable?
- How can I support you?
- Who might help you (in completing a specific action step that was stated)?

Set Milestones for Follow-up and Accountability

- When should we touch base on this again?
- What would you like from me in terms of accountability?

Notes

CHAPTER 4

1. A. S. Tannenbaum and W. H. Schmidt, "How to Choose a Leadership Pattern," *Harvard Business Review* 36 (March–April 1958), 95–101.
2. Philip Zimbardo, *The Lucifer Effect: Understanding How Good People Turn Evil* (New York: Random House, 2007).
3. D. Michael Abrashoff, *It's Your Ship: Management Techniques From the Best Damn Ship in the Navy* (New York: Grand Central Publishing, 2002), Chapter One.

CHAPTER 5

1. What are the mechanics of this 360-degree feedback process? Several people selected by the participant are asked to serve as raters. They would usually include all direct reports, several peers, and the boss.

    The questionnaire includes 50 to 60 questions and is completed on-line. Raters are asked to provide written comments in addition to answering the scaled questions.

    Confidentiality of respondents is maintained. Unless there are results from 3 people in a category, that category is not reported and those responses are combined with another group. Nearly all organizations use the data for development purposes, not for evaluation or promotion.

    Organizations that have measured the impact have found remarkably high percentages of leaders who change their behavior in significant ways.

CHAPTER 7

1. Brad J. Bushman, Angelica M. Bonacci, William C. Pedersen, Eduardo A. Vasquez, and Norman Miller, "Chewing on It Can Chew You Up: Effects of Rumination on Triggered Displaced Aggression," *Journal of Personality and Social Psychology* 88, no. 6 (2005), 969–983.

CHAPTER 9

1. Norman R. F. Maier, *Problem Solving Discussions and Conferences* (New York: McGraw-Hill, 1963).

CHAPTER 11

1. Barry Duncan and Scott Miller, www.talkingcure.com, and Barry Duncan, Scott D. Miller, Bruce E. Wampold, and Mark Hubble, eds., *The Heart and Soul of Change: Delivering What Works in Therapy*, 2nd ed. (New York: American Psychological Association, 2009).

CHAPTER 12

1. Robert F. Mager and Peter Pipe, *Analyzing Performance Problems*, Center for Effective Performance, Item 434.

CHAPTER 13

1. This study was conducted by Monster.com in conjunction with Development Dimensions International (DDI). "Thanks but No Thanks: Why Top Candidates Are Turning Down Your Job Offers and What You Can Do about It," 2007.
2. Frederick Herzberg, "One More Time: How Do You Motivate Employees?" *Harvard Business Review*, 1968; reprinted in *Harvard Business Review on Motivating People* (Boston: Harvard Business Press, 2003).
3. Robert Kegan and Lisa Laskow Lahey, *How the Way We Talk Can Change the Way We Work* (San Francisco: Jossey-Bass, 2001), pp. 99–100.
4. Barbara L. Fredrickson and Marcial F. Losada, "Positive Affect and the Complex Dynamics of Human Flourishing," *American Psychologist* 60, no. 7 (2005), 678–686.

CHAPTER 20

1. Atul Gawande, *The Checklist Manifesto* (New York: Metropolitan Holt, 2009).
2. David Allen, *Gettings Things Done: The Art of Stress Free Productivity* (New York: Penguin, 2001).

Index

About the Authors

JOHN H. (JACK) ZENGER

John H. (Jack) Zenger is the cofounder and CEO of Zenger Folkman, a professional services firm providing consulting, leadership
development programs, and implementation software for organizational effectiveness initiatives. Considered a world expert in the
field of leadership development, Jack is also a highly respected and
sought-after speaker, consultant, and executive coach.

Jack's career has combined entrepreneurial, corporate,
and academic activities. In 1977 he cofounded Zenger-Miller
and served as its president and CEO until 1991. The *Wall Street Journal* named
Zenger-Miller one of the 10 best suppliers of executive development.

Because of his contributions to the field of leadership development and training, Jack was inducted into the Human Resources Development Hall of Fame. His
colleagues in the training industry awarded him the "Thought Leadership Award"
in 2007. Jack is a member of the Board of Regents that oversees higher education
in the state of Utah. Jack received a D.B.A. in business administration from the
University of Southern California, an MBA from UCLA, and a BA in psychology
from Brigham Young University.

Jack has authored or coauthored 50 articles on leadership, productivity,
e-learning, training, and measurement. He is the coauthor of several books on
leadership, including *Results-Based Leadership* (Harvard Business School Press,
1999), voted by SHRM as the Best Business Book in the year 2000; the bestselling *The Extraordinary Leader: Turning Good Managers into Great Leaders*
(McGraw-Hill, 2002); and *Handbook for Leaders* (McGraw-Hill, 2004).

He is also a coauthor of books about teams, including the bestselling *Self-
Directed Work Teams: The New American Challenge* (Irwin Professional Publish-
ing, 1990), *Leading Teams* (Irwin Professional Publishing, 1993), and *Keeping
Teams on Track* (Irwin Professional Publishing, 1996).

He and his wife, Holly, reside in Midway, Utah.

KATHLEEN STINNETT

Kathleen Stinnett is a senior consultant, master trainer, and executive coach with Zenger Folkman. She also serves on the faculty of the Hudson Institute of Santa Barbara, training individuals who are pursuing professional coaching credentials. Kathleen has trained thousands of leaders across many industries, both nationally and internationally. Clients describe her as an energetic, positive force and a role model.

Kathleen has more than 20 years of experience in the field of human performance, helping leaders at all levels to perform with greater fulfillment and improved results. She has worked internally for organizations such as M.D. Anderson Cancer Center, Burlington Northern, and Wilson Learning Corporation. In January of 2000, Kathleen founded FutureLaunch, an organization that provides training, consulting, and coaching services to organizations and individuals. Kathleen was certified as a professional coach by the Hudson Institute of Santa Barbara in February 2000.

In 2003, Kathleen joined Zenger Folkman as a senior consultant and executive coach. Focusing on leadership development, Kathleen coaches leaders at all levels of the organization to understand and improve their personal leadership effectiveness. Kathleen codeveloped the "Extraordinary Coach" program for Zenger Folkman, which equips leaders to coach their employees and colleagues effectively.

In 2005, Kathleen received recognition as a Master Certified Coach (MCC) by the International Coach Federation. She currently serves as a board member of the Coaches Collective International, a nonprofit organization dedicated to matching nonprofit or for-profit organizations with qualified coaches. She is considered a coach's coach, regularly being asked to coach individuals who are learning to become coaches themselves.

Clients that Kathleen has worked with include such best-in-class organizations as AT&T, ConocoPhillips, Fidelity Investments, General Mills, Sandia National Labs, Safeway, and Wells Fargo. She has consulted with organizations in North America, the United Kingdom, Germany, Japan, the Philippines, India, China, and the United Arab Emirates. The principles and practices that she teaches others are proven to work.

Kathleen holds an MS in training and development from the University of Houston and a BS in marketing from the University of Colorado, Boulder.

Kathleen lives in Santa Barbara, California, with Dave and Mocha (a Yorkshire terrier). A pianist and composer, Kathleen recorded an original CD of piano music (*Winter Dream*), which she uses to set the tone of many of her workshops.

Learning to become
a great coach
shouldn't stop
when you
put down
this book

Now that you know the principles behind great coaching, put them to work for the leaders in your organization with *The Extraordinary Coach*—the award-winning development program from Zenger Folkman.

As one of the top ten providers of corporate training in America*, Zenger Folkman built *The Extraordinary Coach* through practical ideas based in hard science that are guaranteed to deliver results. Using *The Extraordinary Coach*, leaders in your organization will:

- understand how great leaders coach others to high performance
- learn how to build trusting coaching relationships that inspire commitment
- learn how to hold powerful coaching conversations that drive action
- use on-the-spot peer coaching and our unique cross-training approach to construct a customized Individual Development Plan

The bottom line? From increasing employee engagement to driving profitability, *The Extraordinary Coach* delivers the tools necessary to make a significant and proven impact on the success of any business.

For more information on The Extraordinary Coach:
Call 801.705.9375 • Visit www.zengerfolkman.com

 ZENGER | FOLKMAN

*according to Leadership Excellence Magazine 2007, 2008, 2009